The South West COAST PATH

1998 GUIDE

THE COMPLETE GUIDE TO THE LONGEST NATIONAL TRAIL BY THE SOUTH WEST WAY ASSOCIATION

Peninsula
Press

THE SOUTH WEST WAY ASSOCIATION

Registered as a charity (No. 266754)

*The Association formed to promote the interest of users of the
South West Way (South West Coast Path)*

CHAIRMAN
Brian Panton, 5 Nicholas Gardens, Ensbury Park,
Bournemouth BH10 4BA
Tel: (01202) 526954

TREASURER
Derek HEXTER, F.C.A.,
Brennels Mead, 40 Highweek Village,
Newton Abbot, Devon TQ1 1QQ
Tel: (01626) 52162

SECRETARY
Eric WALLIS
'Windlestraw', Penquit, Ermington,
Devon PL21 0LU
Tel: (01752) 896237
Fax: (01752) 896237

MEMBERSHIP SECRETARY
Mrs Mary MACLEOD
1 Orchard Drive, Kingskerswell, Newton Abbot,
Devon TQ12 5DG

Published jointly by:
The South West Way Association and Peninsula Press Ltd
P.O. Box 31, Newton Abbot, Devon TQ12 5XH.

Trade Sales and Distribution:
Hamlet Distribution, Moretonhampstead, Devon TQ13 8NA
© South West Association 1998

Printed in England by Swift Print, Dawlish

http://www.gorp.com/gorp/activity/europe/sw-way.htm
also http://www.city.ac.uk/"sa346/sww.html

ISBN 1 872640 43 5

Jacket Design by A&B Creative Services, Kingskerswell, Devon

Jacket Photographs: Top left clockwise - Scarnor Point (North Cornwall),
Near Polperro (South Cornwall), Talland Bay (South Cornwall),
and Hooken Cliffs (East Devon) by Eric Wallis

South West
Coast Path

CONTENTS

Introduction 4

Weather 5

Long Distance Walking Advice 6

Books and Leaflets 7

National Trust 9

Railways 11

Bus Services 12

Sea Transport and Coastal Services..................... 14

Useful Addresses...................................... 14

Maps 15

Banks 16

Telephones 16

Tide Tables 17

Suggested Itinerary 19

The Trail Description 21

Accommodation Section 85

Association History................................... 115

Offa's Dyke 118

The production of this annual guide has been made possible by the support of the Countryside Commission for the Association's computer facilities

INTRODUCTION

The South West Coast Path is a 'National Trail' funded by the Countryside Commission and maintained on its behalf by County Councils and National Park authorities. The route is waymarked by the distinctive acorn symbol. It is by far the longest of all the Long Distance trails; it runs from Minehead in Somerset right round the South-West peninsula to South Haven Point on the south side of Poole Harbour in Dorset We ourselves reckon this is 613 miles, others differ but all agree it is a fair step. A recent contour count indicates you will climb over 91,000 ft which is three times Mount Everest.

This Guide attempts to provide in one single unit all the basic information you need to walk the path. The information is updated annually and members are advised by newsletters of important changes during the year. We try to provide the basic information, that is sometimes so difficult to assemble for other long trails, in just one small book.

A survey established that one of the chief joys of those accomplishing the Pennine Way was the sense of achievement; of a challenge met. What of our path which is twice as long and requiring far more total effort? Because of its length, few will be able to undertake to walk it as a whole. That is why as much as possible of this guide is written to be just as useful to those who only wish to walk parts of the path.

The splendid idea of making this old path around the South West Peninsula one of the first of a series of Long Distance Paths came from a war-time committee of the Ramblers Association. The idea was put into effect by being included in the National Park and Access to the Countryside Act of 1949. In other words, Long Distance Footpaths have an equal basis in law with the much better known National Parks. Unfortunately, for the Long Distance Footpaths, they have largely been treated as poor relations ever since. The proof of this is, despite being authorised by Act of Parliament so long ago and despite several Opening Ceremonies, the South West Coast Path is still UNFINISHED.

The South West Way Association was formed after some months' preliminary work in May 1973. It is an independent body but works in co-operation with the Ramblers Association. The South West Way Association's first aim is to secure completion of the path, and we do believe we have been responsible for many path alignment improvements and better maintenance and waymarking during our 25 year existence.

Furthermore, the South West Way Association believe the Countryside Commission have been in error in two respects. Firstly they have not made it a continuous path despite their own words: "There should be a continuous right of way along the entire length of the path." (Countryside Commission's National Long Distance Path - Some Questions Answered.)

Secondly, in several places, the Path has been diverted from the coast for no apparent good reason, even on occasions, on to main roads with no pavement. The South West Way Association believe it would be scenically more beautiful, less hindrance to agriculture and physically safer if kept on the coast. Experience has shown that diversions away from it are on the whole not satisfactory.

It seems that no local walking organisations were ever consulted about the path until South West Way Association came into being. Being reasonable people we cannot expect to have everything our own way - in fact there are many legitimate interests to consider. However, to establish a path without discussing it with the people who know it best, which is exactly what the Countryside Commission were apparently trying to do, seems altogether wrong.

The South West Way Association believe that, in a tourist-orientated area such as the South West, a continuous coastal path will be a major asset. It hopes the Path will bring more business to less frequented places and relieve some of the pressure on the South West National Parks. There are a great number of bodies interested in various parts of the Path. The South West Way Association believes it is important that it should represent all sections, and view the Path as a whole.

Members receive a free Annual Guide and two Newsletters a year with up-to-date information of the state of the path.

Enquiries to: The Membership Secretary, (see page 2)

Subscriptions: £8.00; Joint: £9.00; Associations, Local Authorities £14.00;
                     Life Membership: £120.00; Joint: £140.00; Non-UK membership: £12.00

The path passes along some of the finest coastal scenery in Europe and, with its enormous variety and contrast between bustling resort and quiet cove, is a never ceasing source of delight.

This path is the longest National Trail - we think it is the finest and we hope you will too. We certainly know of no other that has as much contrast and variety as ours. Try it.

THE OTHER WAY ROUND

In this book the description of the South West Coast Path is from Minehead-Land's End-Poole. The Association has now written a description of the Trail for those walking the other way. It deals only with the path so this annual guide will be necessary for all the other information. The 'other way round' supplement is available from the membership secretary or secretary at £3.50 including postage.

WEATHER

The South West Coast Path is more exposed to wind than any other Long Distance Trail - Pay attention to gale forecasts as well as rain. Along some sections, strong winds can be dangerous especially when rounding exposed headlands and crossing bridges. A high backpack can act like a sail. Detailed forecasts are available on (0898) 500 405 (Somerset) / (0898) 500 404 (Devon & Cornwall) / (0898) 500 403 (Dorset).

A WORD TO BEGINNERS

Long Distance Path Walking

These words are not for those hardy veterans who have all the gear, have done several paths already, and know all about it. We will only say to them at least read the second paragraph of `Grading' near the beginning of the 'Trail Description' section. However, we do get a number of letters each year from those who have not ventured before on Long Distance Paths and need some advice. This we are pleased to try and provide and we do hope those who read this will find it helpful. However; it is easy to miss out things that folk wish to know, so if you who are new read this, and are still baffled, please write to us and we will try to provide the answers. As well as perhaps helping you, it will enable us to improve this section for another year and so be of help to more people.

For Those Who Have Never Been Walking

Have you been walking at all before? If the answer is no, do not for heaven's sake try and plan several days' continuous walking. You need to do some day walks - there are some very good ones on the coast. Better still, look for the sections marked "Easy" - start at one end and stop and turn back before you have half had enough. We say before half because it is always better to do a bit less and really enjoy it.

You can soon progress to setting out to walk a whole section either by using two cars or using public transport. One point here - if possible use the public transport to go out and walk back to your car or base. This means that you do not get yourself in a position of having to race the clock if you should take a bit more time than you thought.

If you are walking on your own, do please take additional care for, as you will appreciate, if you fall or twist an ankle there can be problems. If you are on your own therefore, you should leave a note with someone to make sure that you arrive at your destination. Not everyone is happy walking on their own and can feel lonely. There is also an added problem that you may try to do too much, so please bear this in mind.

There is no need to buy expensive equipment for the easy sections at the start. A pair of stout shoes and a rainproof is all you need. As you progress, a small rucksack or haversack for 'eats' will be needed next.

Obviously if you can join a walking club and go out with them you will collect lots of friendly advice on all sorts of gear you may care to purchase as you become more serious about walking. Maps, guides, etc., are all listed in their appropriate sections.

For Those Who Have Walked, But Not On Long Distance Trails

Day walking on long distance trails is really no different from any other kind of day walking. It is only when you contemplate several days' continuous walking that other considerations arise and there are some pitfalls which even quite experienced day walkers often overlook.

Do not be too ambitious in the mileage you plan. Do not carry too much weight of gear.

Having stated the two big points, we will elaborate. You will not be able to accomplish in daily mileage the same amount you normally cover in a day walk. You will have to settle for less. The first reason is that you will be carrying more equipment; you must for instance, have a complete change of clothing and footwear, possibly nightwear and toilet kit. For this you need a bigger rucksack so you will be carrying quite a bit more weight than you normally do. Secondly, there is what we call the 'wear' factor. For the first few days until you are really fit, it is just simply more tiring having to walk each day. The last point could be called the 'interest' factor. Usually, if you are walking a long distance path, you are further from your home base in fresh fields and pastures new; there is more to see so you will need more time to look around.

If you usually accomplish 15 miles a day - aim, say, for 12. This is particularly important if you are booking ahead. You can find yourself tied to a treadmill which you cannot get off. Booking ahead has the advantage that you know there is a bed ahead. On the other hand, it does mean even if you are tired, have developed blisters, and the weather is diabolical, you have to go on. Be guided too by our `Trail Description' section, the terrain you are tackling. 6 miles, say, of a `Severe' section can equal in effort 10-12 miles of an 'Easy' one.

We have stated you must carry more gear and this is true. Having said that, think long and hard about every item you imagine you may need. You will be surprised - you may find you will not want it at all. Watch particularly those extras such as cameras and binoculars - they are often a source of considerable weight. One little additional point, many rucksacks, even modern ones, are not as waterproof as you think A plastic liner which can be obtained quite cheaply from rambling shops, etc., as an additional inner layer may save you that most unpleasant discovery after a long day spent in the rain that your only change of clothing is no longer dry We would also recommend that in addition to this liner your dry clothing should then be enclosed in further plastic bags to ensure dryness. Trainer shoes are useful for wearing at the end of the day and can be worn on some parts of the path.

A sensible idea before undertaking a long walking holiday is to take, say, a weekend of two or three days first walking continuously as a practice

We are sometimes asked if you require a map as well as a guide book and our advice is certainly yes. One does not get as badly lost on the Coast Path as you can on inland ones but nonetheless a map is an asset. Furthermore many walkers derive much interest from looking at their route in relation to the rest of the countryside on ordinary walks and the same applies just as much, if not more so, on our coast path The National Trail Guides offer a partial solution with their maps; but even these are not as useful as a Map Sheet.

Another point to watch especially on our coast path is the availability of refreshment. At main holiday times, you will get it nearly everywhere except for the few places we especially mention in our 'Trail Description' section. Out of season, you will find it in surprisingly few places on long stretches of coast. The usual remarks about carrying stand-by supplies, therefore, certainly apply; better to carry an extra couple of bars of chocolate than to go hungry.

Walking Alone

The Association have a scheme that enables single lady walkers who are a little nervous about walking alone to team up with other single lady members. Contact the secretary for information.

BADGES

We offer specially designed badges for the South West Way Association.

Cloth badges for rucksack, anoraks, etc. £1.50 inclusive of postage and packing.

We think these badges are attractive - we hope you will too. Available both for members and non-members alike.

CERTIFICATES

These are now available to persons who have walked the whole path. To members - £1.50 and to non-members - £2.50 including postage. Contact the Membership Secretary.

VIDEO

Aerial Britain - The South West Coast Path. Produced by C21C at £12.99. Available at all branches of W H Smith This is the one we helped to make. Beautiful - the coast path from a helicopter.

SWEAT SHIRTS AND T-SHIRTS

We have sweat shirts (£16.25) and T-shirts (£9.75) with the Association logo. Contact the Membership Secretary.

BOOKS, etc.

This list is not exhaustive, there are a number of other books available but we have tried hard to list all those which are really useful and even those not really useful that you might think would be.

SOME PUBLICATIONS ARE AVAILABLE DIRECT FROM YOUR ASSOCIATION, FOR QUICK SERVICE PLEASE WRITE TO THE MEMBERSHIP SECRETARY (SEE PAGE 2)

South West Way - Minehead to Penzance

South West Way - Penzance to Poole.

Both these excellent pocket sized books are by Martin Collins. We can recommend them as most useful. Available from Cicerone Press, 2 Police Square, Milnthorpe, Cumbria, LA7 7PY at £8.99 each (Postage and packing 75p per book). Also available from the South West Way Association.

National Trail Guides - published by Aurum Press in association with the Countryside Commission and Ordnance Survey. Available from the Countryside Commission Publications, Printworks Lane, Levenshulme, Manchester M19 3JP; The Ordnance Survey, Romsey Road, Maybush, Southampton S09 4DM; most bookshops and our own association from the Membership Secretary. These are good guide books with good maps. An excellent venture by those involved.

Minehead to Padstow by Roland Tarr (3rd Edition 1996)

Padstow to Falmouth by John Macadam (2nd Edition 1996)

Falmouth to Exmouth by Brian Le Messurier (2nd Edition 1996)

Exmouth to Poole by Roland Tarr (3rd Edition 1996)

Price £10.99 + 75p postage from our Membership Secretary.

Walk the Cornish Coastal Path by John Mason. This is a Bartholomew Map and Guide at £5.99. An excellent guide to all of the Cornish Coast. From Membership Secretary (Post 75p).

Falmouth and South West Cornwall Guide including accommodation, available free from: The Tourist Information Centre, 79 Meneage Street, Helston, Cornwall. (Tel: 01326 565431).

Eleven Walks in West Cornwall. Price £1 .00 plus postage from the Tourist Information Centre, 79 Meneage Street, Helston, Cornwall. (Tel: 01326 565431}.

(List continued overleaf.)

Discover Guides - St. Keverne, Coverack, Mullion and Redruth Town Trail. Free of charge. Send SAE to Tourist Information Centre, 79 Meneage Street, Helston, Cornwall. (Tel: 01326 565431).

LANDFALL WALKS BOOKS - Bob Acton of Devoran has written twelve splendid books that contain well over 100 circular walks in Cornwall. These feature sections of the coast path throughout the county. They will enable walkers to progress along the coast path by basing themselves at one location. Write to Landfall Publications, Landfall, Penpol, Devoran, Truro, TR3 6NW for full list, or (Tel: 01872 862581).

Footpath Touring with Ken Ward. Land's End and The Lizard. Price £3.75 including postage. Available direct from 'Sea Chimney', South Down, Beer, EX12 3AE. An excellent guide to this section of the path by one of the co-authors of the well-known Letts Guides.

Walk South Devon Coastal Path and Dartmoor by John Mason and Eric Hemery. This is a Bartholomew Map and Guide at £5.99. An excellent guide to the South Devon Coast. Available from Membership Secretary (Post 75p).

Two Moors Way (now illustrated) - by Devon Area Ramblers Association - Price £3.00. This is not our path. One is enough! But we do stock the Official Guide. This describes the path from Lynmouth in North Devon to Ivybridge near Plymouth - and very well done it is too. (Available from South West Way Association. Postage 75p. Write to Membership Secretary.)

Two Moors Way by John Macadam. This is a new recreational guide published by Aurum Press and Ordnance Survey. £12.99.

Classic Walks Cornwall - 56 half day circular walks involving the coast path. From Cornish Publications Ltd, PO Box 12, Perranporth. £4.99 plus 75p P&P.

Classic Walks Devon - 60 Half-day Circular Walks - Many involving the coast path (as for Classic Walks Cornwall).

SOUTH WEST WAY ASSOCIATION PUBLICATIONS

Path Descriptions by our association are very detailed accounts on all aspects of short sections of the coast path and include maps and illustrations. They cover in great detail what cannot be included in the guide book.

These Path Descriptions are all priced at £1.00 including postage. All are available from the Membership Secretary (see page 2).

PATH DESCRIPTIONS

Minehead to Lynmouth (22 miles)	Lynmouth to Ilfracombe (18 miles)
Ilfracombe to Croyde Bay (13 miles)	Croyde Bay to Barnstaple (16 miles)
Barnstaple to Westward Ho! (11 miles)	Westward Ho! To Clovelly (11 miles)
Clovelly to Hartland Quay (10 miles)	Hartland Quay to Bude (14 miles)
Bude to Crackington Haven (9 miles)	Crackington Haven to Tintagel (12 miles)
Tintagel to Port Isaac (8 miles)	Port Isaac to Padstow (12 miles)
Padstow to Porthcothan (12 miles)	Porthcothan to Newquay (10 miles)
Newquay to Perranporth (11 miles)	Perranporth to Portreath (13 miles)
Portreath to Hayle (12 miles)	Hayle to Pendeen Watch (18 miles)
Pendeen Watch to Porthcurno (15 miles)	Porthcurno to Penzance (11 miles)
Penzance to Porthleven (13 miles)	Porthleven to The Lizard (13 miles)
The Lizard to Helford (24 miles)	Helford to Falmouth (10 miles)
Falmouth to Portloe (13 miles)	Portloe to Mevagissey (12 miles)
Mevagissey to Fowey (17 miles)	Fowey to Looe (12 miles)
Looe to Plymouth (21 miles)	Plymouth (River Tamar) to Wembury (River Yealm) (14 miles)
Bigbury to Salcombe (13 miles)	Warren Point (Wembury) to Bigbury-on-Sea (14 miles)
Salcombe to Torcross (13 miles)	Torcross to Dartmouth (10 miles)
Dartmouth to Brixham (11 miles)	Brixham to Shaldon (19 miles)
Shaldon to Sidmouth (19 miles)	Sidmouth to Lyme Regis (17 miles)
Lyme Regis to Abbotsbury (19 miles)	Abbotsbury to Weymouth (14 miles)
Isle of Portland Circuit (14 miles)	Weymouth to Lulworth Cove (12 miles)
Lulworth to Kimmeridge, Lulworth Range (7 miles)	Kimmeridge to South Haven Point, Poole Harbour (20 miles)
Alternative Inland Route, West Bexington to Osmington Mills (18 miles)	

THE NATIONAL TRUST "COAST OF DEVON" LEAFLETS

At long last a new series of detailed leaflets with maps are becoming available. These each include four walks covering the coastline owned by the National Trust in Devon. Each leaflet contains good maps and information of the history, flora and fauna and general information of the areas.

They are available from National Trust shops in Devon or from the Devon Regional Office, Killerton House, Broadclyst, Exeter, EX5 3LE, at 75p each plus post and packing.

1.   The West Exmoor Coast

2.   Watersmeet and Countisbury

All Long Distance Paths

We recommend the Long Distance Walker's Handbook: 6th Edition: Completely revised and updated. Contact - Brian Smith, 10 Temple Park Close, Leeds, West Yorkshire LS15 0JJ (Tel: 0113 264 2205). (£11.99 inc postage)

Information on Long Distance Routes can also be obtained from the Ramblers Association, 1/5 Wordsworth Road, London SW8 2XX.

THE NATIONAL TRUST 'COAST OF CORNWALL' LEAFLETS

A series of detailed leaflets, with maps, covering the coastline owned by the National Trust in Cornwall. Each leaflet contains information of the history, flora and fauna of the area as well as general information on points of interest.

They are available from National Trust shops in Cornwall or from the Cornwall Regional Office, Lanhydrock, Bodmin, Cornwall PL3O 4DE (please include a donation to cover postage):

No 1	Bude to Morwenstow	70p
No 2	Crackington Haven	50p
No 3	Boscastle	70p
No 4	TIntagel	70p
No 5	Polzeath to Port Quin	60p
No 6	Bedruthan and Park Head	60p
No 7	Crantock to Holywell Bay	60p
No 8	St. Agnes and Chapel Porth	50p
No 9	Godrevy to Portreath	60p
No 10	West Penwith: St. Ives to Pendeen	80p
No 11	West Penwith: Levant to Penberth	90p
No 12	Loe Pool and Gunwalloe	70p
No 13	The Lizard, West Coast	70p
No 14	Kynance Cove	60p
No 15	The Lizard, East Coast	70p
No 16	The Helford River	70p
No 17	Trelissick	70p
No 18	The Roseland Peninsula	60p
No 19	St Anthony Head Battery	60p
No 20	Nare Head and the Dodman	70p
No 21	Fowey	80p
No 22	East Cornwall: Lantic Bay to Sharrow Point	70p

NATIONAL TRUST REGIONAL INFORMATION OFFICES:

Devon Information Office, Killerton House, Broadclyst Exeter, Devon EX5 3LE (Tel: Exeter (01392) 881691).

Wessex Information Office, Eastleigh Court, Bishopstrow, Warminster, Wilts. BA12 9HW (Tel: 01985 843600).

Cornwall Information Office, The Estate Office, Lanhydrock Park, Bodmin, Cornwall PL3O 4DE (Tel: Bodmin (01208 74281)

RAILWAYS

Throughout the year there is a regular service of direct Great Western Trains' linking London Paddington with Taunton, Exeter St David's, Plymouth and Cornwall. There are also regular Virgin Cross Country trains services linking Birmingham, the North West, North East and Scotland with Taunton, Exeter St David's, Plymouth, Cornwall, Bournemouth and Poole. All these services offer a range of on train facilities including catering and on some Great Western Trains' services during the school holidays there is a dedicated coach provided for the use of families. During the high season (May to September) demand for seats is high so it is recommended that seats are reserved in advance to ensure a comfortable journey. On Saturdays, additional services run to and from the West Country to the Midlands, North of England and London with a direct service operated between London and Newquay only during the summer.

There is a regular South West Trains' service linking London Waterloo with Bournemouth, Wareham (for Swanage), Poole and Weymouth for those who intend to walk the Dorset end of The South West Way. East Devon is served by an approximate two hourly service from London Waterloo to Axminster (for Lyme Regis and Seaton) and Honiton (for Sidmouth). During some periods of the day the two hourly frequency is reduced. In addition to these services South West Trains' also offer a service of trains linking London Waterloo, Basingstoke, Salisbury, Exeter Central and Paignton.

Wales & West Passenger Trains Ltd offers a regular service of long distance and local service of trains in the South West. The long distance trains link Cardiff, Manchester, Bristol and Swindon with Penzance, Plymouth, Paignton and Exeter. The local services on the branch lines of Devon and Cornwall offer reasonable connections into and out of Great Western Trains' and Virgin Cross Country services. Most of Wales & West Passenger Trains' local services operate on a Sunday during the summer months with the first four listed below also operating a limited Sunday service during the winter months.

Westbury - Yeovil - Weymouth	Liskeard - Looe
Exeter - Barnstaple	Par - Newquay
Exeter - Exmouth	Truro - Falmouth
Newton Abbot -Torquay - Paignton	St Erth - St Ives
Plymouth - Gunnislake	

A wide variety of attractive reduced-rate fares are often available during the summer months. Details of which can be obtained from enquiry at stations and Travel Centres. The method of obtaining train information, to reserve seats or make general rail enquiries has been simplified with the setting up of a National Rail Enquiries bureaux. The telephone number for all rail matters is (0345) 484950 and contact can be made 24 hours a day.

Private Branch Line Railways

Bishops Lydeard to Minehead - The West Somerset Railway PLC run steam trains through twenty scenic miles to Minehead. Bishops Lydeard is four miles outside Taunton and easily accessible by bus. The service operates between March and October. For details contact the company at 'The Station', Minehead TA24 5BG (Tel: 01643 704996).

Paignton to Kingswear (Dartmouth) - For the rambler who is also a railway enthusiast, the Paignton and Dartmouth Railway is a `must'. This most attractive line runs from Paignton to Goodrington, Churston and Kingswear and operates preserved Great Western steam locomotives and rolling-stock. The line passes through some delightful coastal and river scenery, and a trip on the railway could easily be combined with a walk to make a very pleasant day out. It operates from March to December. For details contact - Queens Park Station, Torbay Road, Paignton TQ4 6AF (Tel: 01803 555872).

Bodmin Parkway to Bodmin Town is a service that could prove useful for those requiring bus transport to the coast. (Tel: 01208 73666).

BUS SERVICES

ACCESS TO THE START OF THE PATH:
Access to the start of the path can be made locally and from outside the region, with Southern National's bus service 28 linking Minehead to the Great Western Rail Line at Taunton.

Service 28 Taunton-Minehead currently operates on an hourly frequency up to the early evenings from Monday to Saturdays. On Sundays service 28 operates less frequently. For service 28 timetable enquiries telephone Southern National - Taunton. (Tel: 01823 272033).

National Express operate direct services to Minehead. For more information about national coach services to the South West telephone National Express. (Tel: 0990 808080) (this is charged at local call rates).

BUS INFORMATION:
Listed below, in path order are details of services and information available from County Councils and local bus operators, it is intended for guidance use only. All information provided is correct at time of going to print, responsibility for any inaccuracies or changes cannot be accepted by County Councils or bus operators. For up to date bus service information telephone the relevant numbers given in the following paragraphs.

SOMERSET:
For services from Taunton to Minehead, Lyne Regis and Weymouth, Southern National Ltd, Bus Station, Tower Street, Taunton, TAI 4AF (Tel: 01823 272033).

ATMOS Ltd Transport Services (part of the W S Atkins Group) on behalf of Somerset County Council produce timetable booklets twice a year in May and October. The 5 booklets are based on the District Council areas and are available from Libraries and T.I.C. offices. A countrywide Bus map is also produced annually listing all the bus services in Somerset. Both the booklets and the map are also available from ATMOS Ltd Transport Services, The Crescent, Taunton TA1 4XE, telephone (01823) 358299.

NORTH DEVON:
The North Devon coast has a range of bus services, which may be of use to coastal walkers. The greatest choice of coastal destinations are provided from Barnstaple. The principal services are: 311 Barnstaple to Lynton; 3, 301 & 302 Barnstaple to Ilfracombe; 308 Barnstaple to Georgeham (and Woolacombe in the summer); 1, 2, & 301 Barnstaple to Bideford and Westward Ho!; 2 Barnstaple to Appledore and 3I9 Barnstaple to Bideford, Clovelly, Hartland to Bude 119 - two trips on Tuesdays and Fridays. Note that the number prefix refers to the bus route number. During the summer service 300 operates daily from Barnstaple to Ilfracombe, Lynton and Minehead, with glorious coastal views along much of the route.

From Bideford there are frequent services to the coast. The principal services are 2B Bideford to Appledore; 1 &301 Bideford to Westward Ho! and 3I9 Bideford to Clovelly, Hartland to Bude 119 - two trips on Tuesdays and Fridays.

For those who are not walking the entire path in one go, may find the Western National x 9 service from Exeter to Bude a useful link to or from the coast.

The above services are operated by Red Bus North Devon Ltd., Filers Travel Western National for timetable enquiries telephone Devon County Councils DEVONBUS ENQUIRY LINE - Barnstaple (Tel: 01271 382800) or Exeter (Tel: 01392 382800) or Plymouth (Tel 01752 382800) or Torquay (Tel: 01803 382800), Monday to Friday 0830 - I700hrs.

Devon County Council produce timetable guides summer and winter entitled 'North Devon Public Transport Guide'. They are available from Tourist Information Centres, Libraries, bus operators or by telephoning the DevonBus enquiry line (number given above).

CORNWALL:

Cornwall County Council produce a comprehensive public transport timetable, published annually in June. Available from the Passenger Transport Unit, Cornwall County Council, Camel Building, County Hall, Truro TRI 3AY (Tel: 01872 322142) - price £1.50, with cheques made payable to Cornwall County Council. The timetable can also be obtained locally in Cornwall from Tourist Information Centres, bus stations and libraries, price 75p.

There is no comprehensive county bus enquiry number in Cornwall. Western National bus information is available from Western House, 38 Lemon Street, Truro TR1 2LS. Their enquiry lines are West Cornwall (Tel: 01209 719988), Central Cornwall (Tel: 01208 79898) and East Cornwall (Tel: 01752 222666). Information on other operators can be obtained from the Cornwall County Council's Passenger Transport Unit.

Western National 1 - Penzance to Lands End; Western National 16/17 - Penzance to St Ives; Truronian T1 - Truro to The Lizard/Truro to St Agnes; Western National 88/89 - Truro to Falmouth; Western National 86/87 - Truro to Newquay; Western National 24 - St Austell to Fowey; Western National 26 - St Austell to Mevagissey; Western National 55 - Bodmin Parkway Railway Stn to Bodmin to Wadebridge to Padstow; Western National 124 - Wadebridge to Port Issac; Western National 73 - Liskeard to Looe; Western National 122 - Wadebridge to TIntagel to Bude; Western National X9 Exeter to Bude.

SOUTH DEVON:

The coastline between Plymouth and Exeter is accessible by bus from many inland towns. The principal services are:

80 Plymouth to Torpoint; 81 Plymouth to Cremyll; 7 Plymouth to Mountbatten (and Bovisand in the summer); 49 Plymouth to Heybrook Bay; 48 Plymouth to Wembury; 94 Plymouth to Noss Mayo; 93 Plymouth to Kingsbridge & Dartmouth; X80 Plymouth to Paignton & Torquay; X38 Plymouth to Exeter; 87 Ivybridge to Bigbury on Sea; 164 Totnes to Kingsbridge; 89 Totnes to Dartmouth; 162 Kingsbridge to Hope Cove; 606 Kingsbridge to Salcombe; 200 Kingswear to Torquay; 22 Kingswear to Brixham; 12 Brixham & Paignton to Torquay and Newton Abbot; 85 Torquay to Teignmouth, Dawlish and Exeter; 85A Newton Abbot to Teignmouth, Dawlish and Exeter.

The above services are operated by Western National, Tally Ho! and Stagecoach, for timetable enquiries telephone Devon County Council's **DevonBus enquiry line -** Plymouth (Tel: 01752 382800) or Torquay (Tel: 01803 382800), Barnstaple (Tel: 01271 382800) or Exeter (Tel: 01392 382800), Monday to Friday 0830-1700.

Western National produce timetable guides summer and winter, for the South Devon area. They are available from the Travel Office at Plymouth Bus Station or by telephoning the DevonBus enquiry line.

EAST DEVON:

The East Devon coastline is accessible by bus from Exeter, Ottery St. Mary, Honiton and Axminster. The principal services are:

57 Exeter to Exmouth, Budleigh Salterton and Sidmouth; 52 Exeter to Sidmouth; 382 Ottery St. Mary to Sidmouth; 340 Honiton to Sidmouth; 885 Axminster to Seaton; 31 Taunton to Axminster & Lyme Regis (and continues to Bridport, Dorchester and Weymouth); 899 Sidmouth to Lyme Regis. On Sundays (all year round) service 378 operates along the East Devon coast from Sidmouth to Seaton, Axminster and Lyme Regis (with the first journey commencing from Exeter and the last journey returning to Exeter).

The above services are operated by Stagecoach, Red Bus Services, Axe Valley Mini-Travel and Southern National. For timetable enquiries telephone Devon County Council's **DevonBus enquiry line -** Exeter (Tel: 01392 382800) or Torquay (Tel: 01803 382800) or Plymouth (Tel: 01752 382800) or Barnstaple (Tel: 01271 382800), Monday to Friday 0830-1700.

Devon County Council produce timetable guides summer and winter, entitled `East Devon Public Transport Guide' they are available from Tourist Information Centres, libraries, bus operators or by telephoning the DevonBus enquiry line.

Bus Map - Other useful information provided by Devon County Council includes the public transport map. This depicts all bus routes and railway lines throughout the county and gives a summary of service frequency. It is available from Tourist Information Centres, libraries and bus stations or by telephoning the DevonBus enquiry line.

DORSET:
The Dorset Coast is accessible by bus from various inland points. The principal services are:

Service 31 operates from Lyme Regis to Bridport and continues to Dorchester and Weymouth on Mondays to Saturdays. Please contact Southern National Ltd., 80 The Esplanade, Weymouth DT4 7AA. (Tel: 01035 783645).

Service 1 50 operates from Bournemouth to Swanage via Sandbanks Ferry with Service 142/3/4 operating from Poole to Swanage via Wareham and Corfe Castle. Both services run Monday - Saturday and Sundays. Please contact Wilts & Dorset Ltd, Travel Office, Bus Station, Poole BH15 1SN. (Tel: 01202 673555).

Dorset County Council annually produce a series of local public transport guides listing bus services and companies by area A county-wide Bus and Rail Map listing all services in rural Dorset with frequency guide is also produced These are available from Tourist Information Centres or The Passenger Transport Group Dorset County Council County Hall Dorchester DT1 1XJ. (Tel: 01305 225165)

SEA TRANSPORT AND COASTAL CRUISES

The famous pleasure steamers Waverley and Balmoral provide both cruises and transport, to - and from - the Exmoor Coast.

From May until late September these big, and fast, sea-going ships provide transport between South Wales, Bristol, North Somerset, and the Exmoor Coast.

Sailings are to - and from - Ilfracombe, Lynmouth & Minehead. The timetable is subject to the Bristol Channel tides which have the second highest rise and fall in the world. Free copies of the full programme are available from Waverley Excursions Ltd., Gwalia Buildings, Barry Docks, CF62 SQR - telephone 01446 720656, or from Tourist Information Centres in West Somerset and North Devon.

USEFUL ADDRESSES

Countryside Commission, South West Region, Bridge House, Sion Place, Bristol, BS8 4AS. (Tel: 0117 973 9996).
Country Wide Holidays Association, Grove House, Wilmslow Rd, Didsbury, Manchester M20 2DR. (Tel: 0161 448 29930).
Exmoor National Park Authority, Exmoor House, Dulverton, Somerset TA22 9H1 (Tel: 01398 23665).
HF Holidays Ltd, Imperial House, Edgware Road, Colindale, London NW9 5AL (Tel: 0181 905 9556).
Ramblers' Association, 1/5 Wandsworth Road, London SW8 2XX (Tel: 0171 582 6878).
South East Cornwall Discovery Centre, Millpool, West Looe, PL13 2AF (Tel: 0l503 262777).

COUNTY COUNCILS

Somerset County Council, County Hall, Taunton, TA1 4DY (Tel: 01823 51227).
Devon County Council, County Hall, Exeter, EX2 4QW (Tel: 01392 382000).
Cornwall County Council, County Hall, Truro, TR1 3BE (Tel: 01872 322000).
Dorset County Council, County Hall, Dorchester, DT1 1XJ (Tel: 01305 251000).

Addresses of Ramblers' Association contacts in the West Country

All path obstructions or other problems not on the Coast Path itself should be addressed to the relevant County address.

Devon - Mrs E. M. Linfoot, 14 Bladen Cottages, Blackborough, Cullompton, EX15 2HJ.
Cornwall - Mrs S. Oliver, Trenoweth, Viaduct Hill, Hayle TR27 5HT.
Dorset- Mr B. Panton, 5 Nicholas Gardens, Ensbury Park, Bournemouth, BH1O 4BA.
Somerset - Mr S. Barnard, 11 Gordons Close, Taunton, TA1 3DA.

MAPS

1:50,000 Map. Ordnance Survey

The Metric 1:50,000 Landranger Series needed to cover the coast from Minehead in Somerset to Studiland in Dorset are as follows, working round the coast from Minehead.

181	Minehead & Brendon Hills	200	Newquay & Bodmin
180	Barnstaple & ilfracombe	201	Plymouth & Launceston
190	Bude & Clovelly	202	Torbay & South Dartmoor
200	Newquay & Bodmin	192	Exeter & Sidmouth
204	Truro & Falmouth	193	Taunton & Lyme Regis
203	Land's End & The Lizard	194	Dorchester & Weymouth
204	Truro & Falmouth	195	Bournemouth & Purbeck

The two tourist 1" maps of Dartmoor and Exmoor available are of no advantage except that Exmoor could be used instead of Map 181 and nearly all 180.

1:25,000 Maps. Ordnance Survey

In path order, from Minehead the coast path on $2\frac{1}{2}$" maps.

Outdoor Leisure 9	- Exmoor
Explorer 139	- Bideford, Ilfracombe and Barnstaple
Explorer 126	- Clovelly, Hartland and Bideford
Explorer 111	- Bude, Boscastle and Tintagel
Explorer 9 (109 on reprint)	- Bodmin Moor (depicts coast path from Boscastle to Portgaverne)
Explorer 106	- Newquay, Padstow, Wadebridge and Port Isaac
Explorer 104	- Redruth, St Agnes, Camborne and Perranporth
Explorer 7 (102 on reprint)	- Land's End, Penzance, St Ives
Explorer 8 (103 on reprint)	- The Lizard
Explorer 105	- Falmouth and Mevagissey
Explorer 107	- St Austell, Fowey and Looe
Explorer 108	- Looe, Rame Head
Outdoor Leisure 20	- Plymouth and South Devon
Explorer 31(110 on reprint)	- Torquay and Dawlish
Explorer 30 (115 on reprint)	- Exmouth and Sidmouth
Explorer 29(116 on reprint)	- Lyme Regis and Bridport
Outdoor Leisure 15	- Purbeck and South Dorset

Alto Explorer Series

Penwith-Land's End - Map Guide - £3.75. The Coast Path from St Ives to Penzance. Clear, large scale and all paths clearly marked. Available from membership secretary.

TAXIS

Coast Path walking can be arduous in places but some of the hard work can be eliminated. We have been informed that the use of local taxis can ease the muscles. Transport is not for the walker, naturally, but for rucksack transfer from B&B to B&B. Local taxi firms will be pleased to give a price for the service. Consult yellow pages or ask the locals for details of taxi operators.

NATIONAL TAXI HOTLINE

Many taxi operators subscribe to the "National Taxi Hotline" which works on a Freephone number - 0800 654321. When you dial that number your call will be automatically routed through to the subscribing taxi operator nearest to your location and you have your taxi.

We think it a grand scheme. It is free so no worries about having the appropriate coins when you are tired, wet through and fed up.

BANKS

We suggest you contact your own bank for a list of where their branches along the trail are located. Probably a Girobank account would prove to be the most convenient as there are small Post Offices in most villages.

TELEPHONES

We urge you to consider buying BT Phonecards or chargecards for use in the larger towns. Life is easier when you do not have to seek change for a call box.

DOGS

We have identified about 35 instances where the official coast path makes use of beaches for lengths varying from a few yards to about three miles. Walkers should be aware that the County Councils enforce dog bans on some beaches from late Spring to early Autumn. Whenever walkers with dogs approach any beach which is used as the official route they should look out for official notices and observe the requirements.

Dog owners should exercise strict supervision over their pets along some sections of the coast path. There are places that can be dangerous for boisterous uncontrolled dogs.

RIVER CROSSINGS

The walker tends to view that feet are the only certain method of progress - and why not? Unfortunately, the absolute purist would need to be an olympic-class swimmer not to have to use ferries on the South West Way. However, a certain amount of scepticism is helpful, absolute reliance on ferries is not advised.

There are other ferries available on the Path which walkers may wish to use for diversions or shortcuts. We have attempted to list those directly necessary.

Tide Tables

The tide tables included in this edition refer to the times of low water at Devonport. These tables will act as a guide for those wishing to wade across the Gannel (Newquay), Gillian Creek, and the Erme and Avon (Bigbury on Sea). Please be sure to read the warnings given under each section. We have been criticised for being too cautious over the times we suggest for wading the rivers, and know that some walkers cross at other times. We believe our attitude is correct as there are certainly dangers', but you may wish to try at low tide on other occasions to see if conditions will permit a safe crossing. Variations in barometric pressure can affect tide levels. Remember there are different levels daily of low water, if in doubt seek local knowledge.

Newquay (The Gannel)	Deduct 30 minutes	Gillan Harbour	Deduct 15 minutes
R. Erme	As at Devonport	Bigbury/Bantham (R.Avon)	As at Devonport

*The following Tide Tables are Crown Copyright. Produced from Admiralty Tide Tables with the permission of the Controller of Her Majesty's Stationery Office.

MARCH 1998
From 29th add 1 hour for BST

Days	Low Time a.m.	Low Time p.m.
1 Su	0134	1357
2 Mo	0214	1437
3 Tu	0252	1515
4 We	0330	1553
5 Th	0414	1638
6 Fri	0506	1737
7 Sa	0622	1914
8 Su	0816	2054
9 Mo	0930	2154
10 Tu	1022	2242
11 We	1106	2324
12 Th	1147	-
13 Fr	0002	1223
14 Sa	0037	1256
15 Su	0107	1324
16 Mo	0132	1348
17 Tu	0155	1409
18 We	0217	1430
19 Th	0241	1455
20 Fr	0312	1530
21 Sa	0357	1624
22 Su	0514	1808
23 Mo	0703	1941
24 Tu	0821	2054
25 We	0929	2157
26 Th	1028	2253
27 Fr	1120	2344
28 Sa	1209	-
29 Su	0030	1254
30 Mo	0114	1338
31 Tu	0155	1417

APRIL 1998
Add 1 hour for BST

Days	Low Time a.m.	Low Time p.m.
1 We	0234	1455
2 Th	0313	1533
3 Fr	0354	1617
4 Sa	0445	1711
5 Su	0554	1834
6 Mo	0743	2021
7 Tu	0902	2126
8 We	0954	2214
9 Th	1038	2256
10 Fr	1117	2334
11 Sa	1154	-
12 Su	0008	1226
13 Mo	0039	1253
14 Tu	0104	1318
15 We	0129	1343
16 Th	0155	1409
17 Fr	0221	1437
18 Sa	0255	1513
19 Su	0340	1607
20 Mo	0453	1735
21 Tu	0633	1911
22 We	0753	2027
23 Th	0902	2132
24 Fr	1003	2229
25 Sa	1056	2321
26 Su	1147	-
27 Mo	0009	1233
28 Tu	0054	1317
29 We	0136	1357
30 Th	0217	1437

MAY 1998
Add 1 hour for BST

Days	Low Time a.m.	Low Time p.m.
1 Fr	0258	1516
2 Sa	0339	1558
3 Su	0426	1649
4 Mo	0527	1756
5 Tu	0649	1922
6 We	0813	2040
7 Th	0912	2133
8 Fr	1000	2218
9 Sa	1039	2257
10 Su	1117	2334
11 Mo	1151	-
12 Tu	0006	1222
13 We	0037	1253
14 Th	0108	1322
15 Fr	0139	1353
16 Sa	0211	1428
17 Su	0249	1509
18 Mo	0337	1603
19 Tu	0442	1716
20 We	0605	1839
21 Th	0724	1956
22 Fr	0834	2105
23 Sa	0936	2204
24 Su	1032	2259
25 Mo	1124	2348
26 Tu	1212	-
27 We	0034	1257
28 Th	0119	1341
29 Fr	0202	1421
30 Sa	0242	1501
31 Sun	0323	1541

JUNE 1998
Add 1 hour for BST

Days	Low Time a.m.	Low Time p.m.	Days	Low Time a.m.	Low Time p.m.
1 Mo	0407	1625	16 Tu	0334	1557
2 Tu	0456	1717	17 We	0429	1656
3 We	0555	1820	18 Th	0535	1806
4 Th	0703	1929	19 Fr	0650	1924
5 Fr	0809	2034	20 Sa	0803	2037
6 Sa	0905	2129	21 Su	0911	2141
7 Su	0953	2215	22 Mo	1011	2239
8 Mo	1035	2257	23 Tu	1104	2331
9 Tu	1116	2337	24 We	1155	-
10 We	1154	-	25 Th	0019	1241
11 Th	0013	1230	26 Fr	0105	1325
12 Fr	0051	1308	27 Sa	0148	1404
13 Sa	0129	1346	28 Su	0227	1442
14 Su	0207	1424	29 Mo	0305	1519
15 Mo	0248	1508	30 Tu	0341	1554

JULY 1998
Add 1 hour for BST

Days	Low Time a.m.	Low Time p.m.	Days	Low Time a.m.	Low Time p.m.
1 We	0419	1635	16 Th	0412	1634
2 Th	0504	1726	17 Fr	0507	1734
3 Fr	0601	1827	18 Sa	0615	1850
4 Sa	0704	1932	19 Su	0735	2011
5 Su	0806	2035	20 Mo	0851	2125
6 Mo	0904	2132	21 Tu	0956	2225
7 Tu	0956	2222	22 We	1050	2319
8 We	1043	2309	23 Th	1141	-
9 Th	1128	2354	24 Fr	0006	1226
10 Fr	1213	-	25 Sa	0050	1308
11 Sa	0037	1257	26 Su	0131	1346
12 Su	0121	1338	27 Mo	0207	1420
13 Mo	0202	1420	28 Tu	0240	1451
14 Tu	0244	1501	29 We	0309	1519
15 We	0326	1544	30 Th	0337	1549
			31 Fr	0410	1625

AUGUST 1998
Add 1 hour for BST

Days	Low Time a.m.	Low Time p.m.
1 Sa	0455	1724
2 Su	0604	1840
3 Mo	0717	1952
4 Tu	0823	2055
5 We	0923	2153
6 Th	1018	2246
7 Fri	1109	2335
8 Sa	1156	-
9 Su	0023	1243
10 Mo	0108	1326
11 Tu	0150	1407
12 We	0231	1448
13 Th	0311	1527
14 Fr	0351	1611
15 Sa	0439	1706
16 Su	0540	1818
17 Mo	0707	1955
18 Tu	0837	2115
19 We	0944	2214
20 Th	1039	2304
21 Fr	1126	2349
22 Sa	1208	-
23 Su	0030	1247
24 Mo	0108	1322
25 Tu	0141	1353
26 We	0209	1420
27 Th	0234	1442
28 Fr	0255	1502
29 Sa	0315	1529
30 Su	0346	1611
31 Mo	0441	1741

SEPTEMBER 1998
Add 1 hour for BST

Days	Low Time a.m.	Low Time p.m.
1 Tu	0630	1914
2 We	0749	2026
3 Th	0856	2127
4 Fr	0956	2224
5 Sa	1049	2316
6 Su	1138	-
7 Mo	0004	1225
8 Tu	0050	1310
9 We	0132	1350
10 Th	0213	1430
11 Fr	0251	1509
12 Sa	0330	1551
13 Su	0414	1642
14 Mo	0511	1754
15 Tu	0644	1943
16 We	0826	2104
17 Th	0930	2200
18 Fr	1021	2246
19 Sa	1104	2327
20 Su	1145	-
21 Mo	0006	1222
22 Tu	0041	1256
23 We	0111	1324
24 Th	0136	1348
25 Fr	0157	1407
26 Sa	0217	1427
27 Su	0238	1454
28 Mo	0308	1532
29 Tu	0353	1636
30 We	0533	1839

OCTOBER 1998
Until 24th add 1 hour for BST

Days	Low Time a.m.	Low Time p.m.
1 Th	0717	1957
2 Fr	0830	2104
3 Sa	0932	2201
4 Su	1026	2253
5 Mo	1117	2341
6 Tu	1204	-
7 We	0027	1249
8 Th	0111	1332
9 Fr	0152	1411
10 Sa	0231	1452
11 Su	0311	1534
12 Mo	0354	1624
13 Tu	0449	1734
14 We	0616	1921
15 Th	0800	2041
16 Fr	0906	2134
17 Sa	0956	2219
18 Su	1038	2300
19 Mo	1117	2337
20 Tu	1154	-
21 We	0011	1225
22 Th	0039	1253
23 Fr	0104	1318
24 Sa	0126	1341
25 Su	0150	1404
26 Mo	0216	1433
27 Tu	0247	1512
28 We	0332	1612
29 Th	0448	1759
30 Fr	0640	1925
31 Sa	0759	2034

NOVEMBER 1998

Days	Low Time a.m.	Low Time p.m.	Days	Low Time a.m.	Low Time p.m.
1 Su	0905	2134	16 Mo	1004	2226
2 Mo	1001	2228	17 Tu	1045	2303
3 Tu	1053	2319	18 We	1121	2337
4 We	1142	-	19 Th	1155	-
5 Th	0005	1229	20 Fr	0008	1225
6 Fr	0050	1312	21 Sa	0036	1254
7 Sa	0134	1356	22 Su	0104	1322
8 Su	0214	1438	23 Mo	0134	1353
9 Mo	0255	1520	24 Tu	0204	1427
10 Tu	0339	1610	25 We	0240	1508
11 We	0429	1709	26 Th	0325	1603
12 Th	0583	1833	27 Fr	0429	1721
13 Fr	0710	1957	28 Sa	0558	1847
14 Sa	0826	2058	29 Su	0722	2002
15 Su	0919	2144	30 Mo	0834	2106

DECEMBER 1998

Days	Low Time a.m.	Low Time p.m.	Days	Low Time a.m.	Low Time p.m.
1 Tu	0936	2204	16 We	1007	2225
2 We	1031	2256	17 Th	1048	2303
3 Th	1123	2345	18 Fr	1126	2340
4 Fr	1211	-	19 Sa	1202	-
5 Sa	0033	1257	20 Su	0015	1237
6 Su	0118	1342	21 Mo	0049	1311
7 Mo	0200	1426	22 Tu	0124	1348
8 Tu	0241	1508	23 We	0200	1424
9 We	0323	1550	24 Th	0238	1505
10 Th	0405	1638	25 Fr	0320	1551
11 Fr	0456	1734	26 Sa	0412	1650
12 Sa	0559	1843	27 Su	0519	1802
13 Su	0714	1956	28 Mo	0637	1922
14 Mo	0824	2055	29 Tu	0759	2037
15 Tu	0920	2144	30 We	0911	2141
			31 Th	1012	2239

SUGGESTED ITINERARY

For some the fun of planning their own itinerary is a major part of the enjoyment of their holiday. If you are one of these DO NOT READ THIS SECTION.

On the other hand there are some who have been put off tackling our path because they just could not see how to pack over 600 miles walking into a normal holiday. The answer is, of course, you cannot! Offa's Dyke or the Coast to Coast Walk, to take just a couple of examples, work out well in a fortnight. Other paths such as The South Downs or The Ridgeway conveniently occupy a week.

Our Path, we reckon, needs about seven weeks to accomplish. That being so, we have tried to divide it up sensibly into seven roughly equal sections. Obviously, if we are going to suggest weekly stages, the beginning and end of each one must have reasonable accommodation and public transport. That presents a problem in itself; so after some thought we have broken it down into six 7-day and one 6-day week. As usual, we would be very glad to hear from anyone who has tried one of our weeks and to hear their comments on it.

If you are a seasoned walker then there is a lot to be said for walking the whole path albeit at different times in our usual anticlockwise order. However, if you are not experienced, then obviously we should point out that the South Cornwall week, the fourth one in our schedule, is much the easiest if you want to start with something less demanding.

To keep the weeks set out below in a simple format the information is only an outline. IT IS ESSENTIAL TO CONSULT THE DETAIL IN THE REST OF THE GUIDE TO EFFECTIVELY PLAN YOUR HOLIDAY. Mileages can vary depending on where you actually stay. Furthermore, our mileages are only approximate because they are all "rounded".

After some of the place names we have added 'River Crossing'. You are advised to consult the appropriate section in this book for ferry and low tide suggestions.

Kilometres	Miles	Week 1 (Seven days)
		MINEHEAD Rail Services to Taunton & S. National to Minehead Direct Nat. Express coach services.
14	9	PORLOCK or PORLOCKWEIR
21	13	LYNMOUTH/LYNTON
21	13	COMBE MARTIN
21	13	WOOLACOMBE
28	17	BRAUNTON
18	11	INSTOW (River Crossing)
16	10	WESTWARD HO! Filers/Red Bus to Barnstaple & Rail services to Exeter. Direct Nat. Express coach services.
139	86	

Kilometres	Miles	Week 2 (Seven days)
		WESTWARD HO! Rail services to Barnstaple & Filers/Red Bus to Westward Ho! Direct Nat. Express coach services
18	11	CLOVELLY
16	10	HARTLAND QUAY
22	14	BUDE
27	16	BOSCASTLE
21	13	PORT ISAAC
27	17	TREVONE
27	17	NEWQUAY Rail services to Par (the Great Western main line) Direct Nat. Express coach services
158	98	

Kilometres	Miles	Week 3 (Six days)
		NEWQUAY Rail services to Newquay (from Par) Direct Nat. Express coach services (River Crossing)
18	11	PERRANPORTH
20	13	PORTREATH

28	17	ST IVES
21	13	PENDEEN WATCH
24	15	PORTHCURNO
18	11	PENZANCE Rail services (Great Western main line)
		Direct Nat. Express coach services
129	80	

Week 4 (Seven days)

		PENZANCE Rail services to Penzance
		Direct Nat. Express coach services
21	13	PORTHLEVEN
22	13	THE LIZARD
18	11	COVERACK
20	13	HELFORD (River Crossing)
16	10	FALMOUTH (River Crossing)
20	13	PORTLOE
19	12	MEVAGISSEY W. National to St. Austell & Rail services from St Austell (Great Western main line)
136	85	

Week 5 (Seven days)

		MEVAGISSEY Rail services to St. Austell & W. National to Mevagissey
18	11	PAR
21	13	POLPERRO
21	13	PORTWRINKLE
21	13	PLYMOUTH (Cremyll Ferry)
22	14	WEMBURY POINT (River Crossing)
22	14	BIGBURY ON SEA (River Crossing)
21	13	SALCOMBE Tally Ho! to Kingsbridge & W. National to Totnes & Rail services from Totnes (Great Western main line)
146	91	

Week 6 (Seven days)

		SALCOMBE Rail services to Totnes & W. National to Kingsbridge & Tally Ho! to Salcombe
20	13	TORCROSS
16	10	DARTMOUTH (River Crossing)
18	11	BRIXHAM
18	11	BABBACOMBE
24	15	DAWLISH WARREN (River Crossing)
19	12	EXMOUTH (via Starcross/Exmouth Ferry)
21	13	SIDMOUTH Stagecoach to Exeter & Rail services from Exeter (Great Western main line and Waterloo line)
136	85	

Week 7 (Seven days)

		SIDMOUTH Rail services to Exeter & Stagecoach to Sidmouth
15	9	SEATON
23	14	SEATOWN (Dorset)
19	12	ABBOTSBURY
23	14	WEYMOUTH (River Crossing)
19	12	LULWORTH
21	13	WORTH MATRAVERS*
23	14	SOUTH HAVEN POINT Ferry-Sandbanks, Wilts & Dorset to Poole or Bournemouth & Rail services Nat. Express coach services from Bournemouth to London.
143	88	

* See pages 77 & 78 for opening times of Army Ranges and alternative routes.

THE SOUTH WEST COAST PATH

General

This is a series of notes on the state of the path which we hope will help you in your walking. Obviously it is very difficult to keep something as extensive as this both up-to-date and concise. Suggestions for improvement or amendments will always be welcome. We can only keep you right up-to-date with the state of the path if YOU will keep us posted about conditions as you find them on any stretch of the path. Your fellow members will be grateful, and so will we.

If you have any complaints about ordinary maintenance or signposting on the path, please write either to the Exmoor National Park Authority or the relevant County Council, Devon, Cornwall or Dorset. They should see this is done, and what is generally not realised is that any work carried out is 75% Grant aided from Central Government for official National Trails such as the South West Coast Path. If you have any major problems or difficulties we would always be glad to be advised as well.

Each section has a reference to the Ordnance Survey map relevant to it. Outdoor leisure (OS OL) and Explorer (OS E).

Towns and villages are now marked T or V respectively but the places at the end of each section appear as the first entry in the next one. We obviously stick our necks out to try and classify towns and villages. To us a town should have a reasonable range of shops, maybe even something as exotic as a laundrette. Villages should at least have a pub and a village store open all the year round, and a bus service. There are, of course, numerous other places you can get refreshment in season, but precious few out of it. Please note that all sections end at reasonable access points, usually having parking facilities.

Places which can be reached by rail are marked.

Distances: Explanatory Notes

The distances shown are in four columns:

The first column is the distance of the section to the nearest kilometre.
The second column is the cumulative distance in kilometres.
The third column is the distance of the section to the nearest mile.
The fourth column is the cumulative distance in miles.

We aimed to keep the actual distances in a simple form and not pretend to a degree of accuracy that is not inherent in them. To this end we have rounded every section to the nearest kilometre or nearest mile and we have done the same to the cumulative distances.

Members will notice that our estimate of the total mileage of the route has shot up from 570 to 613 miles. We have always said it was longer than any of the authorities' ideas. With the advent of National Trail Guides, the Ordnance Survey have now made an official distance estimate - 594 miles. We have examined this figure closely. They do not include the City of Plymouth or Topsham Ferry to Exmouth. These have to be walked if one intends to cover the whole official route. Bearing in mind the whole path we feel 613 miles is nearer to the total than their 594.

The distances are of course, always marked along the Official Path, however bad a route it may be, unless we tell you to the contrary at the beginning of the section in the Footpath Guide.

Grading

Each section is graded as Easy, Moderate, Strenuous or Severe. Please note we no longer take into consideration lack of escape routes, distances from public transport, etc. It is purely a question of physical difficulty. We will try to highlight in the sections other considerations when they apply.

We would like to underline one point; the whole of our path is certainly not easy. Some parts of it are but other parts are not. We have had a number of letters from people who have walked The Pennine Way and who have been literally amazed at the severity of some of our tougher sections. Perhaps as a further comment we may add that recently we walked two 6 mile adjacent sections. The time taken for one was 50% more than the time taken for the other. This may give additional emphasis to the importance of studying terrain if you wish to compute time.

THE OTHER WAY ROUND-POOLE TO MINEHEAD

In this book the description of the South West Coast Path from Minehead-Land's End-Poole. The Association has written a description of the Trail for those walking the other way. It deals only with the path so this annual guide will be necessary for all the other information. The 'other way round' supplement is available from the membership secretary or secretary at £3.50 including postage.

THE TRAIL DESCRIPTION - Minehead to Poole
FOLLOW THE NATIONAL TRAIL WAYMARK (THE ACORN SYMBOL)

This guide book describes the 'official' route of the South West Coast Path. Where you find we have very little to say about the path we consider that it is extremely unlikely that the walker runs the risk of going off route.

Now and again we suggest 'alternative' paths away from the official route. Invariably these are for better views and a much more enjoyable experience. Also these choices can mean a reduction of a less attractive section.

In either case you will find that our alternatives take the line of Rights of Way. This Association recommends that walkers should NOT wander off from established paths. YOU CAN FALL A LONG WAY IF YOU DO.

FOOTNOTES

In certain sections we have added footnotes commenting on nine books where you may be led astray. These are as follows:

'BMG' - John Mason's Bartholomew Map and Guide Books.
'CP' - Martin Collins' two South West Way books by Cicerone Press.
'NTG' - Four National Trail Guides - published by Aurum Press in association with the Countryside Commission and the Ordnance Survey.
'AFG' - Aerofilms Guide,

1	Minehead to Porlock Weir			OS OL9 (T) Minehead

Grading: Official Route - Moderate	Distance -	14	14	9	9
Alternative - Strenuous					

See also our Minehead to Lynmouth Path Description.

The official path does not start where you would expect it to at the western end of the sea front road. Look for an inconspicuous opening between two cottages on the sea front a little to the east of the harbour.

Keen photographers please note the splendid official signs have unfortunately not been put at the start of the path. There is one on the opposite side of the road on the promenade about 100 yards after you have started. Nonetheless, if you want your picture by a sign you had better get it here. Despite their promises the Countryside Commission have still not provided one at the other end at Poole Harbour, so do not postpone your photo 'til you get there - it would be a long way to go to be disappointed. There is no need to tell us that the wrong mileage is shown. We know and we have told them about it often enough.

The official route, although a good moorland walk, does not follow the traditional coastal route. Strong walkers, looking for something better, can start at the westerly end of the sea front road, proceed via Greenaleigh Farm to Burgundy Chapel and then make a steep ascent up North Hill. An easier alternative to this first piece is at Greenaleigh Farm, immediately before the house and the signpost 'To Burgundy Chapel and Beach' to fork left and then turn back, sign post 'North Hill'. This path zig-zags back to pick up the official route so avoiding the steep climb after Burgundy Chapel.

When taking the steep ascent from Burgundy Chapel at the T junction go left, the path to the right goes only to a view point, and at the next junction go forward.

When you have gained the summit of North Hill, there is a sign, with the acorn, pointing to Selworthy and Bossington. Follow the line of this until you come to the next coast path sign, where there is a right fork marked 'Rugged Cliff Top Path'. Ordinary walkers should proceed forward on the official route but the more adventurous can fork right and proceed walking seaward by what is a well defined path.

The 'Rugged Cliff Top Path' is a splendid alternative to the official path with good views to seaward and is well marked and warning signs 'No Dogs'. At the stile take the left fork and soon follow the rough track down by a boggy stream to the bottom of Grexy Com be at 937 481. From here take the well-defined diagonal path leading up the hill to the wall which is the National Trust boundary. This wall can be followed towards the sea at first and then along parallel to the sea all the way to Western Brockholes. After Western Brockholes the path swings inland but is well signposted and rejoins the official path behind Hurlstone Point.

Those who have taken the official route, when reaching Bossington Hill should take the definitive Right of Way which goes around Hurlstone Point rather than the signposted official route. This is much more spectacular and, apart from gale force conditions, is not at all unsafe despite warning signs. If you stay on the official path take care to descend the path to the left of Hurlstone Point and do not be tempted to take the more obvious path to the left (no signpost) contouring round Bossington Hill.

The official path goes inland from Hurlstone Point via Bossington and then out to the sea again. However, because of high storms the pebble ridge has been pushed back over the path and at high water it is flooded, and at low water you will have to wade across part of the ridge. You should take the alternative path that has been signposted to Porlock from the road to Bossington Beach, missing the pebble ridge.

2 | Porlock Weir to Lynmouth   OS OL9

Grading: Moderate   Distance -   21   35   13   22

See also our Minehead to Lynmouth Path Description

The path leaves Porlock Weir in front of the Anchor Hotel, turn left at sign marked Culbone.

This path is well marked. At Culbone turn right if you want to visit the small church. There is also a refreshment hut where you help yourself and leave your payment. From the church retrace your steps up the path and turn right on to the coast path, in about 300 yds turn right in to Culbone and Embelle Woods and on into Yenworthy Woods. This section of the path was reopened in 1995. It is well marked.

There has been another landslip beyond Culbone and you could be diverted up a long climb to Silcombe Farm.

The Exmoor National Park authority are waiting for a geological report before deciding what to do with this section of the trail.

When you get to Yenworthy Combe there is a sign to the Pinetum. The official route goes left to Sisters' Fountain. We suggest you take the path to the Pinetum and Glenthorne. At the sign to the beach, unless you want to go to the beach, turn left. At the next turning - right, then left above Glenthorne House, you pass a turreted building on your left which once served as a garage and come to an unusual arch on a hairpin bend. There is a lion on top of the arch and birds on top of the turrets.

There is an arrow forward to the coast path and sign on the actual signpost says Wingate Combe. Go through this arch and follow the zig-zag path up till you come to another path crossing at an angle where you turn right and you are now back on the official path.

At Caddow Combe, the official route is again signposted inland 'Countisbury 11/2 miles'. The sure-footed might prefer the Right of Way signposted 'Lighthouse' which proceeds out to the Foreland Point Lighthouse. Just before the entrance to the lighthouse where the wall commences on the right, the path takes off up the bank to the left. The beginning is clearly marked because the authorities tell you they no longer maintain the path. This path is more exposed than the official route and careful walking is advised. It has magnificent views if you are surefooted and the weather is calm.

The National Trust have a good path which can be taken down the seaward side of the main A39 coastal road so avoiding the upper reaches of Countisbury Hill. Lower down the hill the path joins the road but a new path on the seaward side ensures that you will not get run down.

You come out on the foreshore. Walk along into Lynmouth crossing the footbridge, there turn right down to the seafront turning left up the steps before the cliff railway, that is assuming you are a purist and are not actually going to use the railway which you can well do if you wish! If you use the railway you do suffer slightly at the top in that you will have to walk nearly into Lynton and then out again to regain the North Walk. After all, it serves you right for not having walked the whole way!

3 | Lynmouth to Combe Martin   OS OL9 (T) Lynton/Lynmouth

Grading: Strenuous   Distance -   21   56   13   35

See also our Lynmouth to Ilfracombe. Path Description.

Please note there is a long, lonely section onward from Heddon's Mouth to Combe Martin without any chance of refreshment.

The path itself out from Lynton is a Victorian idea for a coastal footpath called the North Walk and although to our modern ideas tarmac might not be the ideal footpath medium, it is a very fine high level walk indeed. This takes you very happily out to Castle Rock. Unfortunately, the official route is then on road all the way through to Woody Bay. However, there are diversions which will save you some road walking. The first takes off to the right after the turning circle (roundabout) at the end of the Valley of Rocks and then goes in a loop back, to come out by the Lodge at the beginning of Lee Abbey.

The second alternative is a left turn immediately opposite Lee Abbey which is labelled 'Woodland Walk' (each end) and rejoins the road about three quarters of a mile further along.

This is one of the finest pieces of coastal path in North Devon and should not be missed by anyone who is reasonably sure-footed, or unless weather conditions are very bad. The path takes off just before the Woody Bay Hotel opposite the Red House and the beginning of the path is marked by a signpost on the right which says 'Public Footpath to Woody Bay Beach $^3/_4$ mile'. This path comes out on another road where you turn up left. There will be another sign 'Footpath Hunters' Inn $2^1/_4$ miles'. You will cross a stile with a sign 'Heddon Valley Hunters' Inn'. This is a superb path which is now the new official route. It is much nearer the coast giving splendid views. This path later descends to the floor of the valley and you should turn left along the river, signposted 'Hunters' Inn $^1/_2$ mile', until you get to the lower of the two footbridges. Then you cross the river, and soon turn left, walk $^1/_4$ mile upstream to a gate. Turn sharp right and take a zig-zag path half way up to where there is a wooden bar across the path. Here you turn right towards the sea and wonderful views at Peter Rock. (In strong winds you could step over that wooden bar, continue up the zig-zag then turn seaward at the top). From Peter Rock the route takes a seaward path to East Cleave. Walkers who have been this way before will certainly appreciate the improvement in the official route from Woody Bay Hotel to East Cleave. It was always our recommended alternative route. Needless to say, whilst in the valley of Heddon's Mouth, those requiring refreshment have easy access to the Hunter's Inn and the National Trust shop selling very good ice cream.

Just west of East Cleave you will regain the old official route passing along High Cliff and North Cleave. Another of our recommendations has now been implemented. At map reference 628 482 take the short walk across open heathland to avoid the walk up to the old Trentishoe Down Road.

As there are many sheep tracks by Sherrycombe we suggest you follow the grass track along the top of the combe to the inland end of it to pick up the path down.

When ascending Great Hangman from Sherrycombe you reach a seat. Keep alongside the wall on your left. There are a number of well-walked paths going out to the right but they are all wrong! From Great Hangman the path is clear to Little Hangman where more stunning views are available.

When you come to the shelter above Combe Martin, turn right on the unmarked path. This has the better views.

C.P. - The official route no longer goes to Hunters Inn and Trentishoe. See fourth paragraph above.

4 | Combe Martin to Ilfracombe Harbour   OS OL9 (T) Combe Martin

Grading: Moderate	Distance-	9	65	5	40

See Also our Lynmouth to Ilfracombe Path Description.

The path leaves the Kiln car park up Seaside Hill Road above the beach. Turn right onto a narrow tarmac lane, which climbs steeply to rejoin the main A399 road.

Walk on the slightly raised path along the road side, through two gates, then along a path at the top of the fields, to a flight of wooden steps.

Turn left at the top onto a slip road to join the new section of the A399. Walk along the side of the road on a path, up hill for about 250 yards, turn right just past a bus shelter. Then down hill on a road to cross over the now disused section of the A399, into a lane by the side of the Sandy Cove Hotel. This lane becomes a tree lined track until you can see a high stile on the right. Climb this and you are onto open fields with a sight of the sea again. Watermouth Castle, built 1825, comes into view. At Watermouth it is possible to cross the foreshore at low tide to a flight of steps. Take care the rocks can be slippery. This is not possible at high tide when one has to continue along the road with no pavement for approximately 200 yards and there is then a stile off right into the woods. Take care whilst walking this road section.

The next section of the path is very pleasant on the western side of Watermouth and now happily continues out and around Widmouth Head. This new section provides some very spectacular walking; we particularly commend the view back from Widmouth Head over Watermouth, whatever the state of the tide or sea. This will be your last good viewpoint of the dramatic setting of the Great Hangman and the Little Hangman eastwards above Combe Martin. After Widmouth Head the path continues in front of the coastguard cottages going to Rillage Point.

This fine section ends with a road walk down into Hele. Turn right and look out for some steps on the far left of the beach. The path then zig-zags passing Beacon point with a fine view of Ilfracombe until it reaches the top of Hillsborough. There are several paths to choose from here but they all end up in Ilfracombe.

5 | Ilfracombe to Lee   OS E139 (T) Ilfracombe

Grading: Easy	Distance-	5	70	3	43

See also our Ilfracombe to Croyde Bay Path Description.

Walk along the edge of the harbour, bear left at the slip and then right into Broad Street. At a T-junction! turn left into Capstone Road next to the Sandpiper Inn. After about 1 50m (170 yards), turn right and walk around Capstone Point. The route through the town is well waymarked with blue coloured Devon County Council signs.

Follow the coast around Wilders Mouth beach, along the promenade, in front of a parking area. Turn inland, then climb steeply behind some gardens above the Museum. You are now in Granville Road. Pass through a gate, turn right, walk along this cliff road, before bearing right onto an unmetalled road that takes you to the Torrs Walk. It is well waymarked. The National Trust have made a further small loop of coastal path just beyond the Tors whereas the official path is signposted inland and over the top of the hill.

We suggest you now take the National Trust path round Flat Point and not the official route along the old coach road. You will however have to come back up the cliff slope to rejoin the official path, to pass through a field gate This gate takes you onto a narrow rather pleasant road down into Lee.

Refreshments are available all year round at the Grampus Inn in Lee village, which is only a minor diversion from the coast.

6 | Lee Bay to Woolacombe   OS E139 (V) Lee Bay

Grading: Moderate   Distance -   7   77   5   48

See also our Ilfracombe to Croyde Bay Path Description.

This section will take you longer to walk than you think as it includes some up and down work but is a lovely piece of path to walk.

Proceed up the road from Lee, turn right onto a path by the National Trust sign 'Damage Cliff'. To the left of the path are the remains of a pre war golf course. Before Bull Point the path crosses two steep valleys, Hilly Mouth and Bennets Water. The lighthouse is one of the few manned stations left in the country. Rockham has a fine stretch of sands that are very popular in the summer. Morte Point is a spectacular jagged slate ridge rather like a dinosaurs back emerging from the sea. Offshore is the often submerged Morte Stone and this 'Rock of Death' was aptly named in the last century. At certain states of the tide an awesome tidal race can be seen. Many ships have been wrecked off here.

7 | Woolacombe to Croyde Bay   OS E139 (T) Woolacombe

Grading: Moderate   Distance -   8   85   5   53

See also our Ilfracombe to Croyde Bay Path Description.

This section starts rather poorly along the road south from Woolacombe and tries hard to lose itself in the enormous dunes. Waymarking, however, has been improved and one should not go astray. A possible alternative is to walk the Marine Drive which gives fine views. If the tide is out it is easier to walk Woolacombe Beach but it should not be attempted on a flood tide as you may not be able to get off the beach at Vention.

. If you have used the official path it leaves the Warren by a set of steep steps. At the top turn right and after 500 yds a path leaves the official route. This takes you down to a car park (refreshments and toilets). Pass to the left of the caravan site, over a stile and up the cliff slope to rejoin the official route to Baggy Point.

The high level path out to Baggy Point is pleasant. If the visibility is good you will get a good chance as you turn the corner to look at the path for a number of miles ahead across Bideford Bay. At Baggy Point itself, when you have turned the corner, do swing right on to the lower path. It is no further and provides much better sea views.

8 | Croyde Bay to Barnstaple   OS E139 (V) Croyde

Grading: Easy   Distance -   25   110   16   69

See also our Croyde Bay to Barnstaple Path Description

Distances are measured walking via Crow Point, and around Horsey Island, through Velator to join the disused railway track all the way to Barnstaple.

The path crosses the top of Croyde beach, and on to the low cliffs at Down End, turns left and after reaching the old coastguard lookout, one has to cross the main B3231 road. This is a very busy road so take great care as you cross over the road which has to be done at this point.

Turn left and walk downhill a short way to reach some stone steps. After a short climb, the path contours round Saunton Down, parallel to and above the road.

From this path there are some spectacular views down the length of Saunton Sands, and if clear, across the estuary to Appledore. On the hillside to the left can be seen some ancient cultivation terraces.

The large flat-roofed building is the five-star Saunton Sands Hotel owned by the Brend family. Wonderful food; they welcome all, including walkers.

At this point you are confronted with three routes from which to choose:-

1. _The official route_ crosses the B3231 road and passes around the hotel and descends to the large Saunton Sands car park. (The refreshment hut is open from Easter to the end of September). Continue in an easterly direction across the car park and pick up a sandy lane near some holiday chalets. At the end of this lane you return to the B3231 road.

   Take care now as there is 400 yards (365 m)of that road to walk along until a red brick house is reached. Turn right here. The path then wanders around the landward side of the golf course. It is well marked.

2. This route does not involve crossing the B3231. At the bottom of the slope before the road, take off left onto a public footpath. You climb steeply with the path bearing right. It passes near to Saunton Court and continues on to the B3231 road opposite the red brick house. You then follow the official route as described in Option 1 above.

   This diversion eliminates 400 yards (365 m) of the very dangerous road walking. The Heritage Coast Service suggest this route and we have asked for signs to be installed.

3. This third choice is probably the one preferred by most walkers. Cross over the B3231. Pass around the Saunton Sands Hotel and descend to the large car park. Walk south along the beach via Airy Point to Crow Point. After $3\frac{1}{2}$ miles ($5\frac{1}{2}$km) along the beach just after the groyne watch out for a slatted wooden cat walk on your left. This is your beach exit so walk along this to Broad Sands. As you do so you will have regained the official route.

The official route after options 1 and 2 now enters the Braunton Burrows nature reserve.

These burrows are renowned for their great wealth and diversity of their plant life and over 400 species of flowering plants have been recorded here.

When the Burrows car park is reached the path uses the so-called American road to Broad Sands.

Arriving at Broad Sands, either by the Burrows walk or the beach walk (Option 3), the path becomes a little vague, but keep the estuary on your right hand side and you cannot go wrong. Head for the white cottage on the estuary side.

The route now follows the estuary side on top of the Great Sea Bank. The path keeps to the top of this sea wall all the way to Velator If you wish to visit Braunton turn left at Velator and walk along the old railway track into the village.

From Velator, the route now follows the old Barnstaple to Ilfracombe railway track closed in 1970 into Barnstaple

In the summer months the walker has a problem on this section of the path. Not only is it the South West Coast Path, it is also a cycle track and is used by many hundreds of cyclists. Few bikes seem to have any audible means of warning you of their approach. So walking can become very hazardous. After leaving Velator you will pass the old railway station at Wrafton and after about 1 mile the path suddenly emerges onto the estuary side. When the tide is high it presents a very fine picture and in the winter months there are many duck and waders to observe.

After Heanton Court, a possible place for refreshments, the path soon loses its scenic quality. It passes a sewage treatment works, an industrial estate, before it leaves the railway track to lose its identity by a football ground and Mill Street.

By crossing the Rolle Bridge over the River Yeo you are in Barnstaple.

Grading: Easy	Distance -	28	138	17	86

See also our Barnstaple to Westward Ho! path description.

Distances are measured walking through to Bideford, 6 miles can be avoided by using the Instow to Appledore Ferry, but this is seasonal and subject to the tide.

The official route through Barnstaple is via High Street There is a riverside walk. After crossing the Rolle bridge aim to walk behind the Civic Centre and the bus station, and you will arrive at the Barnstaple Long Bridge. Cross the river Taw, pass by two mini roundabouts and Shapland yard, and you will see a sign Bideford Coast Path', pointing down the road on the right, this then links up with the old railway track. The path then uses this track, again part of the Tarka Trail, and again used by cyclists. Just before you reach the site of the old Yelland power station, turn right and pass the seaward side of the site. At Instow there is the option of using the Ferry.

Contact Mr Ommanney	Easter to end September 7 days per week
The Sea Chest	Two hours either side of high tide
Market Street	
Appledore EX39 1 PW	
Tel: 01237 476191	

If the ferry is not running rejoin the old railway track by the old level crossing and signal box

Continue on to Bideford under the new Bideford bridge. The old Bideford railway station is the base of the Hartland Coast Heritage Service. Refreshments are available in season in the reconditioned railway carriage.

Cross the Bideford long bridge, turn right and walk along the quay. Continue walking by the riverside path now named Landivisau Walk (Bideford's twin town in France) keeping the car park on one's left. At the end of the car park there is a waymarked lane passing the Bideford R.F.C. stadium. Continue walking on a road to pass under the new high level road bridge, then up a rough track, turn right by the waymark, and walk down a narrow track. This rejoins the river side by a small beach at Lower Cleave. There is some more road walking passing the Yeoldon House Hotel. Be sure to keep to the waymarked lane, do not stray up any of the many private drives. After the second war tank traps, fork right and the route enters the National Trust property of Borrough Farm. This is a very pleasant section through some riverside woods with fine views back up the river to Bideford.

There is now a steep descent to another small beach with stepping stones over a marshy area. After the second National Trust sign turn right. There are now two options here. A high tide inland diversion has been installed due to a breach in the sea wall but at low tide, continue on along the sea wall. These routes are both well waymarked. With the steps now provided it is not difficult to negotiate the breach in the sea wall. Having done that the path turns inland to meet up with the high tide route. Follow the waymarked route around the Appledore shipyard to reach the road, turn right and into Appledore via Myrtle Street.

At Appledore plenty of accommodation and refreshment places are available. Along the Quay we meet the ferry slipway from Instow. The route now continues into old Appledore, passing the homes of the old sailing captains to near the lifeboat house. Due to a cliff fall, there is an inland diversion, but at low tide the beach can be walked passing the ruins of Hinks' boat yard, to reach the road by the entrance of Northam Burrows Country Park. Walk along the side of the road past the D.C.C. recycling centre and out towards the mouth of the Taw/Torridge estuary.

Here for some distance you are walking on the seaward side of the dunes turning to the golf links side to pass Sandy Mere, then it is a straight walk into Westward Ho!. At most states of the tide it is possible to walk the beach, but be warned, the sand can be rather soft in places. Westward Ho! has plenty of accommodation but refreshment places are limited out of season.

10 | Westward Ho! to Clovelly

OS E126 (T) Westward Ho!

Grading: Strenuous	Distance -	18	156	11	97

See also our Westward Ho! to Clovelly Path Description.

After passing the last of the holiday chalets the path follows the track of the old Bideford to Westward Ho! railway. This is a fine stretch of the coast path over Cornborough and Abbotsham cliffs. At Greencliff a very poor coal was once mined. The path now climbs steeply over Cockington cliffs only to drop again to sealevel to cross a pebble beach before climbing again via a wooden staircase, to cross Babbacombe cliffs. At Peppercombe turn inland to cross the stream and then the path meanders through Sloo Woods, to join the new section through Worthygate Wood.

At Bucks Mills refreshments are available, a walk down to the old Quay is worthwhile. After the climb out of Bucks Mills the path now no longer passes through the holiday village. A new path has been created by the Hartland Heritage Coast Service, avoiding the holiday complex completely. Take care not to lose the path coming out of Barton Wood. Waymaking is not very clear. The walk along the Hobby Drive is nearly 3 miles long, and takes longer than you think. There is a new path which takes you off the Hobby Drive down to the harbour, and by walking down to it and then up the village street again you can rejoin the coast path. The official route is the Hobby Drive.

11 | Clovelly to Hartland Quay

OS E126 (V) Clovelly

Grading: Moderate	Distance -	16	172	10	107

See also our Clovelly to Hartland Quay Path Description.

This is a very fine section indeed. What coastal walking is all about! Allow yourself plenty of time to really enjoy it. Whilst this section is graded moderate overall it could perhaps rate strenuous after Hartland Point.

You leave Clovelly through a large gate which now says 'Please Close All Gates and Keep to Cliff Path'. It is then well signposted for most of the route. You generally follow the fence along until you reach a fourth metal kissing gate which is of double height.

Passing through the tall kissing gate keep on keeping right, you pass an unusual summer house, Angels Wings, but when you reach an arrow pointing left and inland you have a choice. Left is the official and easy path; right are the views and you can always retrace your steps if you do not like the steep path towards. the end of the diversion. Following the diversion the first set of steps on the right is a loop with some views, the third set should not be passed without exploration. They lead through a mini tunnel to a surprise view of the sea. You pass another summer house this time on your left - stone built with a pointed green door and you come out on a platform on the clifftop - another superb view point. From this point a very steep but not dangerous path leads down to rejoin the official path at Mouth Mill. It is very steep - you can always return to the official route if you want.

There is now a good path up through the wood and a stile at the top. The path proceeds through one field and over another stile which is multistepped on the eastern side and then across another field to two stiles: at the right hand one go right, then proceed down the steps, across the bridge at the bottom, turning left, and then take the first turning on the right. This is the more seaward route and is now the official path. We asked for this path and are grateful to the National Trust for having provided it. At Becklands there is a small memorial plaque in memory of the crew of a Wellington bomber that crashed into these cliffs in April 1942.

The route now continues practically on the coast all the way to Eldern Point and then on to Shipload Bay. The true coastal path from Shipload Bay to Barley Bay seaward of the radar station is now open and freely available. (Seasonal refreshment hut - Hartland Point car park.)

The path down into the Smoothlands Valley and out to Damehole Point is a wonderful part of the coast path. Those requiring further exercise may like to walk over the cliff top on the North of the Smoothlands Valley and it does give wonderful views, but it is not the official path. We confidently recommend Damehole Point itself to the sure-footed as not only being one of the most dramatic pieces of definitive Right of Way in the whole country but also as an ideal picnic spot.

To cross Abbey River the path goes inland behind the cottage to a stone bridge.

After crossing Abbey River, those who want the most scenic route should not turn left as directed at the next coastal path sign. Continue right out to the coast at Dyer's Lookout and then turn left up the cliff edge. It is a little further but scenically much better. Those reaching the Rocket House on the road inland to Stoke and not intending to break their journey may like to be advised that a short distance below them by footpath is the Hartland Quay Hotel which in summer operates a shop, confectionery not grocery! This is a good stopping point for refreshment and accommodation.

12 | Hartland Quay to Bude — OS E126 and E111 (T) Bude

Grading: Severe Distance - 22 194 14 121

See also our Hartland Quay to Bude Path Description.

This is a most rewarding but very tough section. It will almost surely take you longer than you think although the beginning is comparatively mild. Before reaching Bude you will have crossed ten river valleys.

The path from Hartland Quay is largely track and becomes a grassy footpath behind St Catherine's Tor. There is then a climb up and down to the waterfall at Speke Mill's Mouth. In our opinion this is the most dramatic waterfall on the whole of the path and we do not forget Pentargon ahead.

The path keeps to the eastern side of the stream for about 1 50 yards then crosses it by a new wooden footbridge. Follow the signs up the valley to the east of Swansford Hill. The path over Swansford Hill is still walkable but should not be attempted in strong wind conditions. Care should be taken on the section over Milford Common as erosion is making the path extremely narrow and it's a long drop into the sea.

Take care at Sandhole Cliff, after joining the metalled road, to watch for the signpost after about a third of a mile directing you to turn right to rejoin the coastal path. If you miss this you may find yourself doing about a two-mile walk down the road to Welcombe Mouth. Our Association has been urging Hartland Heritage Coast Service to install a true coast path along Sandhole Cliff. Those who have been this way before will notice that they have installed half of what we requested.

On the descent into Marsland Mouth look out for a little stone building, once the seaside lookout of the author, Ronald Duncan. It will provide a shelter from the elements.

As you come across the Cornish Border you will start to find a series of extremely helpful and well-thought-out posts. You might smile at the first which says "Cornwall" but thereafter not only do they point the way in each direction, but they also tell you where you are down the shank of the post. Our thanks and appreciation to whoever had this idea - surely the best yet!

The diversion to visit Morwenstow Church is worth consideration. In season refreshments are available at the old rectory. The eccentric Parson Hawker was vicar here in 1830. Look out for his hut which he constructed out of driftwood on Vicarage Cliff.

At Steeple Point there is a tendency to keep too far inland. The official path and the most spectacular one keeps well to seaward. The stream in Combe Valley used to give problems in times of flood, but now, thanks to help from the National Trust and the Countryside Commission's new maintenance scheme, there is a new alternative route with a bridge. In normal times the best proposition is to cross the stream at the mouth across the boulders. By doing so you will miss the chance of refreshments and toilets.

At Sandy Mouth the National Trust have taken over the cafe and improved it. In season it is a welcome refreshment point, but watch the daylight as there is no electricity and the cafe surely closes at darkness at the latest. At Maer Cliff, the official path has fallen into the sea and a diversion has to be made behind the bungalow.

The walking now becomes easier. Soon after Northcott Mouth, Crooklets Beach is reached. Keep to the cliffs passing the cricket pitch. This is the official route and the best way into Bude.

13 | Bude to Crackington Haven

Grading: Strenuous   Distance -   15   209   9   130

See also our Bude to Crackington Haven Path Description.

A colourful free guide to the coast is available at the Bude Tourist Information Office.

Bude is quite attractive and has good shops and accommodation, being a fair-sized town. But before you leave do try a short beach walk to the north on the falling tide and look at those cliffs. Alternating bands of sandstone and shale in beautiful curving waves and with eroding continuations of the strata extending out across the beach. This pattern has been with us since Hartland, but as we go south there will soon be a series of changes - from tightly compressed folds to violent crumplings and igneous intrusions of a much more complex nature.

The southbound path starts from the sea lock on the historic Bude Canal, climbs to the cliff top at Compass Point and on to Efford Beacon. Looking back if the tide is out the magnificent beach stretches before you for several miles going absolutely due north, with the dish aerials of the satellite tracking station visible beyond. To the south east if the weather is clear can be seen the high tors of Dartmoor, and to the south west the prominent outline of Cambeak on the south side of the Crackington Haven inlet.

The path over Efford Down and on to Upton is easy enough to follow, and then it is sandwiched between the cliff edge and the road to Widemouth. The beach at Widemouth is popular for swimming and surfing. Toilets, cafes and accommodation are available, but apart from the fine beach with its prominent Black Rock, an unusual stack of slump breccia Widemouth is not attractive. But be prepared, there will be no more facilities until you reach Crackington Haven.

South of Widemouth the path follows the low cliff for a short distance and then diverts inland slightly at Wanson Mouth to join the coast road by the stream valley. Turn west and climb up to Penhalt Cliff. Major subsidence is occurring and the coast path has long gone, but don't blame the County Council, you will see that the road is going as well! At the southern end of the clifftop car park the coast path proper recommences through a field and then descends steeply into Millook Haven.

Those with a geological interest should go on to the stony beach to view the remarkable chevron folded rock strata in the cliff on the north side - a classic textbook photograph and in sharp contrast to the curving folds to the north beyond Widemouth.

Follow the steep road beyond the stream crossing in Millook for a short distance then branch right on to the cliff top path at Ravens Beak. From here the path climbs steadily but is fairly easy going all the way to Chipman Point. Note the ancient stunted oak wood in the area of Dizzard Point. The stream valley at Chipman Point is steep and deep, one of a series ahead, some with spectacular waterfalls cascading over into the rocky beach below. A tough ascent, then a further drop into the valley at Cleave Strand followed by a ridge walk at Castle Point giving tremendous views. The descent to the Coxford Water stream is severe and the climb onwards to Pencannow Point will certainly exercise the heart/lung system. Pause to recover and enjoy the views before the descent into Crackington Haven.

CP - Dizzard Point - The path is nearer the coast then the map suggests. The variant - Fire Beacon Point to Pentargon is now the official route.

BMG - Page 22. Path just south of Wanson Mouth is on the road.

14 | Crackington Haven to Boscastle

Grading: Strenuaus   Distance -   12   221   7   137

See also our Crackington Haven to Tintagel Path Description.

At Crackington Haven it is usually safe for a swim, but never go out of your depth on Cornwall's north coast. There are toilets and a seasonal shop, pub and cafe, and a long, tough, remote stretch ahead. The folds in the rock strata are remarkable, with interesting patterns down on the beach at Tremoutha Haven. Take particular care at Cambeak, the cliff edge all round is terrifying, but just look at the view. Hartland and Lundy Island to the north; Tintagel and Rumps Point to the south.

The path is now relatively level and generally stays above the massive landslip zone at Strangles Beach. There is a good path down through the landslip to the beach, which is interesting and pleasant at low tide, but it is an arduous climb back. At the northern end of the beach is the conspicuous Northern Door rock arch. There is access to the road and car parking at the National Trust Trevigue Farm (Refreshments and Coast Information Centre).

Ahead looms High Cliff, the highest point on the coast path in Cornwall and best avoided when a gale is blowing. Just before High Cliff the path goes round the back of a small stream valley where there is a diversity of minor paths, but then just aim for the top. The southbound descent from High Cliff is precipitously steep so take it slowly, then the path up through the massive landfall at Rusey Cliff twists and turns through the brambles and gorse. This is a major geological fault zone. The path is easier to follow than it used to be, but the ground here is soily and the vegetation grows rampantly in summer which presents a continuing problem to the County Council who have difficulty keeping it cleared back.

Once at the top of Rusey Cliff there follows an easier stretch through grassy sheep fields, with the approach to Buckator now being more coastal than shown in earlier guides.

The sheer black cliff of Buckator hangs over the sea inlet, with impressive white bands of quartz running through, quite different from the brown and grey cliffs of predominantly sandstone to the north. The path dips slightly to cross a marshy stream where stepping stones provide firm footing, then continues on at high level to Fire Beacon Point. Here the descent is steep but there are attractive slate steps on the most precipitous part. The path then keeps close to the cliff edge and into the Pentargon inlet where an impressive waterfall cascades down to the sea. The best view of this is now from the southern side, cliff falls having caused the path on the north side to be diverted and the old viewpoint has been lost.

Further cliff falls seem imminent on the south side of Pentargon, but from here on it is easy going into Boscastle. Aim for the white mast atop Penally Hill, then follow the path to the beautiful harbour inlet and past the Youth Hostel into the village of Boscastle. Penally Point is well worth the detour, an exciting viewpoint, but the slate rock is dangerously slippery when wet. Note the extraordinary small scale distortions in the strata alongside the path.

NTG - Pages 125 and 127. Show incorrect route at Buckator. Follow the cliff edge around.

15 Boscastle to Tintagel   OS E9 (E109 on reprint) (V) Boscastle

Grading: Moderate	Distance -	8	229	5	142

See also our Crackington Haven to Tintagel Path Description.

There are shops, pubs, toilets, accommodation and an excellent Heritage Coast Centre in Boscastle, and the old village up the lane by the Wellington Hotel is well worth exploring.

The next section on to Tintagel is shorter and easier then the two previous sections. The path leaves from the south side of the harbour and climbs steeply past the gully to Eastern Blackapit to the Willapark headland with its prominent white watch tower. Go up to the watch tower, or take the short cut across the back of the headland past the ancient Forrabury strip field system now preserved by the National Trust. The path soon descends into the stream valley of Grower Gut - there are some granite stepping stones to help you if the water is in flood. Further on the path turns sharp right to keep to the seaward side of the Manor House and onto a prominent headland which overlooks Short Island. If you are a birdwatcher here is a good place to stop, picnic and observe through binoculars. Both Short Island and its neighbour Long Island are densely populated with breeding seabirds during the early summer, including Guillemots, Razorbills and a few Puffins. Always look down on the water, they tend to float around in groups when off duty.

As you go on past Firebeacon Hill look for the Ladies Window rock arch in the gully to the right. From here to Rocky Valley the going is level, but do look back to the dramatic pinnacles below Trevalga Cliff. Soon on your left you are confronted by a conspicuous cliff top caravan/camp site, but perhaps you are planning to stay there! Trewethet Gut is a dangerous and eroding inlet that has necessitated a slight diversion of the path, and then you descend into the exquisite Rocky Valley. Look for seals in the surging sea as you cross the footbridge, and for the Dippers that feed in the water of the stream. There is a path through Rocky Valley to the coast road, where cars may be parked.

From the footbridge a steep climb to high level again, and you find yourself overlooking Bossiney Haven. There is a cross-road of paths giving access to the beach from Bossinney village, and indeed this is an excellent place for a swim just after low tide. But the coast path goes on straight ahead and bears right to another prominent headland called Willapark, the second in just two miles. Again birdwatchers should go to the end and scan The Sisters and the ocean through binoculars. There are often Terns, Gannets and even Shearwaters further out. But beware the precipitous cliff edge as you return to the path. Then on to Barras Nose headland, dominated by that awful hotel eyesore, and down to Tintagel Haven below the Castle ruins. Here there are toilets and a cafe.

16 | Tintagel to Port Isaac   OS E9 and E106 (T) Tintagel

Grading: Severe   Distance -   13   242   8   150

See also our Tintagel to Port Isaac Path Description.

Tintagel has many shops, cafes and guest houses. The Old Post Office, owned and restored by the National Trust, dates back to the fourteenth century when it was no doubt a house of some importance.

Around The Island and down in Tintagel Haven there is some interesting and complex geology with older rocks (Devonian) overthrust on top of more recent rocks (Carboniferous), and bands of Lava and Tuff. The severe erosion, which is no doubt compounded by these faults and thrusts, is making access to The Island increasingly difficult to maintain. In the shelter of Tintagel Haven sailing ships used to be loaded with the high quality slate that is still extracted from several quarries inland away from this highly disturbed coastal zone.

The path to Trebarwith Strand climbs up from Tintagel Haven below and to the left of the Castle entrance and gives an excellent view of the rocks on the south face of The Island. From here on and past St Materiana's Church it is easy going. The Youth Hostel at Dunderhole Point was once a quarry office building. The best route, for glorious views, is the National Trust path out around the headlands of Penhallic Point, rather than the boring official route across three fields. There are further old quarries ahead as you approach Hole Beach and Trebarwith Strand, and surprisingly sailing ships were loaded under the cliffs at Penhallic Point where the remains of the wharf can still be seen The path drops down by the toilets in Trebarwith Strand, and opposite is a welcome pub serving hot food. The beach is worth exploring at low tide, but watch that you don't get cut off, and do be warned that swimming can be dangerous here.

From here to Port Isaac the path is long and in parts very tough. The descents to the valley streams and up again on the other side are about the steepest on the whole of the Coast Path. Do not leave Trebarwith Strand unless you have food, energy and plenty of time in hand. The climb up out of Trebarwith Strand, which is stepped almost all the way, will give you a foretaste of what lies ahead. And having reached the top, you must go all the way down again into Backways Cove, then up again to a more restful level stretch for about one mile to the stream valley behind Tregardock Beach where you are confronted with a detached and eroding piece of the cliff known as The Mountain. As you descend on the inland side of The Mountain you will meet a cross-roads of paths from Tregardock village to the beach., The beach is worth a visit at low tide but your route lies straight ahead and you have quite a long way to go.

From here the stretch marked on the maps as Tregardock Cliff is easy enough, but at Jacket's Point the deepest and steepest valley of all lies before you, the commencement of The National Trust Dannonchapel property. An excellent job has been done on the path, the stream crossing and the staircase of steps on the ascent on the south side. But having reached the top, just past the ugly wartime lookout you drop down again into yet another deep valley. A short diversion out to the cliff edge just before you make the descent reveals a dramatic and dangerous rocky scene with a mineworking tunnel cut through from the valley side. More steps up on the south side of the valley, then over to the Barretts Zawn stream valley where another mineworking adit faces you. This gave donkey access to the Barretts Zawn beach - our advice is don't try it.

On the climb up round the Barretts Zawn cliffs you will certainly see that there have been massive rock falls and that another will occur any time. Then you descend very steeply on the south side into the next stream valley at Ranie Point, and as you slide down the stony slope you may well feel that the path here could be improved. Some walkers evidently complain about the staircases of steps on these valley sides, but they are so exceptionally steep we believe that steps are the best option and we have been urging the hard-pressed County Council to put some here.

Now at last the path levels out through the sheep meadows with just a small valley to cross at St Illickswell Gug where a boardwalk takes you across the marsh. When you reach the road at Cartway Cove the official path is directly opposite and drops down by the side of the hotel at Portgaverne. But, for the best views, take the path to the right and go round the headland and if the tide is out walk along the old harbour quay where sailing ships were once loaded with slate. Either way there is then a short road walk up to the cliff car park at Port Isaac. Go through this past the public toilets and follow the well signed path round to overlook the attractive inlet and hence the village street.

17 | Port Isaac to Polzeath   OS E106 (V) Port Isaac

Grading: Strenuaus	Distance -	14	256	9	159

See also our Port Isaac to Padstow Path Description.

Port Isaac is a gem, with narrow streets and tiny cottages which are no doubt easier to look at than to live in. There are two excellent pubs and one of the cafes is in an extremely old and crooked little building. Do take time to explore the back streets and the small fish market, and see if you can find SqueezEe-belly Alley!

Another tough walk lies ahead and there are no facilities until you reach Polzeath, but the scenery is superb. Take the road to the right behind the fish market and past more toilets. The path bears right along the cliff in front of two prominent guest houses and takes you on past Lobber Point then down into Pine Haven. From here on the path is relatively new and apart from an unpleasant fenced corridor cutting off Varley Head, it really is magnificent, and keeps close to the cliff edge all the way to Portquin. The fence stays on your left for over a mile of steep ups and downs, but it does protect you from the enormous herd of beef cattle that generally roam the meadows behind during the summer. Watch out for the Peregrines that hunt along this stretch and for the occasional Adder basking in the sun quite close to the path!

At Kellan Head The Rumps promontory faces you at the far end of Portquin Bay. Then as you turn the corner the path overlooks the beautiful Port Quin inlet and descends to the village, once a busy little pilchard port, but there are no facilities here now. Follow the road westbound until half way up the steep hill where a new slate stile gives access to the south side of the inlet. You are on National Trust land and free to explore Doyden Point, formed from rocks of Greenstone. The new path follows the stream valley some distance in front of the old Prison Governor's House, and soon passes two fenced mineshafts where you might still find interesting mineral samples amongst the loose spoil material nearby - but keep away from the dangerous cliff edge!

At Trevan Point there is a sharp descent to Epphaven Cove which with its neighbour Lundy Bay has a beautiful beach at low tide. You then enter a surprisingly wooded valley where in late spring you will hear the delightful call of the Willow Warbler. As you climb up out of the valley look out for the startling Lundy Hole behind a protective fence on your right. On the cliff top again as you approach The Rumps you will see the earth ramparts of an Iron Age Fort in the lower ground in front of the headland. When you get there the detour through the entrance and on round the rocks overlooking The Mouls island is well worthwhile and can give good seabird watching, Puffins nest on The Mouls most years.

Then quite easy going on to Pentire Point, another headland formed from pillow lava. A perfect cross-section can be seen in the small vertical rock face on your left as you leave The Rumps headland, the rounded hollow shapes having been formed of molten lava under the sea. The walling stone alongside the path reveals the structure of small holes in the rock caused by gases and steam, but do not remove pieces as samples, The National Trust spend much time and money maintaining these walls and they provide wind shelter for the sheep.

There are many good viewpoints on the Coast Path, but that from Pentire Point is one of the best. In clear conditions south to Trevose Head and beyond, and north to Bude, the satellite tracking station and even Hartland Quay and Lundy Island, but you will need binoculars! Then follows an easy descent into Polzeath with the Camel Estuary before you and Stepper Point with its Daymark Tower on the opposite side. In contrast to the last 20 miles of perfection, the cliff top housing and car parking in New and Old Polzeath are unfortunate, but the sea, the sand and the surf are magnificent. There are toilets on the left as you reach the road beyond Pentireglaze Haven. The path continues along the cliff edge to the village centre and gives access to the beach on the way.

18 Polzeath to Padstow   OS E106 (V) Polzeath (V) Rock

Grading: Easy   Distance -   5   261   3   162

See also our Port Isaac to Padstow Path Description.

Polzeath is a surfers' paradise with several shops, cafes, accommodation and campsites. On the left by the park is a small Tourist Information Office and there are toilets opposite.

Follow the road past the beach car park and take the path right by the cottages where the road bends sharp left on the steep hill. The path follows the edge of Tristram Cliff where you can watch the expertise of the surfers. From here to Daymer Bay the path along The Greenaway is intensively walked throughout the year and measures have had to be taken to discourage people from wandering off the route and scarring the fragile turf with alternative tracks. In fact the newly laid path is so good it is now classed as suitable for the disabled in wheelchairs, which is almost unique on the Coast Path. There are houses on your left, but the coastal scene is beautiful with a rocky sea washed platform below, the haunt of Curlews, Redshanks, Grey Plover and Oystercatchers, and the headlands of Stepper Point and Pentire Point in the background. Many fishing and pleasure boats can be observed entering and leaving from Padstow some two miles up the Camel Estuary.

Just off Trebetherick Point is the Doom Bar, noticeable only at low tide when the waves are breaking over the sand. There were many wrecks here during the days of sail when ships were largely at the mercy of wind and tide. The rusted remains of a capstan used for winching sailing ships in over the bar can be seen on the rocks below the path, and there were others across at Stepper Point. Alongside the path near Trebetherick Point are the hardened remains of an older beach which is now about 25 feet above the present high water line. And on rare occasions in Daymer Bay during the winter the sea scours out the sand to reveal preserved tree stumps and roots in a bed of peat. There was woodland here some 4,000 years ago when the sea level was lower. All to do with natural warming and cooling and the amount of ice at the poles! There are toilets and a cafe in Daymer Bay car park and the beach is one of the safest for a swim - but keep out of the estuary channel at low tide.

The coast path goes down the steps on to the beach and then through the dunes and over a footbridge just below Brea Hill. To visit little St Enodoc Church which was once buried beneath the blown sand, turn left midway along the dunes and follow the white markers across the golf course. You must then retrace your route back to the dunes, or you can go on through the golf course to rejoin the coast path in the dunes on the far side of Brea Hill, but this is a busy golf course and you may wish you had a protective helmet and visor. Your route through the golf course is marked by large white painted rocks. From the footbridge you can go either way round Brea Hill, or straight over the top! Alternatively, if the tide is out you can walk along the beach to Rock and the Padstow ferry. All routes are pleasant and the sheltered estuary surroundings make quite a change from the exposed cliffs that you have been used to. The official path goes through a hollow just behind the dunes on the south side of Brea Hill, a Site of Special Scientific Interest for the rare plant life that thrives on the calcium rich sand. At the southern end the path branches left to a higher level and on to Rock car park, but you can continue on along the beach except at very high tide. There are toilets in the car park and the ferry landing is on the shore below. Be warned however that at exceptionally low tides the ferry may sail from quite some distance downstream in front of the dunes, so keep a lookout as you walk.

Rock/Padstow (River Camel)
Black Tor Ferry
Padstow Harbour Commissioners,
Harbour Office, West Quay,
Padstow, Cornwall PL28 8AQ.
Tel: Padstow (01841) 532239
Fax: (01841) 533346

Ferry operates all year; except Sundays from November to March inclusive at intervals of 15/20 minutes. Times 0750 hrs to 1650 hrs. Last ferry times are extended to 1950 hrs in the summer according to demand.
The last ferry - Rock to Padstow is 20 minutes earlier than 1650 and 1950. There may be a reduction in service during the middle of the day in winter but ferry will run if required, weather permitting.

We understand that this ferry company are no longer keen to issue single fares but we have been told that they will do so for genuine walkers on request and accordingly you should ask for a single fare if that is what you require.

19 | Padstow to Trevone   OS E106 (T) Padstow

| Grading: Easy | Distance - | 8 | 269 | 5 | 167 |

See also our Padstow to Porthcothan Path Description.

Normally the Padstow ferry will take you into the harbour; but at low tide it will deposit you a short distance downstream at St Saviour's Point, just below the path to Stepper Point. Do not take this as an opportunity to cut out Padstow, you must go into the town and explore. The harbour area, the narrow lanes in the old town and up to St Petroc's Church are attractive and fairly traffic free. A glass of beer and a genuine Cornish steak pasty make an excellent traditional lunch. A visit to the Tourist Information Centre on the harbour is recommended, and on your way it is interesting to look at the places of origin of the many fishing boats - all ports from the Hebrides to the Channel Islands!

The coast path starts on your left at the north end of the harbour and is wide and well trodden. In the early summer Blackcaps and Warblers sing in the wooded stream valley at St George's Cove. From Gun Point you can, if the tide is out, take a short cut across the beach to Hawker's Cove by the prominent old Lifeboat House. If the tide is in you can enjoy a quiet swim, this is a very pleasant and usually wind sheltered beach. Round the back of the old pilots' houses from Hawker's Cove and then a climb up to Stepper Point with its disused Coastguard Lookout and the stone built Daymark Tower. From this high ground there is a remarkable panorama behind you and on a clear day you will see the granite tors of Bodmin Moor in the distance.

So now we are back on the exposed Atlantic Coast. Approaching the precipitous inlet of Butter Hole Cove look out for the small Pepper Hole a few yards to the right of the path. There follows a long easy stretch to Gunver Head followed by a steep descent to the small stream valley. The rocky pinnacles of the Merope Islands just behind you are spectacular. A short climb up again and soon you will see ahead the Marble Cliff and Porthmissen Bridge. The cliff comprises many bands of hard limestone and softer shale on which Razorbills, Guillemots and Kittiwakes nest in the summer. At Roundhole Point the path skirts the impressive Round Hole collapsed cave which should be approached with caution, and then descends to the car park at Trevone.

20 | Trevone to Porthcothan   OS E106

| Grading: Easy | Distance - | 12 | 281 | 7 | 174 |

See also our Padstow to Porthcothan Path Description.

There are toilets, a cafe and a good beach in Trevone, but little else of interest to the walker except perhaps some bed and breakfast accommodation. The path passes behind the little headland on the south side of the bay and follows the cliff edge round rocky Newtrain Bay. There has been a cliff collapse here causing the path to be re-routed round, but then it returns to the cliff edge and on to St Cadoc's Point and Harlyn Bay. Here again there are refreshments, toilets and a beautiful beach.

The stream generally has to be crossed via the road bridge, and then the path follows the beach for about 300 metres before climbing slightly into the dunes and so on past the end of the bay to Cataclews Point. The hard erosion resistant dolerite rock here was used to make the polished font in Padstow Church. In Mother Ivey's Bay there are some unpleasant man-made features which mar the coastal scene, including an often foul smelling sewage discharge which frequently contaminates the nearby beaches. There is a huge and conspicuous caravan site near Trevose Farm, and access to the headland by the new Padstow Lifeboat Station is barred by an ugly concrete and mesh fence reminiscent of prison camps which is in sharp contrast to the old Tamarisk hedges nearby. How sadly all this compares with the painstaking remedial and conservation work that has been carried out by the National Trust on long stretches of the coast to the north of the Camel Estuary.

At Trevose Head you can generally visit the immaculately kept lighthouse, but keep away when the fog horn is blowing On a clear day you will see the granite hills of West Penwith behind St Ives to the south and the satellite tracking dish aerials beyond Bude to the north. Turning south, the path passes yet another large Round Hole as it descends to Booby's Bay. There is something of a rocky scramble to get through to Constantine Bay, but it is beautiful here with a particularly attractive beach at low tide. Not really safe for swimming unfortunately. Beyond the dunes the path leaves the beach to go round Treyarnon Point, revealing another attractive beach at Treyarnon Bay. The Youth Hostel is on the left, and in the car park area there are toilets and refreshments. If you are intent on swimming, observe the safety notices which will certainly tell you not to do so at low tide.

An unusually indented coastline follows beyond Trethias Island, but the path cuts across the narrower headlands. Between Pepper Cove and Warren Cove are the ramparts of an Iron Age Fort, and in Fox Cove you may see the remains of a ship which ran aground in 1969. Minnows Islands and the cove beyond are quite spectacular; then the path turns into Porthcothan Bay, descending through the protected National Trust strip which contrasts with the housing development on the side opposite.

21 Porthcothan to Newquay   OS E106

Grading: Moderate   Distance -   **15   296   10   184**

See also our Porthcothan to Newquay Path Description

Porthcothan has toilets, a shop and limited accommodation. The path leaves past the shop and keeps in front of the houses and on round the headland overlooking Trescore Islands. There is a steep descent into Porth Mear valley, a popular spot for birdwatchers, and an equally steep climb up again, then an easy walk to Park Head, another spectacular viewpoint. Ahead lies the famous Carnewas property of the National Trust, with a beautiful beach at low tide. As you leave Park Head you will see that the cliff is slowly sliding down, although it has been like this for many years. Bedruthan beach itself has a recurring accessibility problem due to the dangerous condition of the cliffs, but a great deal of money is being spent on the long flight of steps down. If the tide is on its way out it is worth going down to explore the rock stacks, Bedruthan Steps, but don't get cut off and don't even think about swimming. The National Trust cafe and Information Centre in the car park are open throughout the summer.

Bedruthan Steps can be a busy place, but few people stray far from their cars and you will soon find yourself on a quieter stretch of path to Trenance Point. A steady descent into Mawgan Porth follows, where the road must be used for a short distance in order to cross the stream. There are toilets and shops here. The southbound path leaves to the right on the sharp road bend on the hill out of Mawgan Porth. Then follows a long high level stretch to Watergate Bay, with minor descents at Beacon Cove and Stem Cove, between which across Griffin's Point headland are the ramparts of another Iron Age Fort. Just inland is the airport and RAF station at St Mawgan, and you may find yourself being targeted by high powered military jet aircraft as they come in to land. Ahead lies the magnificent Watergate Beach, but the path remains at high level until it crosses to the road behind the Watergate Hotel.

After crossing the stream bridge by the car park, where there are toilets, the path leaves to the right from the road to Newquay and again climbs to the high clifftop where it remains all the way to Whipsiderry. Here some ugly clifftop development has been permitted, but the coastal scene is great, with Newquay and Towan Head in the background. The cliffs at Whipsiderry are high and precipitous, but there are steps down to the beach and some caves to explore. The path just manages to squeeze between a guesthouse and the cliff edge, and then takes you on to Trevelgue Head.

We recommend that you cross the footbridge on to the island, where a rough sea can be most spectacular. Then you must return to the road at Porth Beach where there are toilets and cafes. You may then walk out along the southern edge of the beach rather than taking the official road route, joining the path by more toilets. From here it crosses the headland between Porth and Lusty Glaze, a hotel having claimed the old path round the headland. This short cut avoids the road and takes you round the cliff edge at Lusty Glaze Cove and into the Barrowfields Park. Then you are on the road into Newquay town centre, but if the tide is out you can walk along the magnificent beach from Lusty Glaze or from Barrowfields all the way to the harbour. The Youth Hostel is across the road from Barrowfields.

BMG - Does not cover total mileage through Newquay.

22 Newquay to Holywell   OS E104 (T) Newquay (Trains) (V) Crantock

Grading: Moderate   Distance -   8   302   5   189

See also our Newquay to Perranporth Path Description.

Newquay is the biggest town on the north coast and the pedestrianised shopping centre is quite attractive. There is no shortage of restaurants, pubs and accommodation here, and there is even a railway station! But do explore the beaches and the harbour before you leave, and if the tide is out you can gain access to the coast path by the steps at the back of the harbour.

The path leaves just above the harbour and climbs past the old Huer's Hut to Towan Head. In the cliffs below the Hut is a noisy Kittiwake colony and this is a very good spot to observe the differences between Kittiwakes, Fulmars, Black-headed Gulls and the rest. Towan Head is particularly good for seabird watching, with binoculars you may spot Gannets, Petrels and Shearwaters further out.

From Towan Head the path follows along the back of Fistral Beach. This is probably the most popular surfing beach in the British Isles, international competitions are held here. The path climbs to the cliffs at the southern end, passing in front of the housing development at Pentire, then across the headland at The Warren over to The Gannel river estuary. The proprietors of the Fern Pit Cafe on Riverside Crescent operate a summer season only ferry service to Crantock Beach, supplemented by a low tide portable footwalk.

Newquay/Crantock (River Gannel)   End of May to mid September
Fern Pit Café and Ferry   1000 -1800
Proprietor - G.A. Northey   Continuous 7 day week.
Fern Pit, Riverside Crescent, Newquay TR7 1 PJ
Tel: Crantock (01637) 873181

The official crossing of the Gannel is from Pentire to the eastern end of Crantock Beach via the Fern Pit Ferry. This is the most comfortable and scenic way to cross and we would recommend it, there is even a cafe on the Newquay side so that one can while away one's waiting time with refreshment. The snag is that in winter there is no ferry running. Information for those using the other crossings is shown in sequence below.

Up river there is an alternative ferry and a tidal footbridge off Trevean Lane which crosses over to Penpol Creek. If you are at Fern Pit and need to go upstream go east (inland) along Riverside Crescent, Riverside Avenue, Fistral Crescent, turn right into Pentire Crescent, continue along Penmere Drive and turn right into Trevean Way, then turn right at the C.P. sign. Be warned there is an earlier footpath sign to Crantock DO NOT take it because you may find it is under water. Having crossed the Gannel, turn right to follow an estuary side path. Presently it becomes a track and you pass a house on the right, then some bungalows and can soon turn right down into the N.T. car park at Rushey Green. Take the exit practically opposite where you came in. There is a seasonal cafe close to the car park.

Further up stream again, just before the estuary becomes a river, there is another footbridge which we call `Trenance'. This has recently been heightened so that it is more often useable than was once the case. It is beside the new A3075 Gannel Road just before the boating lake on the left and its junction with Trevemper Road. If you are in Newquay and know the tides are against you the quickest way to get here is to walk down the new Gannel Road (A3075). On the other side of the footbridge, walk forward until you reach the first tree, as opposed to bush on your left. This is decision time. There are splendid new maps about, which offer a new permissive path along the south side of the estuary. Be warned if the tide is high you may well have been able to use this bridge but a lot of the permissive path may be under water! So at that tree, an ash, either turn right through the pedestrian gate that is the permissive path or if you have any doubts you are advised to take the old bridleway, through the big gate, going towards Trevemper. Proceed forwards uphill and having gone over the brow, turn right before you get to the tarmac. You walk via Treringey coming to Penpol Creek and so on, to Rushey Green as described above.

However if all these crossings fail there is the A 3075 main road itself, which is the only all-states-of-the-tide and all-seasons route. Those taking the A3075 should proceed along it until just after the roundabout where the A392 branches off. In about 20 yards (18 m) take the little unsigned lane, on the right. You immediately pass a partly ruined barn on your right and soon you pass a house on the outskirts of Trevemper. Then as the road bears left, go forward and right. Pass through a gate and turn left to go via Treringey to Penpol Creek and so, on to Rushey Green.

Crantock Beach is attractive at low tide and can give good views of Terns fishing in The Gannel below the cliffs of Pentire Point East. The path passes behind the dunes to the National Trust car park at Rushy Green, then westwards through the dunes to the cliffs of Pentire Point West. Alternatively you may walk along the beach to gain access to the path by scrambling up at the western end of the dunes

Porth Joke is a sheltered sandy inlet then follows a climb to Kelsey Head another Iron Age site. From here in the distance can be seen St Agnes Head with Bawden Rocks offshore Holywell Beach lies before you and the path descends to the dunes and then into Holywell. Those continuing onwards can take advantage of the splendid new National Trust footbridge across the river seaward of the village.

NTG Page 35 (Map) The official path goes out onto Towan Head and back.

| **23** | **Holywell to Perranporth** | **OS E109** |

Grading: Moderate, but if the tide is close in and one has to use the sand dune route to get to Perranporth it certainly becomes strenuous.   Distances -   10   314   6   195

See also our Newquay to Perranporth Path Description.

The path cuts across Penhale Point headland and then skirts the seaward edge of the rather ugly Penhale Camp where there is a short fenced section. The army presence here however has served to preserve the beautiful wild dunes area inland from being overrun by campsites and chalets, and it now deserves to be protected as a nature reserve. Then out to Ligger Point and the first good view of the long Perran Beach.

The easiest path, if the tide permits, is now along the great stretch of firm beach to Perranporth rather than over the dunes. Even if, as is sometimes the case, one can only walk part-way along the beach it is worth going down to do this, there being a number of 'escape routes' up from the beach gong south. The important point to watch if you want an easy descent to the beach is to fork left along the sandy path after the old wooden stile, the right fork is quicker but much steeper.

The official path takes you towards the dunes where will see the rusty coloured Perran Iron Lode in the cliff quarry. The path descends behind this and follows the back of the beach for almost a mile then climbs up through the dunes behind the rock cliff at Cotty's Point. The incoming tide will reach the foot of the cliff here but there are escape steps to the dunes at each side and if the tide is out you can continue on along the beach rather than going over the top. The path descends to the back of the beach just south of Cotty's Point, crosses the stream by a footbridge and so takes you into the town or the car park where there are toilets.

| **Grading: Moderate** | | Distance - | 6 | 320 | 4 | 199 |

See also our Perranporth to Portreath Path Description.

Perranporth is a busy holiday centre during the summer and has good shops and accommodation. The eroding rock stacks at the southern end of the beach are interesting, and may be explored using the beach access at the far end of the car park in front of the hotel terrace. Round the corner you will find a staircase from the beach up to the cliff car park at Droskyn Point. The official route leaves west from the town car park and follows the hill up Cliff Road, but just to the left of the Atlantic House Hotel there are some steps up and a footpath which takes you past the Droskyn Point car park. Whichever way you have chosen, keep inland of the prominent castellated building and on along Tregundy Lane to the end of the houses. The southbound coast path is signposted half left at the entrance drive to the Youth Hostel and the new South West Water sewage pumping station. It then descends slightly to the right before climbing to the cliffs overlooking Shag Rock.

From here on you will see increasing evidence of mining activity. The path is fairly level going, passing the small outcrop of granite at Cligga Head which has been quarried and displays conspicuous stripes of greisen (for the chemistry of which you must consult the textbooks!). The mineralisation along the coast here and to the south is attributable to the intrusion of the granite which extends over a considerable area below the surface. Southbound through the quarry and mineworkings you are unlikely to lose the path. Hanover Cove is named after a shipwreck. The Hanover was lost in a storm in December 1938 on route from Lisbon to Falmouth, all hands were lost plus a cargo of gold. It is rumoured that there is £50m of gold still onboard.The rock formations around the cove are dramatic and green copper stains the cliffs. There are many mineshafts hereabouts capped with conical steel mesh which allows access for bats.

The long stretch to Trevallas Porth is level easy going alongside the airfield perimeter, you will progress much faster here than you did further north. There is a sharp descent into Trevellas Coombe where there are many mine workings with their decaying buildings. Go upstream to the bridge which crosses the stream in front of the Blue Hills engine house and then half right over the top to Trevaunance Cove. The path passes perilously close to the precipitous cliff edge, but there is another track slightly further back. Past the waste tips and the capped mineshafts still at high level the path forks, left direct to St Agnes avoiding the road and right down to the road at Trevaunance Cove. Cross over the road and turn right behind the four storey grey rendered housing block and the official path takes you past the toilets. If you go down into the cove where there is a seasonal cafe, there is a footpath behind the Jubilee Terrace and steps back up to the path near the Trevaunance Point Hotel. This has a pleasant garden where you can enjoy the view and a glass of beer.

It is possible to cross the beach from Trevellas Porth to Trevaunance Cove at low tide, but be warned that the boulders are dangerously slippery. Surprisingly there was once a harbour under the cliff on the west side of Trevaunance Cove, but all you will find now is a tumbled mass of granite blocks.

BMG - Path loops inland at Trevellas Porth.

| 25 | **St Agnes to Porthtowan** | | | | OS E104 (V) St Agnes |

| **Grading: Moderate** | | Distance - | 8 | 328 | 5 | 204 |

See also our Perranporth to Portreath Path Description.

Beyond the Trevaunance Point Hotel the path climbs left past some unusual mine workings. From the top it stays at high level out to St Agnes Head, passing many mineshafts and waste tips on the way. Here you are circumnavigating St Agnes Beacon, a small outcrop of granite half a mile back from the coast. As the path turns south you will see Godrevy Lighthouse across the bay, with St Ives and the massive granite of Penwith beyond. The going is relatively easy and soon you will pass the much photographed Towanroath Engine House, part of the Wheal Coates tin and copper mine and now preserved by the National Trust. The path then descends into Chapel Porth where there is a car park, toilets and a seasonal cafe. At low tide if you walk some distance north along the beach you will see a streak of copper ore in the cliff beneath the Towanroath shaft.

The southbound path climbs steeply out of Chapel Porth past more mineshafts and waste tips on Mulgram Hill, then follows a good clifftop walk to Porthtowan. The path descends to the back of the beach and on past the car park where there are toilets. The transition from mining to tourism here has produced some unattractive features but the beach is beautiful and extensive at low tide, from Tobban Horse in the south to Chapel Porth in the north.

BMG - Path loops inland at Porthtowan.

26 | Porthtowan to Portreath   OS E104 (V) Porthtowan

Grading: Strenuous   Distance -   6   334   4   208

See also our Perranporth to Portreath Path Description.

Porthtowan is popular for surfing and has accommodation and a few shops and seasonal cafes. To find the southbound path turn right along West Beach Road then left up the narrow road to the cliff top. You will see a steep path up from the west beach, but parts of this seem to be in imminent danger of slipping away so we do not recommend it. On the headland the path turns south, passing many mineworkings, and keep some distance back from the crumbling and dangerous cliff edge. At the steep valley drop to Sally's Bottom steps have been installed on either side, then on reaching high level again you find yourself walking alongside the unattractive Nancekuke fence which encloses the large military establishment just inland. You may not be convinced, but the new fence is lower and less intimidating than the one it replaces. It stays with us for over a mile and almost to Portreath, where the Daymark above the harbour entrance can be seen ahead. The path turns south just before you reach the Daymark, avoiding another dangerous cliff edge, and joins the road down to the harbour. The long narrow inlet is unusual, but the protective pier which extends over the rocks on the south side is now out of bounds, too many people have been swept off by waves breaking over.

27 | Portreath to Hayle   OS E104 and E7 (102 on reprint) (V) Portreath

Grading: Strenuous in parts   Distance -   19   353   12   220

See also our Portreath to Hayle Path Description.

There are shops, cafes and bed and breakfast accommodation in Portreath, but the beach is small in comparison with most on this coast. To gain the southbound path go round the harbour to the beach car park then to the right up Battery Hill. Where this road drops to the beach again at the western end, the coast path branches left up the valley to the clifftop The surface can be wet and muddy, it is far better to climb to the right by the National Trust sign and go over Western Hill, this path continues through to join the coast path overlooking Western Cove.

You soon enter Western Hill National Trust property where there is a choice; the old official route is forward and misses out the fine views from Western Hill and the possibility of seeing seals out by Gull Rock. There is a minor path going right and this is the official route up to those fine views.

At Bassett's Cove you go through a big car park and start several miles of easy cliff top walking. There are practically no signs but only two places you are likely to go astray. For a mile and a half you get closer to the road and then start to get away from it again; after a further half mile you should observe a small field ahead and to your left, here you have to fork right and then turn right.

You pass Hell's Mouth which has a seasonal cafe just across the road, then when you are approaching another field you come out on to a track where you turn right but this time do not take the next right as it is a beach path only. We have asked the National Trust for signing in both these places.

There is then a very pleasant walk around Navax and Godrevy Points, there are good views out to sea, ahead to St Ives and what to many is a surprise southwards. You then have to negotiate a big car park but by keeping well to seaward you can miss most of it and the road that leads to it.

You cross the Red River by a new bridge in front of Godrevy Cafe (open every day of the year except Christmas Day from 10.00 to sunset). Cross over the bridge and walk due west towards the dunes.

You now have a 'spot the post' competition amongst the dunes. There is certainly no logic in the route and unless it is cowslip time you will be regretting the tide was in.

The route becomes beset by caravans and chalets and, eventually when you have given up all hope, arrives in a big open car park area. Go out the other end and down a broad track. Here swing right in front of Hayle Bulk Supply Point; if you think the area is grotty take comfort from the fact it was once worse, they had a coal fired power station here! Go ahead to cross the bridge to swing right into Hayle.

28 | Hayle to St Ives   OS E7 (102 on reprint) (T) Hayle (B.Rail) (V) Lelant (B.Rail)

Grading: Moderate	Distance -	9	362	5	225

See also our Hayle to Pendeen Watch Path Description.

Distance is measured from Hayle, around the estuary to Lelant then along the coast to St Ives.

Note between Lelant and Marazion there is a cross peninsula path, St Michael's Way. This could be used to make a circular round trip around Penwith by walking round the coast and then coming back inland from Penzance or Marazion to Carbis Bay.

In Hayle you can walk along the grass on the right hand side of the road. Just before the viaduct turn right to join the main road again on the other side of the creek. The quickest but dreariest route is straight along the main road, 'Carnsew Road'. There is a longer but somewhat more attractive alternative not to be missed by bird watchers. Go along the road passing the 30 decontrol sign and at the end of the long building on the right is a footpath sign-posted 'The Weir 1/2 a mile'. At the end of tall hedge swing right, then swing left by a bridge. Then as the ground widens swing left again to walk along a lagoon embankment. Presently you come out again on the main road and have to turn right. Whichever way you did that first stretch from Hayle, turn right on the A3074 signposted St Ives passing the Old Quay House.

Here again is decision time as for some incredible reason the official path continues along the A3074 road through Lelant. At the end of the main street, where the main road swings left, you go ahead on a minor road to the church. If you wish to do this O.K. but we suggest a quieter and no further distance alternative below.

After the Old Quay House go carefully along the main road passing under the railway bridge. Then turn right signposted BR St Ives Park and Ride. You go along a minor road and pass through a car park passing Lelant Saltings Station. You can then walk either along the road north eastwards or for a while through the playing fields. If the tide is out you can go right to the end and use the poor stepping stones. If the tide is in join the road earlier because the stones get covered by the tide. Then follow the road which turns inland coming out by the church.

At the church continue on the same line go ahead across the golf course and under the railway again. Here turn left to proceed along the seaward side of the railway.

Just before Carrack Gladden where you are close to the sea there are several paths going down on to the beach. If the tide is well out you can go down and save yourself several ups and downs by walking along the beach to Carbis Bay.

If you stay on the path you come up by a pedestrian level crossing and then swing right, on the descent avoid two beach paths on your right

About two hundred yards before Carbis Bay there is another opportunity to go down to the beach and save yourself one last hill. If you stay with the path you go up to join a road, turn right down this. Circle round on the inland side of the cafe complex to leave Carbis Bay on a tarmac path above the beach but to seaward of the hotel.

Ascend, crossing a railway footbridge then keep ahead avoiding path on left. Continue along ignoring 'Private road pedestrians only' on right. The path becomes a minor road where road swings left and there is another private road on your right go ahead. Cross the railway again on a more substantial old fashioned bridge to swing right and downhill. You come down to Porthminster Cafe and then you can walk either side of the little park, continuing along below the railway station.

29 │ St Ives to Pendeen Watch   OS E7 (102 on reprint) (T) St Ives (Trains)

| Grading: Severe | Distance - | 21 | 383 | 13 | 238 |

See also our Hayle to Pendeen Watch Path Descriptions.

You are now starting on the longest and most deserted stretch of coast on the whole South West Way. Therefore think about accommodation. Out of season you will have to walk three whole sections, 22 miles, even in season two sections, 17 miles, before you find refreshment on the path. You can divert as listed below inland but this will increase the mileage and all suggestions are subject to some seasonal closing and opening hours. There is not even a telephone box on the path. It is magnificent walking but do not start out unprepared.

Refreshment possibilities are, Zennor; Bosigran Farm, Pendeen/Botallack and St Just. Then sometimes on the path is a mobile snack wagon in Cape Cornwall car park.

One other warning, the path is often rough and rocky and the terrain is severe and in places after rain surprisingly boggy, few will average 2 miles an hour; in other words it will take you longer than you expect.

Many use St Ives as a staging post, if however you should just wish to walk through continue along the path below the railway station by which you enter. This becomes a tarmac lane which proves to be called `The Warren' at its end. Keep as close as you can to the harbour until you reach its north west corner. Here you have a choice; the purists will stay with the harbour and walk out round what is called The Island or St Ives Head, it is a pleasant walk. The less pure or perhaps those with still a lot of miles to cover can cut the corner by following signs to 'Tate Gallery' this will bring them out behind Porthmeor Beach. Those going out to The Island can walk right round the harbour to turn left signposted 'The Museum'.

You can walk round The Island but the interesting little St Nicholas Chapel is on the high point in the middle. When you have completed your circuit you turn right to pass along in front of the 'Tate Gallery'.

Go along behind the beach passing the `Tate Gallery' ignoring the ramp going down to the beach. The road starts to rise, there is a car park on your right and the path you want starts to bear off right by some public conveniences. You pass a bowling green and continue along the deteriorating tarmac path out into the country.

One place where it is easy to go wrong, because of inadequate signposting, is shortly after Clodgy Point on Burthallan Cliff a path goes inland here and currently it is better marked than the main coastal path.

The coast path cuts behind the National Trust property of Pen Enys Point if you should have time on your hands it is a pleasant extension.

If the weather is clear Carn Naun Point is the place to look back and gloat at what you have done. Be careful though a little later just before the stream, where there is a path down to the beach which you should avoid, and, just after the stream a path running inland which ignore. Look for seals out on the Carracks they are often there.

You pass the old mine building at Treen Cove and come out behind Gurnard's Head. Here again if you have time it is a splendid diversion out to the Head but so often folk are pressed for time and cut across the neck.

The area around Porthmeor Cove is particularly spectacular if you can take your eyes briefly off where you are putting your feet!

Bosigran is difficult to negotiate and we have asked the National Trust for better signing As you drop off Carn Veslan look ahead to the ridge of Bosigran Cliff and aim for the inland high point.

(Not the big hill inland with the tower.) The path drops then starts to bear left uphill, crosses through a ruined wall then forks right (not the obvious path going up left). Shortly you do go left up another clear path but in only a few yards turn right up a more indistinct path heading for the inland high point. As you get nearer you pass round to the left of it to drop into the valley. Here you go across a main track used by the climbers and on across a little stone bridge. You go straight up the other side only bearing right again as you approach the top wall.

On Rosemergy cliff there is a currently unmarked four way junction, go straight ahead.

30 | Pendeen Watch to Cape Cornwall   OS E7 (102 reprint) Inland (V) St Just

Grading: Moderate   Distance -   6   389   4   242

See also our Pendeen Watch to Porthcurno Path Description.

Remember what was said about refreshment in section 29.

The official path from Pendeen Watch goes along the road to the end of the next block of buildings and here turns right. There is a better unofficial coastal route which you can find by walking along to the right of the road and going down along the cliffs as the road bears away from the coast.

Naturally avoid the marked and fenced off mineshaft. Presently you come opposite a close inshore islet The Avarack with a big cairn on the to p. Here take the mid path going downhill, not the one right on cliff top. Towards the bottom the path bears left again up a stream valley to rejoin the official route at a bridge over the stream This brings you to the old Levant Mine dressing floors. A minor inland diversion is recommended to Geevor Mine (museum, refreshments and toilets).

After the Levant Mine the path bears right along tracks which are not coastal and what few signs there are you may trip over but are unlikely to see! Watch for the turning out to Kenidjack Castle it is now properly signed. We recommend the most seaward paths to the Kenidjack turn off path.

Out on Kenidjack Castle the path goes down across a stile and reaches a track where you are signed left. The adventurous may prefer to turn right a couple of yards and go down across the old spoil heaps, later keeping close to the cliffs on the right to reach the stream. Cross the stream, circle round the right side of the spoil heaps on the other side and go up a faint path to an old leat, dried up stream bed. Turn briefly right along this to clamber up a few more yards to another leat unfortunately more overgrown of late but passable. Turn right along this to reach the road just before Cape Cornwall.

If you are not adventurous turn left as signed presently veering right downhill Continue up the valley by a cottage to bear right and cross a footbridge. The path then bears right to a junction by a ditch. The official path bears left, zig-zagging uphill to turn right at the top. An easy but somewhat overgrown in places alternative continues right. If you take this proceed along the path, just before a small piece of ruined wall on your left, scramble up a few yards to turn right on a similar path above which leads to the road.

When you reach the road whichever way you came you must turn down it. The official path goes down towards Cape Cornwall but does not go out on to it. Therefore those in a hurry may prefer to turn left just before the car park, but careful if you want refreshment, the snack wagon, if it is there, will be down in the car park. Alternatively if you have the time, go out on the Cape it is a wonderful spot owned by the National Trust for 57 good reasons and open to all. It was once considered to be 'Land's End' so may be it has had a lucky escape!

31 | Cape Cornwall to Sennen Cove   OS E7 (102 on reprint)

Grading: Moderate   Distance -   8   397   5   247

See also our Pendeen Watch to Porthcurno Path Description.

After Cape Cornwall you climb up the track to Ballowal Barrow, the road bears off left but the Coast Path goes ahead. This is probably one of the grandest sections of the whole cost path.

In the Porth Nanven valley you cross the stream; do not turn seawards but head up opposite towards the little col. The path then goes straight ahead above the sea.

At Cam Barges the path takes a little inland loop to avoid the worst of the sand dunes. If the tide is out a quicker option is to walk along the firm sand to Sennen Cove. (All year round refreshments available).

32 | Sennen Cove to Porthcurno   OS E7 (102 on reprint) (V) Sennen Cove

Grading: Moderate   Distance -   **10   407   6   253**

See also our Pendeen Watch to Porthcurno Path Description.

Leaving Sennen Cove you pass the Round House; go on into the car park area and turn left at the public toilets. Proceed ahead shortly to turn right and then head for the battlemented look-out.

Paths from Sennen to Land's End and for several miles beyond are so ubiquitous that it is impossible usually to give precise directions, you just follow the coast and your fancy and are unlikely to go seriously astray. There has in time past been publicity in the national press about footpath access to Land's End. This in no way concerns the Coast Path which is as freely available as it has been for years past.

Regarding the Land's End complex itself, you have two choices, if you want to use the cafes or other facilities head straight for it. If you wish to pretend it is not there, though that may be difficult, keep right out on the coast and only look out to sea! For what it is worth the official route goes via Gleeb Cottage with its collection of animals rather than using the path nearer the sea.

The short length just before Nanjizal Cove is perhaps the best bit of a very fine section, if you are lucky enough to pass that way in early spring you will see that it was once a bulb growing area. After you have crossed the stream do not turn right at once but proceed ahead for 30 to 40 yards then turn right.

After a climb you are heading out to Gwennap Head and Tol-Pedn-Penwith. Tol-Pedn means the holed headland and it is spectacular. To find the hole proceed up to the look-out house and just pass it to stand in front of the old rocket practice wooden pole. From here walk on a bearing of approx 140 and go for about 40 yards over the brow, the path then bears right 190, you drop down over a natural bridge with the hole on your left. Walk round it do not fall down it! and then leave again on the obvious path which soon climbs back on the clifftop, you do not have to go back the way you came.

At Porthgwarra, if you turn down the slipway it is possible to make a short diversion by way of a tunnel through which boats were once hauled. The only snag with this innocent entertainment is that you will have by-passed the seasonal cafe above! If you use the cafe turn first right afterwards.

Although the path from Porthgwarra leaves by an inland route you can walk out round Carn Scathe if you wish. To do this when you have turned down from the cafe bear right just before granite gate posts between the cliff top and a garden. The first few yards are overgrown but you will soon be glad you went that way. When you get back to the main path turn right of course.

After climbing out of Porthgwarra the path levels off and stays with the cliff tops. As you descend towards Porth Chapel Beach take a short excursion out onto a granite point for glorious views of the beach. Returning to the path it descends to the back of the beach passing by St Levan's Holy Well. Do not continue down to the beach, unless you want a swim, but turn off left above it. Another rewarding diversion from the official path is out and around the headland of Pedn-mên-an mere.

You come out into the car park behind the Minack Theatre through an unusual kissing gate. Go through the car park to leave at the other end on a path parallel to and behind the Theatre entrance. There are various warning notices but you would need to be very infirm or suffer from vertigo not to be able to go down the steps. At the bottom turn left and do not, unless you want a swim, go down to the beach but keep along the path contouring above the beach.

In Porthourno there is a good cafe usually open from Easter to the end of the season but you will have to make a short detour left up the valley to reach it. Also, further up the valley, is an excellent museum to celebrate that Porthcurno was once the world centre of communications.

33 | Porthcurno to Lamorna   OS E7 (102 on reprint)

| Grading: Strenuous | Distance - | 8 | 415 | 5 | 258 |

See also our Porthcurno to Penzance Path Description.

There is again fine walking in this section and some of it easy going, however parts of it are not easy and it may well take longer than you expect.

If you have visited the cafe you can take the old path and miss out Percella Point but the views from it over Porthcurno are spectacular. After Percella Point the official path is way inland with fields between it and the cliff top. How it can be named 'the coast path' is anybody's guess. However, you will not be cheated out of a more seaward path because the National Trust have a splendid coastal route. So before you get to those fields watch out for a path on your right leading seaward of the official route. That is the one this Association calls 'a coast path'. You can even divert from that to drop down to Pendvounder Beach for a swim. Further east along Treen Cliff this path rejoins the official one.

The next chance of a diversion is Treryn Dinas which is an extra not to be missed by anyone who likes a scramble, up and on to the famous Logan Rock.

Unfortunately you have to go back inland again to continue on your way to Penberth, a scenic gem. Cross the slipway, passing the old capstan and go up the other side outside the house to climb a cove side path. You come up to headland which is worth another ten minute stop.

Around St Loy the authorities have so far failed to make the good path they should, you therefore get shunted inland then have to use what in wet weather can be a very mucky path to get to the beach. There is no path at all for a few yards, but in response to representations by the Association a path of sorts has been formed by the authorities along the bouldery beach but watch out for the turn inland again after about 50 metres. We have had reports of a walker missing this in misty weather and getting cut off by the tide.

After Boscawen Point and before Tater-du Lighthouse you come to a junction; do not turn left but proceed ahead to go through two large metal green gates, neither of which were signed on the last check.

Be careful on Carn Barges not to be diverted onto the inland path to Lamorna, the official and better route is round the coast. Look for the cross just before Lamorna unless you are in too much of a rush to get to the seasonal cafe, right on the path!

34 | Lamorna to Penzance   OS E7 (102 on reprint) (V) Mousehole (V) Newlyn

| Grading: Strenuous and then easy | Distance - | 10 | 425 | 6 | 264 |

See also our Porthcurno to Penzance Path Description.

After the cafe you bear right behind the harbour and cross the bridge. You go up past a most complicated waymark which, unless you look at it carefully, almost sends you the wrong way. However keep right but with only one house still on your right.

The path is then good out around Carn-du and on to Kemyel Point. The route from there to Mousehole is not good because the authorities have ignored the old coastal path with its still extant stone stiles in favour of a sinuous new route and then a rural lane.

You climb the hill to pass a onetime look-out on your right. The path steadily improves underfoot and eventually you come out on to a road where you turn right.

Few find the right route into Mousehole because it is never signed properly. We will describe it here in case you would like to join that exclusive bunch. Descend the hill passing the Wild Bird

Hospital on your left. There is a post box on your right with a Coast Path sign pointing the way you have come but not the way you are going! Turn right at an acute angle opposite Kemyel Cottage. Go down a narrow tarmac lane 140 degrees part way down bear slightly left heading towards the rocks, St Clement's Isle, you can see out to sea. Just before the foreshore bear left along a terrace and fork right into a car park. Go to the bottom right end of the car park to continue briefly along the harbour side. You then have to turn in again left and then first right. However those with an interest in history before turning right should go forward past the house with pillars to read the plaque on the other side. The turn right brings you out on to a busier street bear right along it to come behind the harbour again.

The official route leaving Mousehole goes up a narrow road without pavements but we suggest you do not. At the other end of the harbour go in and pass through the car park there, down a ramp and along a concrete path. Go round the corner and up steps past a lifebuoy at the top turn right along the pavement.

Approaching Newlyn part of the official route is on a road with no pavement so take take and as you are a pedestrian you can use the No Entry or, even better, if you watch closely there Is a footpath on the right going down a slope just before it and you can go safely the same way at low level.

Go round the back of Newlyn Harbour passing the War Memorial then bear right over the little bridge, Seaman's Mission on the right. A diversion a few yards upstream takes you to the award winning Pilchard Works, a working museum. Over the bridge bear right to come out once again behind the beach. After you have passed the tennis courts or remains of them the path comes back to the road, here go across the corner of the beach to go up steps and walk along the promenade.

At the end of the Promenade pass the swimming pool and continue round to pass Penzance Harbour and on to the railway station.

BMG - Does not cover complete path or mileage through Penzance.

35	Penzance to Marazion	OS E7 (102 on reprint) (T) Penzance (Trains)

Grading: Easy	Distance -	5	430	3	267

See also our Penzance to Porthleven Path Description.

Note between Lelant and Marazion there is a cross peninsula path St Michael's Way. This could be used to make a circular round trip around Penwith by walking round the coast and then coming back inland from Penzance or Marazion to Carbis Bay.

Before leaving Penzance it is recommended you have a look at the state of the tide because seaward of the sea wall near the Tourist Information Centre is a new seaside walkway. If the tide is low enough, and you will see if it is, you should use it and the beach to avoid the authorities dreadful idea of a coast path for the first $3/_4$ mile.

The official route is from the bottom of Market Jew St. going out on the main road alongside the railway station, however the pavement runs out on the seaward side so it is better for a while to keep to the landward When you get to B3311 cross over later joining the A30 at the end of the Penzance ring road. Soon on your right just before the heliport is a footbridge, cross this and the coast path goes along the top of the sea wall, if the tide is out you can walk along the beach as an alternative.

At Long Rock where the station is now a restaurant you emerge into the car park. Go through this and continue along the road towards Marazion. There is a roadside car park and then the path goes up on the sand dunes, although at the last check there was no sign and no apparent way up. Press on between the beach and the road, if you get this bit right you will cross a pedestrian bridge just seaward of the road bridge. You now go through field/car parks, at the end going up a side road to join the main road.

36 | Marazion to Prussia Cove

Grading: Moderate   Distance -   6   436   4   271

See also our Penzance to Porthleven Path Description.

Walkers are treated badly at the beginning of this section, there is no path at all for a while and then the first coastal length is on a beach.

You go up the road in Marazion, zig-zagging if you wish to use a pavement and pass the 40 sign. When just ahead is the sign which thanks you for driving carefully turn right into a driveway. At the bottom you are on a beach, walk along to ascend some hideous metal steps.

Shortly above Trenow Beach if you are fortunate you will be able to walk along a cliff top path without trouble.

After that you should have no trouble getting to Perranuthnoe where there are refreshments in season. The path turns inland here behind some houses, comes out on to the road to go up the lane opposite. Go right at the fork passing Blue Burrow Cottage and bear right.

When you get back to the coast do not go down the track to the beach but turn left into the next field At Cudden Point the path cuts slightly inland but then the true coast path goes seaward again before Little Cudden.

At Bessie's Cove the path goes up to join a track by a letter box. Continue ahead bearing right to turn right over a stone stile beside a massive gate. You can go down the track but the path is correct and at the top is traffic free.

37 | Prussia Cove to Porthleven

Grading: Strenuous   Distance -   10   446   6   277

See also our Penzance to Porthleven Path Description.

The path at Prussia Cove is quite a surprise, a sunken lane between two large stone buildings. You continue along a lane with the old coastguard row up on your left to pass through a gate, after which the track becomes a path and you should fork right at the first junction.

The path later becomes a green track down to Praa Sands where there are plenty of opportunities for refreshment in season.

The presently poorly marked route takes you down on the beach to leave it again as soon as you have passed the beach cafes up wooden steps. At the top turn right and proceed along to turn left to the well marked path through the sand dunes, shortly to turn right along the road through the estate.

If you do not wish to go down on the beach there is nothing to stop you turning left after the first cafe you come to, go inland past the public conveniences and then turning back right through the car park to reach the coast. Then proceed as above from the top of the wooden steps. If you like beach walking and the tide is out you can walk the length of the beach.

Assuming you have gone through the estate bear right at the other end to pick up the path just inland of the big stones in the road.

At Rinsey Head the path bears inland cutting off the point. You pass an old railway coach and at the top turn left and then immediately right going through the National Trust car park. As you drop down you should see two paths ahead, one going uphill which you do not want, the other going down, which you do. Pass the restored engine house to pick up the path below it on the other side.

At Trewavas Head the path bears inland of the old mine ruins, this used to be difficult to follow but recently way-marking has been improved.

As you approach Porthleven the path becomes semi-tarmac. You pass a cross erected in memory of those buried on the cliffs in unconsecrated ground. You go through a gate, or round the gatepost to join a lane, swing right as you reach the main road to go down to the harbour.

38 | Porthleven to Mullion Cove — OS E8 (103 on reprint) (V) Porthleven

Grading: Moderate   Distance -   12   458   7   284

See also our Porthleven to The Lizard Path Description.

At Porthleven as so often you have to walk right round the back of the harbour and out the other side. You go beyond the battlemented tower like building to keep up the coastal road using Mounts Road although it says it is a cul-de-sac.

Shortly after the last building on the right turn left off the track into the National Trust property Parc-an-als Cliff to avoid a landfall. Over the top you pick up the track again to proceed on and down to the beach.

If you have plenty of time there is a walking route right around Loe Pool the biggest natural lake in Cornwall.

As you cross Loe Bar look for the path going up just to the right of the field but divert to see the white cross on your right. You pick up the path you want on 126 degrees from the cross, after the path levels out you pass a wooden seat and about 100 yards after this fork right to pick up the old route.

At Gunwalloe Fishing Cove you come out on to gravelly road, do not take the first right which goes down to the beach but bear right on the second turning to pass inland of a house. At the top of the hill there is a stile where walking gardeners should look left.

Above Halzephron Cove you bear round to join the old road. Turn right shortly before you come to a barrier. You enter National Trust Halzephron Cliff do not turn right immediately but continue ahead to turn right just before the next field gate.

At Gunwalloe Church Cove there is an option. If you want to see the church, and it is interesting, when you join the road go right and after you have seen the church you can usually cross the beach and its stream.

If a church visit is not for you the correct route bears left aiming for buildings which prove to be public conveniences and a very seasonal cafe. There is a sign where you join the road but it is badly sited so is not obvious. Proceed down the road with National Trust Gunwalloe Towans sign on your right. Bear left off the road just before a turning space. Cross a bridge over a stream and turn right round the back of the beach. The path is narrow until you come to a track where you turn left uphill.

At the top there is a small car park; as soon as you have gone through this you can bear right to walk along the cliff tops and so miss a length of tarmac road.

There is a seasonal cafe at Poldhu Cove. You walk round the back of the beach on the road and go up the drive of the residential care home. Turn right off the driveway shortly before you get to the big house.

Skirt around the back of Polurrian Cove to go up the steps, then a track to turn right on a road. Where the road bears left proceed ahead on a path. If you are a purist the coast path goes in front of the old coastguard lookout, but this bit of path is seldom cleared.

Just past the Mullion Cove Hotel the path veers right, through the car parking spaces opposite starting by an old cannon. At the bottom turn left.

39 | Mullion Cove to The Lizard — OS E8 (103 on reprint)

Grading: Moderate   Distance -   10   468   6   290

See also our Porthleven to The Lizard Path Description.

Very spectacular a wonderful section this, with lots of interest. It can be accomplished too, without great effort! Un(ess the weather is beastly you will certainly enjoy this stretch. If you can arrange the transport it makes a spectacular long half day excursion.

You go up the road a very little way turn right and then right again.

After Mullion Cove in several places there are alternative paths but usually it makes little difference which you take, except as mentioned below.

After Parc Bean Cove going up Lower Predannock Cliff you want the higher path not the lower and at the top bear right.

After Vellan Cliff just before Gew-Graze the path veers slightly inland for a stile.

Taking the path down to Kynance Cove, as you go down aim for the further headland you can see which is Lizard Point. Later you will see a sign close to the sea where you have to turn left, go down further to cross a wide concrete bridge by a house.

There is a good, long season cafe at Kynance Cove. Unless the tide is right in, the quickest route is to cross the few yards at the back of the beach and go up the steps the other side. If the tide is right in you have to go up the drive before the cafe and bear right at the top.

Whichever way you came go through the car park and go out again just to the right of the public toilets.

Lizard Town is exceptionally well foot-pathed so if you are lodging there you have a great many options.

40 The Lizard to Coverack   OS E8 (103 on reprint) 1 mile to (V) The Lizard Town

Grading: Moderate but strenuous in parts	Distance -	18	486	11	301

See also our The Lizard to Helford Path Description.

A word of warning; old stone stiles are made of the local serpentine which can prove very slippery when wet, so take care on wet polished rock.

Most will start this walk by turning left above the Most Southerly Cafe, going along in front of the lighthouse. Unless you suffer from vertigo do not miss diverting right shortly after the lighthouse to see the spectacular Lion's Den which although only about 20 yards off the path is still missed by many.

You pass Housel Bay Hotel and later go through a kissing gate. The path is odd in that it keeps to the top edge of the field until the next gate, where it turns to the seaward edge again.

You pass the old Lloyd's Signal Station and come out on a drive by a house. You go along this only a short way and the coast path then takes off right.

At Kilcobben Cove you come just inland of the top building of the life-boat station, walk round it and go down the first little flight of steps but then go forward and not down the long flight of steps to the life-boat.

At Church Cove where refreshment is available, you go across diagonally behind one building to go through beside a big gate. Avoid the next four right turns to go uphill and over a stile.

After Polgwidden watch for a sharp right turn going along in front of an isolated house. The wrong path goes forward and looks more impressive.

Those with a taste for adventure and a resilience to scratches may like to divert down the cliff on the southern end of The Devil's Frying Pan before Cadgwith. It is possible to go over the top of the natural arch and so down to the bottom of the pit. This is the way really to appreciate the size of this natural feature but we stress it is only for the adventurous with nerves of steel.

You pass the National Trust Omega Devil's Frying Pan sign and the true coast path is diagonally ahead, down steps into the car park and out the other end to turn right. In fact it has lately been signposted avoiding the car park; the choice is yours. Whichever way you went you drop down a lovely path through a garden. Watch for the right turn just after you have gone over a stone stile next to a metal gate.

You drop into Cadgwith behind the beach where there is a chance of refreshment, and then start up the hill staying with the road to turn first right just past Veneth Cottage.

After Enys Head there is a poorly marked section, you come to a fork where go left, soon there is another right turn which you ignore, you come down to a gate where you turn right. Go down until you see the National Trust Poltesco sign on the left. Here turn right going down steps and over a bridge.

Avoid both the next right turns unless you wish to see the old Poltesco serpentine works.

At the next junction as you go up bear right and again at the next junction. Later you go through a golf course area at the end of which bear right. You come out on a road where you turn right. If the road is busy you can presently go across and take a permissive path to the beach, but it is not as rewarding as you might hope.

At Kennack Sands (refreshments in season) the path is behind the beach towards the toilets and then is now well marked behind the two beaches. If the tide is well out you can walk along both beaches to the far end but as the proper path at the time of writing is well maintained there is little gained.

What you do need to watch for at the far end of the second beach is that you take the coast path which looks fairly insignificant starting up nearly on the cliff edge, there is a bigger wide path going inland but do not take it. There is another minor junction shortly where you keep right again.

Care should be taken in front of Borgwitha and behind the cliff castle Carrick Luz because you cut across the neck of the peninsula and do not go inland or seaward. Improved waymarking should mean that you do not now go astray.

There is a very steep if scenic drop to Downas Cove and up the other side. After Beagles Point there is another smaller drop, cross a bridge and go up what is almost a stone chute the other side. At the top turn right.

After Black Head there is a very fine viewpoint for looking ahead along the South Cornish Coast. The path has been much improved and for a long way goes along the top of the cliffs. After you pass a piggery the route gets complicated. You come to a track, bear left but after about thirty yards go ahead on a path where the track bears left.

You cross an old stone stile, pass an old fashioned pump and come to a grassy area with caravans*. Here turn sharp right and turn right again when you get to the tarmac drive. Go along the left side of this until just before a sign forbidding access. Here turn sharp left and go down steps; there is a junction here left which is a quick but incorrect route. Right is correct and more scenic. Go down to the next junction where ahead is Chynall's Point, a cul-de-sac but part of the coast path. Left is your route towards Coverack.

As you enter Coverack you reach a tarmac path, turn right and go down to join a road. If you wish to do all the coast path there is then a little loop that many miss. Twenty yards down the road the path goes away right above a children's playground. The path then looks as though it is going to end but press on over a slight rise to go down steps and turn left in front of a house.

Keep right of the back of a pub into the car park turn left and left again to pass the front of the same pub.

*There is a shorter alternative route here if needed. Turn right as above but when you get to the drive turn left along it and very soon divert off right on a field path to Coverack.

41	**Coverack to Helford**			**OS E8 (103 on reprint) (V) Coverack**	

Grading: Moderate		Distance -	20	506	13	314

See also our The Lizard to Helford Path Description.

Note: Evening meals can present a problem in Helford. At busy periods the Shipwrights Arms (01326 231235) will only serve pre-booked meals. The Riverside Restaurant (01326 231443) is an alternative. There is also the Rose Tea Gardens which serves meals but shuts earlier. Think about this before leaving Coverack or you may go to bed hungry.

The statistically minded may wish to be advised that in this section they will pass the halfway mark of the whole coast path.

In Coverack you walk around behind the harbour and the beach and where the main road bears inland go ahead up the small tarmac road. The tarmac ends just before a small rise, go over this and start to drop down, look for a path turning off right just before a gate across the road.

The patch out to Lowland Point is improved but the further you go the less evidence of path there is. However the basic ploy is to keep close to the shore going east until you have to turn north at the point.

After Lowland Point the coast path goes through Dean Quarry. This Association fought hard to get the path on the coast here rather than a long diversion inland. Blasting can take place 1000 to 1030, 1300 to 1330, 1700 to 1830. At these times the path will be closed but you can use the diversion if travelling north.

Most of the quarry area is well signposted, but it is important that when you come up level with the first building you start down the steep ramp to the beach the footpath goes left off this. Towards the end of the quarry area signs are more scarce but keep with the track close above the sea to go down on to the beach at Godrevy Cove.

Walk just over half way along the beach crossing the stream bed which sometimes has water but is often dry, then turn half left to circumvent a marshy area and pick up the path at the back of the beach. Here turn left until you can turn inland through fields. At present the correct path is a sunken, usually muddy, lane on your right, so that most stay in the fields to join the track up to Rosenithon.

At the T junction in Rosenithon turn right, go up the hill the road swings right and just after this the footpath takes off left into a field. Cross one field and a traditional Cornish stile, surely the forerunner of the modern cattle grid. Cross two more fields in the same direction and surprisingly the stile is just below the gate you come to.

Turn left on the road then first right down into Porthoustock. From Porthoustock to Porthallow the official route again goes inland to avoid the now unused quarries around Pencra Head and Porthkerris Point. However, there is a coast path.

Coastal Route
This long time unofficial route is now freely available thanks to the landowner. Even the high tide route is infinitely superior to the inland route. Warning, check state of tide at Porthoustock, you cannot see what it is at decision point later, low tide route is currently overgrown for about 100 yards south of Porthkerris Cove.

In Porthoustock keep right of the telephone box, pass the entrance to the beach forking left up a bank passing in front of a thatched cottage. You soon come to a big metal gate the pedestrian access is just to the right round the wall.

Continue along the track, there are buildings on the right, a quarry pit down on the left and then two level quarry entrances on the left a big one then a small. Next on the left is a small section of concrete walling about five yards past this there are steps going up, take these. The first few have metal treads, later ones are concrete, they are not continuous and run out towards the top, however proceed steeply up to the trackway on the higher level, where you turn right.

Proceed along, until the track bears half left, decision time.

Low Tide
Proceed straight ahead, it does not look very inviting, over low piles of stones in about twenty five yards look for the overgrown entrance of a path just left of a low bank. You descend an inclined plane which is overgrown in places for about 100 yards. You go down to Porthkerris Cove with a big quarry on your left. Go along the beach, with opportunity for seasonal refreshments behind. Proceed up the road. Just after a little open area on the right the road bears left and there is an entrance on the right to a field, take this. Keep with the right hand hedge to go through a gap into another field. Walk across this on 280 degrees aiming for a sycamore tree and go through the kissing gate.

High Tide
Keep with the track which soon swings fully left, its quite a long walk round, but you have spectacular views across to Falmouth and beyond. The track eventually meets the road by a radar station turn right for a long walk along the road. Watch out for set-aside open access notices on your left. The first is an advanced warning but the second gives access into a field. Go in as the far as the field corner on left then turn left on a bearing of approximately 304 degrees towards a sycamore tree and go through the kissing gate.

At Sycamore Tree Routes Rejoin

Proceed ahead up the path and then steeply down to the beach at Porthallow.

Official Route

You leave Porthoustock going up the hill, but soon, where the road bears right go ahead on a track. You pass houses on your right, the track ends and you keep ahead into a field. Here turn steeply up the field 302 degrees joining the right hand field bank at the top. Keep close to the bank to a sunken stile in the corner then slightly more right 338 degrees to another sunken stile just left of the gate.

Bear left on the road which later bears left to Trenance. Here turn right. At the next T junction look for the footpath ahead and a few yards to your right. Go down alongside a vineyard to join the road where you turn right down to Porthallow. There are seasonal refreshments available here.

You leave Porthallow by taking the second turning on to the beach and immediately turning left to go along the back of the foreshore and up steps, bearing right at the first junction.

As you approach Nare Point ignore a metal kissing gate which you pass on the right to shortly turn left along a one-time track which served the lookout. You go through a gateway and when the track swings uphill proceed ahead across a footbridge.

After the second National Trust property `The Herra', you come to a small beach where you go across the back. You come to a second beach, Flushing Cove, where you turn right on a path behind the beach.

A very short distance beyond the beach a footpath takes off left and it is decision time. If you know the tide is in and you want to walk round, turn left.

Gillan Creek - Walking Round

It is about $2^1/_4$ miles, say an hour, easy walking but nearly all road. This distance is extra to the mileage shown for the section. If time is of the essence you can go via Manaccan and be in Helford in 3 miles but that is of course not walking the coast path.

The route starts as a concrete track, grass centred, becomes tarmac then takes off right as the road bears left to go through one field. In the second the path does not go up to the farm buildings but skews right across the field to run along the far side of the field hedge and then comes back to the farm track to go up to the road. At the road turn right and then right again at Carne at the head of the creek.

Gillan Creek Crossing

No ferry but it can usually be forded from one hour before Low Tide to one hour after. Predicted low water is 15 minutes earlier than shown in the Tide Tables. But do proceed with care!

There are two possible crossing places. Proceed until you can go no further along the path by the river, descend steps to the beach and wade across towards two caravans on far shore.

A little further upstream you can cross part way on stepping stones in two sections. But this is not the easy option it sounds because they are extremely slippery and do not go across the whole river. It is advisable to carry handfulls of sand to scatter onto the stepping stones and even then be careful if you do not use the stepping stones take your boots off and paddle across.

Once across turn right to pass in front of the church Turn left up the hill about ten yards past a mounting block on the left look for a path going off at an angle right, take this and turn first right. You may then see the sign which should be at the bottom.

For the short route you need to turn left just after the house on your right beyond the kissing gate. If you have time the circular route out around Dennis Head is rewarding. To walk this, proceed ahead into the open field along a vestigial track towards a wood, keep to the left of the wood but close to it. Pass round the back of it where you will find a stile on your left you can complete the circuit of the head returning to the stile and then back along the right hand hedge. You pass through several fields but then watch out for the sharp and partially concealed right turn into the wood. (Dogs are not allowed.)

You come out by an old railed hound enclosure to bear slightly right and then go up a tarmac drive with grass in the centre. At the top turn right down the road, turn left up steps just as you get to the drive of a house called Traeth Cottage. It is easy to miss, if you get to the shore you have missed it!

Go along the back of the car park, down the road, crossing the first bridge over the creek. Turn right and go along past The Shipwright's Arms to the ferry point.

For the statistically minded again, if we include the Isle of Portland within the coast path, and the Countryside Commission does not, as you reach the ferry point we estimate you are half way around.

42 | Helford to Falmouth   OS E8 (103 on reprint) (V) Helford

Grading: Moderate   Distance -   15   521   10   324

See also our Helford to Falmouth Path Description.

Helford to Helford Passage use ferry, see details below. If the ferry is not running your alternatives are probably a taxi or a 15 mile walk This is mostly road but you can incorporate Frenchman's Creek.

Helford Passage (Helford River). Seasonal.   Good Friday to 31 Oct incl.Departs Helford Passage
Helford River Boats, Helford Passage,   on the hour and Helford at 10 min. past the hour,
Nr Falmouth Tel Mawnan Smith   9am to 5pm and 9am to 6pm in July and August.
01326 250770   All ferry crossings are subject to tide and weather
                                               conditions.

This section makes a good day walk from Falmouth by using the, admittedly infrequent, bus service to the road turn just above Helford Passage. Be sure you get your bus out and walk back, that way you can enjoy your walk.

At Helford Passage go along the beach eastwards to go up the steps at the end. At Durgan bear sharp right when you reach the track then bear left by the old school. Go up the road past a little grassy area with a seat on the right then DO NOT turn first right, it is the second turning you want.

At the next beach you come to Porth Saxon, you go in front of the boathouse, and the path is then at the back of the shore. At the following beach, Porthallack, the path in contrast stays in the fields to go on to the beach beyond a building.

The true coast path goes out round Rosemullion Head with its fine views but there is a short cut across its neck. You come to the National Trust Nansidwell property and shortly into a big field, go downwards and across to join the bottom hedge. The exit is in the corner. There is another path better walked going ahead but it is the wrong path. The path does not go on the beach but bears left at the last moment.

You come out onto the road at Maenporth (refreshments in season) turn right along the road turning right again at the other end of the beach.

On reaching the road turn right for Swanpool, there walk across the back of the beach to continue on the coast path turning right at the first junction. At Gyllyngvase Beach turn right along the road it will not be most people's favourite walking but it is quite rewarding looking back to where you have previously been.

When you get towards the end of the seafront passing the last big hotel, The Falmouth Hotel, do not go down right but continue on the pavement beside the road until you have passed the cul-de-sac notice, then you can bear right if you wish away from the road. However presently you will need to cross the road for the safety of the pavement around Pendennis Point.

At the point the road turns left, go along this road for about quarter of a mile, passing several seats, then just before another one there are steps going down to the road. Almost opposite there are three entries, take the third one; you come out on a tarmac lane briefly left then turn right on the road. You go down with interesting views over the shipyards.

You come to a T junction where you turn right, there is then a town centre sign pointing left but that is the long way round for traffic so stay with us. Go ahead under the railway bridge the road shortly bears left and there is a pub on the right which still proclaims it has hotel stables and motor garage

The road bears right passing a big car park and soon becomes a shopping street. Continue until Marks & Spencers, and the next turning on the right takes you to the ferry.

BMG - Does not cover the total mileage through Falmouth.

43 | Falmouth to Place House   OS E105 (T) Falmouth (Trains) (V) St Mawes

No Grading   Distance -   0   521   0   324

See also our Falmouth to Portloe Path Description.

In season you can cross by using two ferries, see details below. The only point to watch is that depending on conditions the first ferry takes 20 to 30 minutes for the passage.

The ferry from Falmouth to St Mawes runs the whole year round except for winter Sundays. The scarcity of public transport in winter on Sundays combined with the fact that it is a long hike makes us advise anyone arriving in Falmouth in winter on a Sunday to take it as a day off!

The ferry from St Mawes to Place only runs in season. If you are a purist there is a reasonable walking route round of 8-9 miles two sections of which are very good walking indeed, see below for details. There are about a couple of buses a day from St Mawes to Gerrans, except on Sundays, or you could consider a taxi. If the ferry is not in service you can always ask. We have heard from walkers who have been lucky enough to get a lift from local boat owners.

Falmouth/St Mawes
St Mawes Ferry Co
75 The Beacon Falmouth TR1 1 2BD
Tel (01326)313813 - Nov - March
(01326) 313201 - April - Oct
(0850) 769127 (mobile)

All year round. Weather permitting.
Falmouth/St Mawes (Summer Service) April to October
Weekdays: 0830 hrs, 0945 hrs, then 1/2 hourly
to 1715 hrs. Sundays (commencing May)
1000 to 1700 hrs. Hourly. Depart Falmouth,
Prince of Wales Pier. St Mawes/Falmouth.
Weekdays 0900, 0945, then 1/2 hourly until
1715 hrs. Sundays (commencing May)
1030 to 1730 hrs. Hourly Nov. to March boats daily.
From Falmouth 0830,1015,1115,1315, 1415, 1615hrs.
From St Mawes 0900, 1045, 1145, 1345, 1445,1645 hrs.
No Sunday Service.

The St Mawes Ferry Co. are prepared to land pre-organized parties of 20 or more at Place House. To do this they would need prior knowledge to lay on an extra boat. This is also dependent on the state of the tide and weather.

St Mawes/Place House (St Anthony)
For information please write to:
Mr R Balcombe
Turks Folly, Drump Road
Redruth TR1 5 1 PR
Tel: (01209)214901 or (01326)270553

Seasonal
Daily - 1 May-30 September
St Mawes to Place 1/2 hourly
from 1000 to 1630 hrs. No 1300 boat. Place
to St Mawes 1/2 hourly from 1015 to 1645.
No 1315 boat.

Walking Route
Turn left after leaving the ferry from Falmouth and proceed along the road till you reach the castle, immediately after the castle take a left turn along a minor tarmac road, if you look carefully you will see a footpath sign amongst all the clutter about the Castle's car parks.

Follow this minor road until you come to the National Trust land `Newton Cliff' which you enter. The route follows a very lovely path along the estuary with superb views across to Falmouth and the far shore. You come out on a minor tarmac road just after a footpath sign `Public Footpath St Mawes 2 miles' pointing back the way one has come. Turn right along the road. Continue along this minor road bearing left at the junction to pass in front of a boatyard. Immediately after passing the boatyard buildings the path swings a few yards right to proceed along the bank above the shore.

You come to the gate leading to the yard of St Just in Roseland Church with a large sign 'Dogs on Leads Please Consecrated Ground'. Go through this, keeping left all the way to pass the church on your right. Ignore the turning right marked `Way out' but instead keep left through a lych gate and pass the house 'Lanzeague'. After its second gate the path bears right up hill starting beside a low rail fence backed by trees. You pass through a decrepit metal gate continuing ahead uphill with views of the creek to your left. You go through a wooden gate into a lane in parts muddy in parts green to exit on to the road.

Turn left and walk along the road for about 150 yds, ignore the first footpath on the right immediately past a house but take the second on the right shortly afterwards. For the first field you have the hedge on the right. For the second and third it is on your left. Then for the fourth it is again on your right. In this fourth field look for a sharp right turn shortly before the end. Turn down steps to the road. Here turn right to reach the main A3078.

At Trethem Mill turn left, this is on a bridge crossing the creek, and immediately turn right up some stone steps and ascend through a wood. Coming out of the wood cross a field on approximate bearing of 110 degrees, to leave by a conspicuous tree. Cross the corner of the next field on 140 degrees and leave by a wooded track. At the top there is a stile, bear 137 degrees diagonally across the field to the hedge and follow this to the road. Turn right down the road.

At the next junction follow the road curving round to the right past Polhendra Cottage and then left through a large metal gate as indicated by a footpath sign. Aim across approx. 123 degrees to descend to the bottom of the hedge which you can see on the opposite side of the valley. Here you will find a bridge, cross it and proceed up, with the hedge on your left. At the top ascend some stone steps and cross the next two fields on 125 degrees. On reaching the road turn right into Gerrans.

Walk down to the church and here take the left fork (not left turn) Treloan Lane. You walk via Treloan and Rosteague, at each junction keeping straight ahead to come out on the road just before Porth Farm. The slightly quicker way is then to turn right along the road and left where there is a sign 'Footpath to Place by Percuil River' to come to a wooden bridge. The pleasanter alternative is to go ahead into the National Trust car park and then turn right to get to the same wooden bridge by paths.

Over the bridge the path turns right to follow Porth Creek and then the Percuil River, down to the low tide landing point for the ferry and soon on to Place itself. This last stretch of walking is very scenic.

44 | Place House to Portscatho   OS E105

Grading: Easy   Distance -   10   531   6   330

See also our Falmouth to Portloe Path Description.

The St Anthony Peninsula, thanks to the National Trust, offers a very good half-day circular walk. Most people will start at Porth Farm, walk to Place as already described, and then follow the coast path round St Anthony's Head and on to Towan Beach here turning back inland to Porth Farm.

Some maps show a definitive Right of Way across the front of Place House, this route however is not really practical except at very low tides.

This means that you must walk up the road at Place passing the gates of the house and shortly turn right to go behind the church. You get back to the creekside, soon to leave it again to go over behind Amsterdam Point. The path then is superb with wonderful views across the Carrick Roads. After the footbridge across the top of a one time dam turn sharp right. Shortly turn even sharper left to go up steps and turn right again at the top. Look for the very little path forking right up to the topograph for the best viewpoint.

The path then proceeds forwards without problems to Portscatho, however owing to the lie of the land you do not see the village until the very last moment and it always seems to take longer than one thinks it should.

45 | Portscatho to Portloe   OS E105 (V) Portscatho

Grading: Strenuous   Distance -   12   543   7   337

See also our Falmouth to Portloe Path Description.

You leave Portscatho going through a couple of small fields, if the tide is out you have a choice. You can start down the steps then turn right and go down to cross Porthcurnick Beach, this is slightly shorter. The reward for not turning for the beach but going up the steps opposite is that you then pass a seasonal refreshment hut.

If the tide is out it is easier to walk along Pendower Beach to Carne Beach. You can look forward to see if this is feasible as you walk down by the car park before Pendower Beach.

Having ascended Nare Head, it is possible to short cut it by veering left but unless the weather is poor do not do this or you will miss out on the rewarding views. Study the way the first arrow is pointing and follow its direction along the edge of the gorse. There is an unmarked path going right to the head itself. Shortly afterwards there is a post with an arrow pointing left here on a bearing of 120 degrees, if you look carefully you will see a small path going forward into the gorse, take this. This path gives the best views of Gull Rock offshore. It winds back to join the main track, here turn right.

At the other end of the track about 200 yards on, where it opens up, there are little ventilators, bear across right to pick up the coast again. Do not stay on the track.

Another place you can go wrong is after the very steep descent off The Blouth where the path bears left and then right over a stile. There is a sign but it is badly sited so it is easy to miss and as a result a lot of people go wrong here.

At The Straythe there is a pleasant surprise for those who walked this way some years ago. A new well engineered path zig-zags up to replace the old uncomfortable and nearly vertical flight of steps. At the top the route is well sign-posted through the gardens but you do need to turn right in the field when you get there.

There is a long descent into Portloe but at least you can see it unlike Portscatho. Watch for the sharp left turn just as you draw nearly level with a green seat on your right. Then you want the second turning on the left to pass in front of the public toilets and so down to Portloe.

46 | Portloe to East Portholland   OS E105

Grading: Strenuous	Distance -	3	546	2	339

See also our Portloe to Mevagissey Path Description.

This stretch is rewarding and will give you enjoyment for your efforts.

From the quay at Portloe you can turn first right, scramble along and up some steps, to rejoin the coast path that way. However the true coast path goes up the road, turns right along another road, and then shortly leaves it down some wide steps past cottages. The official route does have the advantage that it passes the Post Office which serves cream teas.

A new path has been made in the landslip area just before West Portholland.

You can, if you wish, avoid the road walk from West to East Portholland by going forward behind the beach at West Portholland and walking along the sea wall between the two settlements. This is a little rocky at the beginning but should present no problems to any sure footed walker.

47 | East Portholland to Gorran Haven   OS E105

Grading: Moderate	Distance -	11	557	6	345

See also our Portloe to Mevagissey Path Description.

The path starts along a one time tarmac lane from East Portholland. Turn right at the end of this lane to descend a field and continue alongside the coast. There is a path forward but if you use it, you simply get a longer stretch of road to walk to get to Porthluney Cove.

There is a seasonal cafe behind the beach in front of Caerhays Castle. Note one point, on leaving the road you cross half the first field joining a rough track close to a projecting corner of waste land. The path does not stay on the track here but turns sharp right along the fence. The badly sited marker post is usually invisible in the long grass.

From Hemmick Beach via The Dodman to Gorran Haven, it is all good walking; there are wonderful views from The Dodman in the right conditions. You can look back on triumphs past and challenges still long to come! Just north of The Dodman Cross is an 18th Century coastguard watch-house which does prove useful shelter in heavy rain.

At Little Sand Cove there is an old path cutting the corner off Pen-a-Maen Point. We do not recommend it - you climb higher and will not have such good views.

48 | Gorran Haven to Mevagissey   OS E105 (V) Gorran Haven

Grading: Easy	Distance -	5	562	4	349

See also our Portloe to Mevagissey Path Description.

This section starts happily enough but you are beginning to leave the most remote and least spoiled section of the South Cornish coast behind.

You come into Gorran Haven on Foxhole Lane, turn right into Canton and just before the beach turn left into Church St. Proceed up this, there is a footpath loop to the right if you want a brief better look at the beach, and turn right at the top into Cliff Road. You go up past the old coastguard row and turn right again at the top, still Cliff Road. At its end Cliff Road turns left and you go up a stile into a field.

From Turbot Point you descend to Colona Beach passing the National Trust Bodrugan's Leap sign. Turn right to pass behind the beach, do not go left when the track bears left but proceed ahead very shortly to cross the tarmac drive to continue ahead on a footpath across the grass. At its start you are heading in a straight line for Mevagissey Harbour; later it veers a little left and you pick up a hedge on your right. Continue along this hedge until it goes up to join the road where you turn right.

At the end you will find the road is called Chapel Point Lane, turn right, bear left at the sea and follow the road round past the Rising Sun.

You bear right on entering Mevagissey on Polkirt Hill. You pass buildings on your right and then enter a park, proceed through this to the other end. Turn right down the first flight of public stone steps on the right to come out on the quay close to some public toilets.

49 | Mevagissey to Charlestown   OS E105 and E107 (V) Mevagissey (V) Pentewan

Grading: Strenuous	Distance -	11	573	7	356

See also our Mevagissey to Fowey Path Description.

In Mevagissey walk along the back of the harbour to turn right and then very shortly bear up left veering away from, and up above, the quayside. You come out into open playing fields, go across but aim for the extreme right end of the terrace of buildings you see opposite. This is where the footpath leaves the field. There have been a series of landslips in the next section but no serious problems currently exist. Continue along, avoiding right turn down steps. The path comes out again into a field and there is a steep descent to cross a bridge. Here turn left.

You descend from Penare Point to walk behind the ruins of Portgiskey, crossing three stiles to turn right. Ignore the next stile on the right but proceed curving right up the hill to cross a stile just before the road, here turn right.

You come out on to the road close to the entrance of a massive caravan park. Here you have the choice of:

1. turning left to the main road B3273, then right towards St Austell and first right again signposted Pentewan and called West End, which is the official route, or;

2. turning right towards the sea, crossing two stiles and left after the public toilets along the front, over a bridge of the St Austell river; then make for a narrow wooden bridge ahead, turn left and take footpath close on the right up through a private garden to rejoin the coast path at the top of the hill. However, this route avoids the shops at Pentewan.

Do not leave Pentewan unrefreshed, you have a long tough section ahead.

Turn right off the road into the harbour area just after the publc toilets, walk along the harbour to the end of the cottages where you will see a path on your left going up through gardens to link up with the coast path behind the cottages. This path is frequently unsigned and does not look like a public Right of Way, but it is at the top of the garden, turn left and then soon right.

Back on the coast path put this book away, you will need your energies for other things! However take it out again when you have crossed a sloping bridge in a sizable wood.

Having crossed the bridge, you soon cross another small stream and come to a T junction. The right turn will take you down to Hallane Mill Beach, a lovely spot for a picnic with a waterfall. The coast path turns left soon to turn right again to start ascending to Black Head, a superb diversionary viewpoint on a clear day. It was once a rifle range but was purchased by the National Trust, helped in a small way with a donation from this Association.

The passage of the wood behind Ropehaven can give trouble if signing is not maintained. On entering the wood you turn right then left at the seat. Avoid the right fork down to a cottage and turn sharp left at the top into a narrow walled lane. Turn right on to the narrow road. The path leaves it to go into a field just beyond the little car park/lay by.

At Porthpean Beach the sign forward can be misleading go down on to the promenade to walk along past toilets and a seasonal cafe. Continue to the end, it does not look likely, but there is a steep set of steps at the end to get you back on track.

Just before Charlestown is a stile leading through a high wall you get a few more yards on the coast by using it.

---

50 | Charlestown to Par   OS E107 (V) Charlestown

Grading: Easy   Distance -   6   579   4   360

See also our Mevagissey to Fowey Path Description.

The official path does not go across the dock gate at the mouth of the harbour but provided the gate is closed most people will go that way. Despite the nearness of St Austell the path is on the whole good until near Par.

You come up from the harbour keeping to the right of a house called Salamander. It is at first a tarmac track and then goes into fields. Later you come out beside a road, walk a few yards along it to turn right and then fork left.

After passing the Carlyon Bay Hotel you come out by a car park area, keep to the right of this to cross the road and continue alongside a golf course.

You become more and more threatened by the clay processing industrial complex ahead, however continue bravely bearing finally left just before a wall/wire netting fence. The next bit could be called different, or interesting, but it is hardly beautiful! Avoid the escape route left under a low railway culvert but continue ahead along what looks like a dead end to the road and turn right to go past the entrance to the ECC works.

Continue north on the road and go under a railway viaduct to turn first right signposted A3082 Fowey, cross a level crossing and under another railway bridge. Proceed up a no entry road, Par Green, with the Cornish Arms on your left. You pass The Good Shepherd Church on your right and Welcome Home Inn on your left. You then take the second path off on the right although the National Trust waymark indicates straight on along the road. To try and make this clearer, the beginning of the path has a low concrete wall and house No. 52 (Sandroy), on the right. It soon comes to a tidal stream, bear left to walk along it, cross a road and come out in a caravan site, keep down the right hand side, to turn left and go along the seaward side of a blue roofed building. You pass a cafe, which claims to be open all the year round, and finally come to Polmear with its seasonal cafe.

If you miss all this you can simply walk along Par Green, bear right at its end to get to Polmear by main road. It is less pleasant, gives less chance of refreshment but it gets you there just the same.

Grading: Moderate   Distance -   **10**   **589**   **6**   **366**

See also our Mevagissey to Fowey Path Description.

It is a fine walk out from Polmear via Polkerris around the Gribbin Head to Menabilly and so on to Fowey. The availability of public transport from Par to Fowey makes this a very practical half day excursion with lovely views nearly all the way.

The path leaves the main road at Polmear just beside the eye-catching Rashleigh Cottages. For a very short while it is also The Saint's Way see note below*. At the first junction keep right and at the second turn right leaving the Saints to their own devices.

As you enter Polkerris you turn right. Go down to the beach and turn left, currently no sign, to proceed up the ramp and join a path.

You should have no problem then until you enter the National Trust The Gribbin property through a field gateway. There is soon a junction, bear right and you come to a pedestrian gate. The official route goes to the Daymark and then sets off downhill inland. There is a better alternative seaward, bear right along the fence from the pedestrian gate to presently go through a second pedestrian gate and the way forward is then obvious passing through a little wood, when you come out proceed downhill to join the official route. If you want the best route but also wish to make a closer examination of the Daymark itself bear left and go and find out. When you have satisfied your curiosity proceed due south and you will come to the second gate already mentioned.

You come down towards Polridmouth Beach and walk around close behind it, the path becomes concrete and there are even concrete stepping stones, this does not sound delightful but this is a lovely little stretch by the house and lake. The path goes steeply up bearing right through woods at the other side.

Again there should be no navigational problems until you reach Allday's Fields (memorial stone on your left). You enter a wood, first right is a loop path out towards the castle and there is a steep path dropping to the beach which can be used as a short cut when the tide is out. On entering the wood the more direct route is to go ahead at the first junction and to turn left at the next. This takes you down an increasingly rock cut lane which has a very sharp elbow about two thirds of the way down.

The path comes out at Readymoney Cove and it is then all road to Fowey. However if you are continuing along the coast path watch for the ferry point on your right before you get into the town. It is down steps just after Fowey Hotel's tea garden.

*The Saints Way is a long distance footpath from Fowey to Padstow and a guide book is available. Quite apart from being a walk in its own right this could make a link enabling walkers to undertake a circular Cornish peninsula walk of approximately 220 miles

---

Grading: Strenuous   Distance -   **11**   **600**   **7**   **373**

See also our Fowey to Looe Path Description.

Leaving Fowey, if you have time on your side, you can go via the higher vehicular ferry to Bodinnick and walk The Hall Walk to Polruan. The more direct route already mentioned is the lower passenger

ferry. This section is very good value for money in two senses of the word. Firstly there is a fine path all the way from Polruan to Polperro with magnificent sea views. Secondly, it is probably the toughest stretch of walking on the South Cornwall coast.

Fowey/Polruan (River Fowey)
Polruan Ferry Co. Ltd
Tomsyard
East Street
Polruan-by-Fowey
Cornwall
PL23 1PB
Tel: 01726 870232

All the year round. Continuous. Summer, 30th April
to 1st October: From Town Quay, Fowey.
0715 to 2300 hrs (2330 during August).
Winter, October - April. From Whitehouse Slip
Fowey. Oct/Apr. Sat starts 7.30 Sunday starts 10.00
No service Christmas Day, limited service Boxing
and New Years Day.

In winter months when the weather deteriorates you may find that the ferry operates to and from the town quay at Fowey rather than the jetty lower down the harbour. There should be sign up to this effect.

From Polruan to Cawsand Caradon District Council will be operating a kit transfer service, 'Caradon Packhorse'. For details telephone the South East Cornwall Discovery at Looe (01503 263266).

Landing from the ferry go along the quay and up Garrett Steps just beside The Lugger, at the top turn right along West Street and then left when you get to Battery Lane. The path comes out in a grassy area, keep with the wall on your left going round the corner. The path goes right, just after an earth bank and then proceed ahead across another open area with a small ruin up on your left. It joins the road beside a school, continue ahead to turn sharp right just before the notice saying 'Furze Park'.

About two miles after leaving Polruan there is a considerable hill behind Great Lantic Beach. You can go all the way to the top and turn right there. The route we recommend turns right about 30 yards before the top, go over a stile and drops down again. Ignore the first two turnings right as there are beach paths. Presently a wide path, the other route, joins from the left. Shortly after that there is another path right this is a spectacular, even more seaward, loop.

Although a definitive Right of Way is shown below the Watch House, at the moment the practical route is the broad path above it. Assuming you are on this path, ignore the stile on your right which goes directly to the house. Just after this is another loop path right but it has little in views to compensate for the extra effort.

When you come to Lansallos Cove, look for West Combe on your map, a sign points you inland for the coast path. Unless the tide is fully in, it is more interesting to go ahead and turn right down to the beach through a small rock cut lane. Go left, cross the back of the beach and climb the little rock cut steps on the other side.

Later you enter the National Trust Chapel Cliff property and there is a series of parallel paths all going to Polperro. You should take the rocky path on your right by an outcrop, on your left, as you get a glimpse of some houses on the opposite cliff. This is the most seaward path and passes several seats and shelters to arrive at a rocky area overlooking the mouth of the harbour. From the rocky area turn left and the official route into Polperro is the first set of steps on the right.

53 | Polperro to Looe   OS E107 (V) Polperro

Grading: Moderate	Distance -	8	608	5	378

See also our Fowey to Looe Path Description.

This next section is particularly well walked and the local bus company is sufficiently commercially minded to put up bus times for cliff walkers between Polperro and Looe actually on the path!

In Polperro you have to walk behind the harbour crossing Roman Bridge to turn right. Leaving Polperro there is a loop path right called Reuben's Walk. If you take this turn left again just before the miniature lighthouse.

Note the spectacularly sited War Memorial on Downend Point A little way past this is another beach path right which you ignore.

There is a seasonal cafe at Talland Bay.

After the cafe go up the tarmac track, turn left past the toilets and then right. Pass a field car park and after about a quarter of a mile turn right into a car park and so back on the path again.

Entering West Looe you have a long stretch along the seafront but presently come to a stretch of road with no pavement. This drops into a dip and watch for a battlemented look-out platform on your right. Just past this are steps down to the harbour area of the river; that is the best way to go. This has a double advantage it keeps you away from the traffic and takes you past the long seasonal ferry to East Looe, certainly if you are walking straight through this is the best way to go.

54 | Looe to Portwrinkle   OS E107 & E108 (T) Looe (Trains) (V) Seaton (V) Downderry

Grading: Strenuous - Moderate in places	Distance -	12	620	8	386

See also our Looe to Plymouth Path Description.

This is a section with several difficulties. You leave East Looe by turning up Castle Street, cross a minor cross roads continuing up the hill. The road peters out becoming a pleasant high level path above the sea.

The path becomes a road again and at the first junction bear right. Pass Bodrigy a seasonal cafe, continue on the road until just after it has veered left. Here a steep tarmac path takes off right just beyond a big electric cable post.

At the top of the path you come to a road again to continue ahead for a while until the road bears left but the path goes forward again between houses. Go down steps, do not turn left or right but continue nearly opposite to go ahead.

The path comes down to Millendreath (seasonal refreshments) pass behind the beach to go up the cul-de-sac road the other side. The road becomes a path in a sunken lane but 1 50 yards after you reach road again turn right into the Bodigga Cliff N.T. property. The path is now greatly improved and you should enjoy this stretch.

The path comes out on the road above Seaton, turn right down what is Looe Hill. Go down to the bottom and turn right into Bridge Road, if time presses the quickest route is along the road, however at most states of the tide there is a better alternative. Where the road starts to go uphill, opposite the Post Office, there is a wall on the seaward side. Behind this wall is the beginning of coastal defence works with a path on top. After a while you have to go down to the beach and then you have two choices. If you turn inland just before the 'Inn On The Shore' you will arrive at the centre of Downderry, shops, seasonal refreshment etc. If you do not want to do this but wish to minimize road walking, and there is a lot in the next section to come, go on to the next stream and turn left there up concrete steps. You come up beside a school to turn right along a road.

Continue with the road until it sweeps inland at a hairpin bend. The path takes off right here, next to a house named 'Downderry Lodge', zig-zagging uphill to come eventually into a field. The coast path should then go right and many people have mistakenly done that finding it hard to believe that twenty five years after the Cornish section of the coast path was opened it is still unfinished! However the dull by-pass route goes forward through a few inland fields and then joins a road where you turn right. You then have a long tedious section on the road before turning right again just after a bungalow named 'The Bungalow' to go down to Portwrinkle to turn left.

BMG - Page 76. Third line from bottom - for 'left' read 'right'.

55 | Portwrinkle to Cremyll (for Plymouth)   OS E108 (V) Cawsand/Kingsand

Grading: Moderate	Distance -	21	641	13	399

See also our Looe to Plymouth Path Description.

If the tide is out and there is no firing at Tregantle Fort, you can in fact walk along the beach the whole way to Polhawn Cove and some find this a better alternative to what is currently offered.

If you do this you need the first path down right to the beach and be warned, the last mile before Polhawn becomes rocky.

The current route takes the second path on the right going up opposite to the entrance to the golf club. It is currently well marked except right at the end of the course, where you need to aim for the pedestrian gate seen on top of a rise.

You come out to the road but the path for a while is just inside the hedge. This travesty of a path ends by the road junction to Torpoint where you have to come down to the road and turn right along it. All this agony is caused by some bureaucrat in M.O.D. who refuses to let you walk through the rifle range when not in use, if it can be done elsewhere, even on a tank firing range in Dorset, with good will it could here.

However back to the road, you pass Tregantle Fort entrance, the road bears left and shortly you turn right signposted Whitsand Bay etc. The road bears left shortly with National Trust properties on your right. Here the National Trust have constructed a splendid new path to the seaward and lower side of the coast road as far as Sharrow Point Car Park, although twice it has to briefly rejoin the road verge at incuts by the cliffs.

There is then another long stretch of road, until you see notices for Whitsand Bay Holiday Park on the left and the coast path starts again on the right, at this point even sharper left is a seasonal cafe. The coast path is now well marked and a great improvement over the road, but it does descend and climb twice. So if time presses you can stay on the road until you see on the left Wiggle Old Farm House, turn right there and within a few yards you will pick up the coast path again.

The path is then clear until you are immediately inland of Rame Head, a diversion to the headland is well worth making if conditions are clear. The path then proceeds across an unmarked junction, go straight ahead, along a good high level path above the sea, when you get to the road keep right.

Continue along the tarmac avoiding the path turn off on the right, the road turns left with intermittent views ahead to Plymouth Sound Breakwater and presently over a quarter of a mile later, takes off into the wood right.

Traversing Cawsand/Kingsand the official and in fact easiest way is not straightforward and only some of it is signposted, so read the next paragraph carefully.

You enter Cawsand from 'Pier Lane', go across the square to pick up 'Garrett St'. As you come towards the end of this street look for the old Devon/Corn boundary mark on a house on your right. Then turn right in front of the Post Office. Soon you will approach a street called 'The Cleave'. Just before you reach it turn left. Then turn first right up what is `Heavitree Road'but they do not help you by telling you that until you are a few yards up it. As you ascend you will presently see 'Lower Row' on your left, here turn right and enter Mount Edgcumbe Country Park.

When you come out on to a road at Hooe Lodge turn right but look, in 20 yards, for the path leaving the road on the left. You continue along a section of the one-time Earl's Drive but shortly after going under an old stone arch turn right. Follow the signs which direct you down to the foreshore for a very few yards but you soon go up again.

You continue through a high deer gate, you come out by a classical summer house keep along right to pick up a concrete driveway, and later right again when the drive goes left to walk inside of a hedge. You pass an old blockhouse on your left.

The path comes out by The Orangery (seasonal cafe), go through an arch go forward to turn right through the park gates to the ferry point for Plymouth.

BMG - Page 79. Most of that road route is now off it.

56	**Cremyll (for Plymouth) to Turnchapel**	**OS E108 (T) Plymouth (Trains)**

Grading: Easy Distance - 11 652 7 406

See also our Plymouth to Wembury Path Description.

The distance for this section is from the River Tamar to Turnchapel along a walking route if the Sutton Harbour - Turnchapel ferry is not operating. If you do use this ferry your total distance will be about two miles.

Cremyll/Plymouth
Cremyll Ferry,
Cremyll Quay,
Cremyll,
Nr. Torpoint,
Cornwall.
Tel: 01752 822105.

All year round at intervals of $\frac{1}{2}$ hr to 1hr. Summer service from 1 May to 18 September: From Mt. Edgcumbe 0650 to 2015. From Plymouth 0720 to 2030 weekdays. Saturdays from Mt. Edgcumbe 0815 to 2100 and from Plymouth 0845 to 2115. Sundays from Mt. Edgcumbe 0900 to 2100 and from Plymouth 0915 to 2115. Winter service from 19 September to 30 April: There are fewer ferries and on weekdays the last ferry leaves Mt. Edgcumbe at 1815 and Plymouth at 1830, Saturdays 1830 and 1845, Sundays 1700 and 1715. Sunday ferries commence at 0900 and 0915.

On landing at Admirals Hard walk up the road and turn second right into Cremyll Street, and continue to the massive gates of King William Yard. Pass them on your right and continue on out to Firestone Bay. At the sea wall you have a fine view to Drake's Island and beyond towards Wembury. A slight excursion could be made by turning right to walk out to Western King's Point and Devil's Point, for River Tamar views. You will have to return. From the sea wall turn inland to walk into Durnford Street, continue along it and walk past the Royal Marine Barracks, turning right immediately after them. This will bring you into Millbay Road where you continue on to the Dock Gates (east) where you turn right into West Hoe Road. Keep to this road. You are now in the West Hoe area and the streets surrounding you have numerous B & B establishments. Fork right into Great Western Road.

As you approach a terrace of three storey small hotels, watch out for a path on your right known as Rusty Anchor. This is a slight diversion from the main road and provides a shore-line walk.

On regaining the main road, turn right and continue along the Hoe foreshore. You stay on this promenade all the way around to The Barbican and Sutton Harbour. But, you could achieve grand views over Plymouth Sound by climbing steps opposite the swimming pool up to the lighthouse, Smeaton's Tower, and passing that to cross The Hoe to have a look at Sir Francis Drake, still scanning the English Channel for the Armada.

Retrace your steps and continue your shore-line walk to The Barbican. A small jetty on your right is of historic significance in that it is the site of the Mayflower Steps, of great interest to our US members.

Whatever you decide upon, ferry or the walking route, it is well worth exploring the ancient Barbican area before carrying on.

Ferry Service
At the time of revising this information we found that changes are being made so we cannot include names or telephone numbers. What we do know is that there is a proposed new service between The Barbican and Mountbatten that should be operational by the time you read this.

We advise you contact the Tourist Information Office at The Barbican (Tel: 01752 264849/264851).

As soon as we have definite information we will include it in our Spring Newsletter.

Walking Route - Sutton Harbour to Turnchapel

Lock gates have now been installed at Sutton Harbour so walk on across them into Teat's Hill Road. As you progress along Teat's Hill Road you will arrive at Breakwater Hill. Turn right here, but do not walk into the scrap yard unless you want to view vehicles being broken up. Carry on up the hill for a limestone, clifftop walk with views over the Cattewater. At a fork in the lane bear left and you will descend to the area of Cattedown Wharf. We will now just supply directions - continue on past warehouses into Maxwell Road, a new road will take you direct to Laira Bridge which you take to cross the River Plym. You have pavements to walk upon. At the first roundabout turn right into Oreston Road.

You now have a choice:-

(a)   Across a piece of grass on your left you will find an old railway line which is now a cycle/walk route through to Radford Lake or,

(b)   Keep on to the top of the road, bear right, then when you reach Rollis Park Road, turn right to descend to Oreston Quay. You are beside the water only for a couple of hundred yards, and at Plymstock Road turn left. Start climbing away from the estuary and at Lower Saltram turn right and carry straight on to Radford Lake.

The 'castle' through which you walk was once the lodge to a large house, now no more. Turning right after the causeway brings you to a path alongside the southern shore of Hooe Lake. At the time of writing it was not waymarked, but you should not go far wrong if you keep to this path. You will join a narrow road which leads to Hooe Lake Road.

Walk straight across the grassy area keeping to the shore and turn right along Barton Road, and by staying with this road you will come into Turnchapel.

BMG - Does not cover any of the walk from the River Tamar to Heybrook Bay. We think you ought to walk it all, especially Plymouth Hoe and the Barbican area.

NTG - Also does not supply walking instructions for this 7 miles of the coast path.

---

57 | Turnchapel to Wembury (Warren Point)   OS E108 and OL20

Grading: Easy   Distance -   11   663   7   413

See also our Plymouth to Wembury Path Description.

Due to the praiseworthy activities of Plymouth City Council over the past twelve months you are about to step out onto welcome coast path realignments. Those who have walked this section before will be amazed at the difference and those who have been Association members for a while will realise that our efforts have been successful.

The start out of Turnchapel is the same as before, a short walk up St Johns road to a car park on a bend. Look to your right for a sign pointing to the new coast path which drops down towards Clovelly Bay. It is a shore line path to Mountbatten Point. The path goes around the point then runs south climbing to Jennycliff.

Keep to the cliff edge and continue south, that is to the end of the grassy area where you will find a signed path entering woodlands.

This up and down new path is a delight and well below the dangerous road that we once had to walk. Within a $1/_4$ mile this new path links in with the original coast path. Turn right for a scenic uncomplicated path to Fort Bovisand, one of the great forts that once defended Plymouth.

Those who have been this way before should now pause to reflect. Since Turnchapel you have not had to set foot upon a vehicular road! We congratulate all responsible for this improvement.

On the descent to a road the path can be seen ahead between hundreds of chalet/huts and the sea. At Heybrook Bay when you reach the road - turn right.

The path passes in front of the guns of HMS Cambridge. When firing is taking place you will certainly hear it. Red flags fly during the shooting and when it is about to commence. Do not walk seaward of them but follow a well marked diversion to the left. This path circles the property of the Royal Navy and will return the walker to the coast safely. Needless to say, if the red flags are not flying then the official coast path is yours but do not loiter along the section.

There is a free telephone - 0800 833608 for prior information of firing times. Firing usually takes place between 0900 and 1800, rarely at night or at weekends and Bank Holidays. The gunnery school is closed at Christmas, Easter and for three weeks in August.

Now follows a low cliff top walk to Wembury Beach. The path passes seaward of the church and climbs to a level path that leads into the estuary of the River Yealm. At a small house, The Rocket House, once used for the storage of life saving apparatus, the official path takes off downhill diagonally towards the river and the ferry point. We suggest you walk down to the ferry point even if the ferry is not running or you do not intend to use it because you can take advantage of a scenic short circular back to the Rocket House. Once the ferry steps have been reached carry on for a few yards then take a wooden stepped path on the left that climbs to good views over

Newton Ferrers and Noss Mayo.

AFG - The inland alternative is around HMS Cambridge, not through it.

| 58 | Wembury (Warren Point) to Bigbury on Sea | OS OL20 |

| Grading: Starts easy but becomes strenuous | Distance - | 22 | 685 | 14 | 427 |

See also our Wembury (Warren Point) to Bigbury on Sea Path Description.

The first obstacle is crossing the River Yealm

Wembury (Warren Point) to Noss Mayo Ferry.
River Yealm

Bill Gregor,	Seasonal, all week.
1 Underhaye,	1st April to 30th September
Yealmpton	1000 - 1600 fine weather
PL8 2JR.	1000 - 1100 and 1500 - 1600 poor weather
Tel: 01752 880079.	

The ferryman is often there outside these hours. Stop at steps at Warren Point or slipway at Noss Mayo. Look towards Newton Ferrers and shout "Ferry" and wave. We suggest you might also telephone ahead to Mr. Gregor to give him an idea of your ETA.

If there is no ferry then this means a walk back to the Rocket House to follow the path described below into Knighton. There is an hourly bus service (number 48) to Plymstock and Plymouth where there is available an infrequent service to Noss Mayo (number 94). For a quicker conveyance around the estuary there are reasonably priced taxis available:-
Wembury Cabs - John Pitcher (01752 862151) and

Tims Taxis - Tim Craig (01752 830225)

From the Rocket House the track leads into a road. At Wembury House a stile leads to a field and to the footpath junction. The path you want is the one to the right which runs alongside a high wall. Follow it to the end of the wall where it goes through two successive kissing gates. It then bears left approximately 330° across fields towards Knighton. As you leave the fields it goes down a few steps. Turn left and then first right. This will bring you out onto the road. Turn left and the bus stop is a little further along on the other side of the road just before the pub. The distance from ferry point to bus stop is $1^1/_2$ miles.

Before reaching the bus stop you will pass a telephone box where you can call a taxi if you want.

For those who contemplate walking around the estuary please take care as the A379 is a very busy road. We have asked the Countryside Commission to start thinking about the installation of a riverside walk around, so in the not too distant future we may get to write a description of how to do it.

At Noss Mayo those who have come around will have a picturesque riverside walk out to where those who have been fortunate enough with the ferry will disembark. The Erme Estuary is about 9 miles ahead. You are the best judge of how long that will take you to get there for low tide, so plan your Noss Mayo departure accordingly. The well marked path climbs through woodlands to pick up Lord Reveistoke's nine-mile drive made for the carriages of his guests at Membland Hall, since demolished.

At Battery Cottage just as you are leaving the woodlands look out for a path going off to the right. You can take this down to Cellars Beach, for a swim maybe. It continues on around the back of the beach then climbs to rejoin the coast path at Brakehill Plantation where you turn right onto Lord Revelstoke's drive.

There is a definitive seaward path at Stoke Down at 560460 just after passing a single stone gate post on the left. Use this if you wish to visit the historic Church of St Peter the Poor Fisherman. This will mean an uphill road walk to regain the coast path. If you do not divert then the path crosses the Stoke Beach road to continue along, passing the ruined 'Tea House'.

You are now in for a very steep descent and further on a steep climb up to St Anchorites Rock and you pass Bugle Hole. The section then to Mothecombe Beach provides superb views to the Erme estuary. It has been fairly described as England's most unspoilt river estuary. We certainly believe it to be the most attractive.

River Erme   No ferry

Low water is at about the same time as the Devonport Tide Table shown here.

It is usually possible to wade the river 1 hour each side of low water along the old ford. Great care should be taken because heavy rains or seas can make the crossing dangerous. On modern maps the old ford is not shown but this in fact ran from Ordnance map ref. 614 476 to map ref. 620 478. In other words, the old ford connected the road by the row of coastguard cottages with the end of the inland road to Wonwell Beach from Kingston

Should you arrive at the River Erme at a time that promises a very long wait for low tide to enable you to wade across then there is an inland alternative. This alternative is of about 7 miles with fairly steep up and down country lanes You are the best judge of your rate of travel so the decision to wait for the tide or continue walking is yours.

If you follow the riverside paths shown on OS map OL20 you will be trespassing on a private estate so follow the narrow country lanes to Holbeton village. Then continue on a northerly route to Ford and Hole Farm. Soon after passing Hole Farm take off on a public footpath on your right. From here to the main A379 road is about $^{3}/_{4}$ mile. Turn right to cross the River Erme at Sequer's Bridge. Stay on the A379 for about $^{1}/_{2}$ mile but take care as this is an extremely busy road. You will see a road on your right signposted to Orcheton. Follow this road south towards the village of Kingston but before you reach that village you will see road signs to Wonwell Beach. Just before the slipway on to the sands you have a choice. If the tide now permits you can continue south along the beach or take to the waymarked coast path in the woodlands on your left.

Beyond the Erme the walking becomes tougher but the all round views will compensate the effort. There is an interesting low tide alternative at Westcombe Beach. Go onto the beach for a walk through the promontory to Ayrmer Cove via one or other of two 15 yard long caves. You will walk on shingle through them but be a little careful on rocks that can be slippery once through the caves. This is a low tide diversion only. The path passes Challaborough with its cafe and caravans to Bigbury on Sea, where the Bay View Cafe' is open all day and the only establishment for evening meals.

Burgh Island can be visited by walking across the sands or by a 'sea tractor' if the tide is in. The pub is very old, the hotel is fascinating art deco modern and the hut at the top of the island stands on the site of a chapel. This hut was used by the 'huers' - pilchard fishermen on the lookout for shoals of fish.

BMG - Page 16. Go further upstream than shown on the map to wade the River Erme. Cross over towards the road on the east side. The woodland route is not shown from that road southwards.

---

59 Bigbury on Sea to Hope Cove, Inner Hope   OS OL20 (V) Bantham (V) Thurlestone

Grading: Moderate   Distance -   9   694   6   433

See also our Bigbury on Sea to Salcombe Path Description.

There are riverside footpaths along both west and east banks of the River Avon to Aveton Gifford.

This makes the inland walking route from Bigbury on Sea to Bantham and vice versa about 9 miles in total. The OS OL20 map show the riverside paths. What you have to watch is that the road between the two words 'Ford' is tidal and therefore is at times submerged.

The official route turns right at the bottom of the road on to what is called Clematon Hill at the western side of the mouth of the River Avon.There are good views here across the estuary but unfortunately you have to walk up the busy road to Mount Folly Farm afterwards. However, again there is compensation because the views southward across the estuary just after the farm are particularly spectacular.

Bigbury/Bantham (River Avon) Seasonal. Not Sundays.
H Cater, Yorick, West Buckland Easter for 1 week then Whitsun until end of August
Kingsbridge, Devon 1000-1100 and 1500-1600.
Tel: Kingsbridge (01 548) 560593

During busy periods and good weather Mr Cater may be around outside these times. We suggest you telephone Mr Cater the day before you require the ferry and give him your estimated time of arrival. Low water is about the same time as the Devonport Tide Table. It is possible at low tide, when not rough, or the river is not in flood, to wade the river.However, we strongly stress we are not advising this as a cheap method of avoiding the ferry crossing. When the ferry is working, you are strongly advised to use it because wading is not easy and you may get a lot wetter than you expect.   You will most likely be up to your thighs in water and in no circumstances should the crossing be attempted if conditions are wrong. The two guide points are just below the ferry crossing. On the true right bank - the western side - there is a well defined hedge running north and south with pine trees. On the left bank - the eastern side - there is a castellated building with battlements and a little flag pole in the middle. (This castle is just above the famous thatched boat house which is so well known from many pictures taken of the River Avon and Bantham.) However, if crossing from the true right to the left - in other words from west to east - take off at the hedge and wade towards the castle-like building. If going the other way, vice versa. Please note it is important that you do wade at this point. The river looks shallow in a number of other places but there are deeper channels and indeed soft sand patches which can make it extremely difficult. Further towards the sea, there is a considerable tidal ebb which can be exceedingly dangerous.

PLEASE NOTE WHEN THE FERRY IS NOT OPERATING A RECOMMENDED WAY TO REACH BANTHAM IS BY REASONABLY PRICED TAXIS:

Arrow Cars - Mr Kemp - (Telephone: 01548 856120) and

D & C Taxis (Telephone 01548 852906).

It should always be borne in mind that the depth of water at low tide and consequently safe passage across is affected by natural: conditions inasmuch that strong south west or westerly winds tend to bank up water in the English Channel and that therefore, there will be a greater depth of water than expected. This will also happen if there is a lot of rain in the catchment areas of the rivers, with consequently more water coming down. Caution: although we know several who have waded the River Avon we do not recommend it; great care is required, especially by those with backpacks.

VERY IMPORTANT - PLEASE TAKE NOTE

EVEN AT DEAD LOW WATER WE STRESS THAT YOU MUST CONSIDER VERY SERIOUSLY WHETHER YOU SHOULD WADE THIS RIVER. IT IS VERY DIFFICULT AND CAN BE DANGEROUS EVEN FOR TALL AND STRONG ADULTS. MANY OF OUR MEMBERS, INCLUDING YOUR SECRETARY WILL NOT VENTURE ACROSS. THEIR OPINION BEING - "WHEN THE FERRY IS NOT RUNNING THEN THE **ONLY** ALTERNATIVE IS TO GO ROUND ".

Inland Walking Route

When the tide is not low (and we urge you to read again our advice about wading) and the ferry is not available the only way to the other side is an inland walk to Aveton Gifford and around This is a pleasant 7 mile (12 km) diversion as it is mostly along country paths. Walking through agricultural land in deep country makes a change from the coast.The paths are shown on OS OL20 and are quite well marked but they are little used and are not always easy to follow. Allow plenty of time for some heavy walking, for straying off route or for a possible delay at the tidal road near Aveton Gifford.

Disregard the coast path where it turns right through Mount Folly Farm and descends to the ferry point, but proceed towards Bigbury for 60 yards to the next footpath sign. Turn right into the field over a stone stile and walk along the field edge. Over a wooden stile will bring you onto the golf course where, after a short distance, you meet a surfaced track. Turn left towards the clubhouse for two hundred yards where you turn right between two Nissen Huts going down a track to Hexdown Farm. Pass through the farm buildings and immediately turn half right as waymarked and continue downhill with the boundary on your left. Proceed along a track through a timber gate down to Villa Crusoe. Follow the footpath sign slightly left along a tarmac drive, into woodland, then through Lincombe and on to the B3392 on a corner. Proceed northwards towards Bigbury for 350 yards (be careful of the traffic) and turn right at the footpath sign to Aveton Gifford (via tidal road). Cross the field to a post and wire fence and enter the top of Doctors Wood. Re-emerge into a field and cross due east to a wooden stile. Proceed along a high level path (beautiful views) then walk downhill to the tidal road which will bring you to Aveton Gifford. There is a viable alternative if the tide is over the road by walking north-westward to Foxhole then north-eastward to Waterhead and Aveton Gifford. The whole path is adequately waymarked.

Cross the Avon on the roadbridge (A379) towards Kingsbridge, and turn right at the end of the bridge into a cul-de-sa named Bridge End. Continue to a gate at a signpost, and straight on to a metalled road, where you turn right at a signpost.

Bear left at road fork, following the footpath sign to a gate; turn right here and follow a fence on the right, and through another gate into a field.

Turn half right down to the bottom of the valley, and bear right to a gate with a waymark 'to Stiddicombe Creek'. Cross this as best you can (not easy) and enter wood on right. Work steadily uphill to top corner and follow waymark signs along the top of the field with a hedge on the left (watch out for herons by the river) to a stile by a gate; over another stile and continue. Bear right and cross a farm track to a gate between walls. Cross the stream ahead with stepping stones, and along to a stile and waymark signs, where you turn right and straight on to Bantham, where you turn right and through the village where you will see the ferry sign. Here you would have stepped ashore had it been operating. The coast path is straight on towards the sea.

Some of this walk is shown in the National Trail Guide.

You should take great care where the path proceeds along the seaward boundary of the Thurlestone Golf Course, watch out for golfers and where they hit the ball. We have had a report of a walker on this section who was hit in the mouth by a golf ball at close range with resulting horrific damage to teeth and lips.

60	**Hope Cove, Inner Hope to Salcombe Ferry**	**OS OL20 V Hope Cove**

Grading: Strenuous	Distance -	12	706	7	440

See also our Bigbury on Sea to Salcombe Path Description.

Excellent coastal walking, some of the finest in South Devon. Before leaving Inner Hope one ought to walk along the inland road to look at 'The Square' and its attractive thatched cottages. To return to the coast path. It is well marked out to Bolt Tail where the remains of an Iron Age fort is marked by a dry stone wall and the remains of a ditch.

The path is obvious to Bolberry Down (refreshments available - Port Light Hotel) and on to a viewpoint overlooking Soar Mill Cove. There is a steep descent to the cove but the climb out is easier. We have heard of walkers going wrong as they near the rocky splendid Bolt Head. The correct route is the coast route, do not divert inland anywhere until the headland is reached. The path then runs due north into and around Starehole Bay. Here, in 1936 the grain clipper Herzogovin Cecille finally sank, having struck the Ham Stone off Soar Mill Cove.

From the bay the path joins the Courtenay Way which was cut out under rocky pinnacles. The way ahead is through woodlands to the roadway below the National Trust's Overbecks House and Youth Hostel. Follow the road to South Sands where, in season, a ferry can be taken to the main ferry point in Salcombe. If it is not running or you are a purist the way ahead to the town and ferry for East Portlemouth is along the most seaward roads ahead.

AFG - Incorrect route shown between Soar Mill Cove and Bolt Head.

BMG - Incorrect route shown between Soar Mill Cove and Off Cove.

Grading: Strenuous Distance - 20 726 13 453

See also our Salcombe to Torcross Path Description.

This is first class walking, some of the best of the whole coast path.

Salcombe to East Portlemouth Ferry
The Salcombe Ferry,
Somerset House,
Devon Road,
Salcombe
Devon TQ8 8HQ
Tel: (01548)842061/842364

All year round Nov-March.
0800 to 1700 hrs half-hourly. April-October
continuous service running to 1930 hrs. July
and August Sundays, Saturdays and
Bank Holidays 0830 hrs start.

Having crossed the estuary the path goes off to the right along the narrow road. Just after the National Trust car park at Mill Bay there is a choice of paths. One goes uphill on the left through trees, but we suggest you stay with the lower one to the right which is, after all, the official path. It is a pleasant walk along Rickham Common and passes below the Gara Rock Hotel (refreshments available).

After Gammon Head a look towards Prawle Point will reveal the wreck of the Demetrios which was smashed onto the cliff in December 1992 when she broke her tow en route to the breakers yard.

The official route is to the very end of Prawle Point, to the Coastguard lookout. It is hoped that the National Trust will mark a path out to the point along the western side of the headland. The path is there and it is a better route than the one on the top. The official route is back inland again but near to the lookout on the east side of the point is a path descending a valley. This is the better one. Prawle Point is National Trust property and there is a true coast path along the top of low cliffs around Copstone Cove to link in with the official route at Western Cove.

It is easy walking for a while along the edges of fields on what is a 'raised' beach. The path then becomes rocky and up and down prior to Lanacombe Beach. The path is straightforward to Start Point and on to Torcross but we do advise leaving yourself time to make the diversion to the old deserted village at Hall Sands. Very few who go down there to see the ruins alongside the sea will not be moved by the experience. An early 1996 cliff fall caused a stop on this path but by the time you read this we hope the Heritage Coast Service will have installed another path for us. However, at the time of writing further falls have not made access possible.

There have been cliff falls between Hall Sands and Torcross but the authorities have made sensible slight adjustments.

| 62 | Torcross to Dartmouth | OS OL20 (V) Torcross (V) Strete (V) Stoke Fleming |

Grading: Moderate Distance - 16 742 10 463

See also our Torcross to Dartmouth Path Description.

The coast path runs along the length of the shingle bank. You can walk either side of the road, the top of the beach for sea views or alongside the Ley for bird watching.

There is no true coast path from Strete Gate to Warren Point and virtually the whole route is inland and some on a busy main road. This is reckoned to be the worst section of the whole of the South West Coast Path and the Association continues it's efforts to obtain an enormous improvement.

If you intend to avoid the busy main road through Strete than as you approach the village look for Hynetown Road on your left and turn into this road to follow the official path to rejoin the main road on the other side of the village. After this follow the main road for about 200 yards and then take care to fork left, signposted 'Southwood' - there is no coast path sign here. Immediately before the entrance to Blackpool Sands you must turn left by the cottages.

At the time of writing we are aware that negotiations are under way between the landowner and the Heritage Coast Officer for a slight alignment improvement from Blackpool Sands eastwards. We have no idea if it will be in place by the time you read this but you should be aware of it and watch for it.

It is believed that an off-road path is to be installed from Blackpool Sands gateway seaward of the A379. If it is then you cross the A379 to its' start. After an uphill walk this new path will cross back over the road and enter the Old Road at Stoke Fleming to link in with the existing, official non-coast path.

If this slight improvement has not been made then after you join the A379 you have to walk along it then turn left into a lane by the cottages.

Follow the inland signed route to Stoke Fleming and the rest of the signs along this poor route. You have about another 2$^1/_2$ miles to go before you regain the coast path proper.

As you stand on the National Trust's Warren Point this is another occasion to pause and reflect. The beautiful path you see ahead of you towards the River Dart estuary could easily be continued behind you nearly all the way back to Slapton Sands if it were not for landowners who do not like you and the Countryside Commission who refuse to support Devon County Council and this Association.

Dartmouth Castle commands the mouth of the River Dart and should be visited, time permitting. In season there is a regular ferry from the castle to Dartmouth and this can be utilised for a pleasant river trip, instead of walking down the road.

BMG - The route shown between Strete Gate and Stoke Fleming is not the official one - see NTG.

BMG - The better route to Dartmouth Castle is not shown.

NTG - Map p118. Contours are at 25ft intervals not metres.

---

63 | Dartmouth to Brixham   OS OL20 (T) Dartmouth (V) Kingswear (Trains)

Grading: Strenuous		Distance -	18	760	11	474

See also our Dartmouth to Brixham Path Description.

Walkers will probably use the lower ferry to cross the River Dart but there are two other regular ferries which also run all year round. Nearby is the passenger ferry, which lands by the steam railway station, and which gives a more comfortable crossing, and if these two are not running then further up the river is the higher ferry taking pedestrians and vehicles. If you use the higher ferry you will then need to turn right along the railway line to the road, then turn right again and descend the hill to join the coastal path by the lower ferry slipway.

Dartmouth/Kingswear
South Hams District Council, Lower Ferry,
Lower Ferry Office, The Square,
Kingswear TQ6 OAA
Tel: (01803) 752342

0700/2255 hrs Sunday start 0800 hrs.
Winter - 12 minutes service.
Summer - 6 minutes service.
Last ferry leaves: Dartmouth 2255 hrs,
Kingswear 2245 hrs.

On landing at Kingswear, by the lower ferry, pass through an arch on the right. Ascend Alma Steps then turn right along Beacon Road. In 1$^1/_4$ miles turn right down steps at Warren Woods.

When you reach the old Battery Buildings at Froward Point do divert inland to see 'The Daymark' navigation tower nearby if time permits but then return to the coast path to continue. The sign here is 8$^3/_4$ miles to Brixham and the path descends steeply going right from the back corner of the derelict look out building and then passes through the World War II gun and searchlight positions. Next at Pudcombe Cove you can obtain access to the National Trust gardens at Coleton Fishacre if they are open.

Now a pleasant walk to Berry Head Country Park, a Nature Reserve with much of interest - do spend time there if you can. The Northern Fort, one of the two Napoleonic Forts contains the Berry Head lighthouse and the old guardhouse is now a cafe, open in the season and sometimes out of season as well.

Having left Berry Head and descending Berry Head Road, when you are level with the Breakwater descend the steps to the new promenade which follows the water's edge past the new marina to the inner harbour.

64 | Brixham to Torquay Harbour   OS OL20 (T) Brixham (T) Paiqnton (Trains)

Grading: Moderate   Distance -   13   773   8   482

See also our Brixham to Shaldon Path Description.

Distances are taken along the official path where there is one, then along the back of Goodrington Sands beach, around Roundham Head, along Paignton and Preston sea fronts and along the promenade at Torquay.

From Brixham to Elbury Cove the path is fair though not as scenic as one might hope. Thereafter it becomes more urbanised with the poorest section from Hollicombe to Torquay Harbour where you usually have quite heavy traffic nearby. Remember, in case of need, there is a very frequent bus service from Brixham to Torquay via Paignton! There is, also, a regular Brixham/Torquay seasonal ferry service.

When departing from Brixham leave by the new path running along the harbour, signposted Coastal Footpath to Oxen Cove and Freshwater Car Park. At the car park continue on past the Zeneca Brixham Environmental Laboratory and on to the Battery Gardens where you follow the lower path to Fishcombe Cove. Ascend from the cove and at the road junction turn right, signpost Public Footpath to Churston Ferrers.

At the far end of Elbury Cove ignore the more obvious path going inland and leave the beach by ascending the steps. Take care at Broadsands beach that you do not follow the path up the cliff at the eastern end, but turn left up the road, pass under the railway viaduct and then turn immediately right where the coast path is signposted.

At Goodrington turn right, under a railway bridge and follow the promenade round and just before the end a zig-zag path takes you up, through ornamental gardens onto Roundham Head.

At Hollicombe Head you can turn right and go through the delightful park that was once the gas works. Bear left to emerge through the main gate onto the road. Then turn right for Torquay.

CP - At Goodrington South Sands the path crosses back under the railway line There is no road walking until Paignton Harbour.

BMG - Does not cover Brixham to Babbacombe. Over ten miles omitted!

65 | Torquay Harbour to Shaldon   OS E31 (T) Torquay (Trains)

Grading: Strenuous   Distance -   17   790   11   493

See also our Brixham to Shaldon Path Description.

You walk on round Torquay Inner Harbour, turning left up Beacon Hill and soon reach The Imperial Hotel. Turn in right here to pass in front of the main entrance to the hotel and then follow the scenic path to the grassy plateau of Daddyhole Plain, which you cross to find the path descending to Meadfoot Beach.

At the far end of Meadfoot Beach turn right through a small car park and ascend to Marine Drive where turn right. There is some subsidence on this road but it does not affect pedestrians. Shortly turn right at a signpost Thatcher Point and follow the track. However, before long, because of an unfortunate diversion you will be forced back onto the road. Due to a cliff fall that is not being dealt with at a speed this Association would like. Here the route follows a path above the left hand side of the road and at the end cross the road and take the Bishops Walk path signposted Ansteys Cove.

As you join the road by the car park above Anstey's Cove you can, time and energy permitting, take the steep path down to the picturesque cove. But you'll have to return the same way; following repeated rock falls the adjacent Redgate Beach has been sealed off indefinitely by

Torbay Borough Council, and it's no longer possible to cross the two beaches and regain the official route by the path up the cliffs. Instead, about fifty yards beyond the turning down to Anstey's take the path through the woods to the right signposted 'To Babbacombe & St Marychurch over the Downs', which takes you up to Walls Hill.

From Walls Hill the path will take you to the road descending to Babbacombe Beach, at the far end of which traverse a wooden bridge structure to Oddicombe beach where the path bears upwards just before the lower station of the Babbacombe Cliff Railway. You shortly pass under the railway and then take care to turn right downwards at the start of a pleasant path leading to a grassy picnic area where bear left uphill to join the track to Watcombe.

(Alternatively, except at high tide, you can walk along Oddicombe Beach and take the cliff path at the far end which leads up to the same sloping stretch of grass. But don't go down again to the next cove - Petitor - because there's no way out at the far end.)

At the valley road linking the main Torquay/Teignmouth Road to Watcombe Beach turn left and immediately right, signpost Maidencombe 3/4 and follow a wooded path until you reach a path junction where the signposting shows the inland route as the coastal path and the more coastal path as an alternative path. We suggest you take the new coastal path which in time will become the official route and then from the car park at Maidencombe go a few yards up the road and turn right, unless you wish to obtain refreshment in the village.

From here there are some quite stiff gradients until you reach the road at Labrador where turn right and in a few yards leave the pavement to take a sunken path on your right and shortly enter a field on your right via a stile by a field gate.

Superb views now as you descend along the coastal side of the field system, then taking the path round The Ness to Shaldon.

66 | Shaldon to Exmouth via Topsham Ferry OS E31 (110 on reprint) (V) Shaldon (T)
Teignmouth (Trains) (T) Dawlish (Trains) (V) Dawlish Warren (Trains) (V) Starcross (Trains)

Grading: Easy	Distance -	30	820	19	512

See also our Shaldon to Sidmouth Path Description.

Distance is measured by diverting inland from the centre of Dawlish along the main road to Holcombe, and also includes the diversion inland to use the ferry at Topsham.

This is a section where you may have problems depending on the time of year and state of the tide.

There is no ferry at winter weekends. Your walking route around is to continue along riverside roads from the ferry point and cross Shaldon Bridge. Immediately after crossing the railway line exit from the bridge into Milford Park. Walk beside the railway line, through Bitton Sports Ground into ParkHill, cross that into Bitton Avenue at Clay Lane turn right into Willow Street. At the end bear left then right which will bring you into Quay Road, into Osmond Street and then straight on to Harbour Beach and the ferry. Keep going on out onto 'The Point' turn north east and once more you are upon the coast path.

Shaldon/Teignmouth (River Teign)
Teignbridge District Council, Resort Managers Office, Forde House, Newton Abbot, TQ12 4XX.
Tel: Teignmouth (01626) 774770 Resort Manager or (01626) 779769 Tourist Information Centre.

All year round. 20 minutes service.
May to October 7 days a week
0800-dusk. November to April
Monday to Friday only 0800-1700.

After crossing from Shaldon by ferry follow the promenade past the pier and shortly you reach Eastcliff Walk forking up on your left and there you must make your first decision. The true route is ahead along the sea wall but at certain states of the high tide and particularly in bad weather it may be impossible after a two mile walk to pass under the railway line at the end of the wall, and if this appears likely a detour is needed. You should ascend Eastcliff Walk which soon becomes a track and will eventually lead you to the A379 where turn right and rejoin the coast path at the top of Smugglers Lane.

If conditions look right enjoy the walk along the sea wall and at the end pass under the railway line and ascend Smugglers Lane to the A379. -Now you have a short walk on this busy main road, although there is a footpath on the left hand side, and after about 150 yards turn right into Derncleugth Gardens, then left into Windward Lane and take the path over a stile on your left. After a field section you are back on the road but immediately follow the Old Teignmouth Road on your right until you reach the main road yet again, turn right and shortly by some railings turn right and follow the path which soon zig-zags down to the boat cove and follow the sea wall to Dawlish Station.

From here it is possible at low tide to walk along the sea wall to Dawlish Warren, then at the start of the new promenade cross the railway by a footbridge to join the inland path and reach the main road. if the tide is high you must take the alternative route up the Exeter Road out of Dawlish and shortly after passing the new Rockstone Flats turn right on the road signposted Dawlish Warren $3/_4$ mile and immediately take the coastal footpath signed on your right to follow the Ladies Mile to Dawlish Warren. (You can in fact take a footpath immediately before the Rockstone Flats, although this is not signposted, then take the left fork to join the coastal path.)

There is no official path along the Warren but if time and energy permit you can enjoy a circular walk round this sandy Nature Reserve.

You are now faced with crossing the River Exe and in the summer months there is a ferry from Starcross to Exmouth reached by walking along the road from Dawlish Warren. However this is a busy road and you can if you wish catch one of the frequent buses to Starcross.

Starcross/Exmouth (River Exe)
Mr B Rackley,
Starcross Pier & Pleasure Company
26 Marine Parade,
Dawlish.
Tel: (01626) 862452

From Starcross Pier.
Seasonal. 7 days a week.
April - end October. 1000 hrs then every hour
on the hour; last ferry 1745 hrs.
From Exmouth, Ferry Steps.
1030 hrs, then every hour on the half hour, last
ferry 1730 hrs. Crossing approx. 15 minutes.

In winter and at other times when the ferry is not running, it is possible to catch a train from Dawlish Warren, changing at Exeter and going to Exmouth or to catch a bus at Exeter and cross over at Countess Wear and catch a bus to Exmouth.

When the Starcross/Exmouth ferry is not running you have the following alternatives.

1. You can catch a train at Dawlish Warren changing at Exeter and going back down to Exmouth.

2. You can do the same thing using the frequent bus services, changing over routes at either Countess Wear or in Exeter.

3. You can use the all year round ferry at Topsham to cross the River Exe. From Starcross continue by road to Powderham Church where a footpath follows the river and then the canal to a bridge across the canal where the ferry then crosses the river. (This ferry is dependent on tide and weather, does not operate at lunchtime or on a Tuesday).

4. A new venture is Exe Water Taxis which will pick up passengers from the tip of Dawlish Warren and take them to Exmouth - contact Bob or Jenny Killick, 60 High Street Topsham EX3 ODY (01392 873409).

Topsham Ferry (River Exe)
Exeter City Council Canals & Rivers Dept.
Tel: (01392) 274306.

Oct./April 0800-1730 hrs. Weekends only.
May/Sept. 0800-2000 hrs. Daily except Tuesday.
Intervals between runs on request.
Dependent on tide and weather.

Once across the river you have to get to Exmouth and we are inclined to suggest the frequent bus service but failing this the walk as far as Lympstone will be on the road except for a small footpath section between Clyst Bridge and Ebford. From Lympstone there is a riverside path to Exmouth, now part of the East Devon Way - look for the mauve markers featuring a foxglove.

BMG - Page 29. The official path goes up and onto the point west of Shaldon - see NTG.

BMG - Page 31. When Starcross Ferry not running you need not go into Exeter - use Topsham Ferry - as above.

67 | Exmouth to Budleigh Salterton   OS E30 (115 on reprint) (T) Exmouth (Trains)

Grading: Moderate   Distance -   **10**   **830**   **6**   **518**

See also our Shaldon to Sidmouth Path Description.

No real problems here for walkers but keep inland of the range at Straight Point.

68 | Budleigh Salterton to Sidmouth OS E30 (115 on reprint) (T) Budleigh Salterton

Grading: Starts moderate but becomes strenuous   Distance -   **11**   **841**   **7**   **525**

See also our Shaldon to Sidmouth Path Description.

The start is along a raised path inland to the River Otter Bridge at South Farm, then a riverside path back to the coast.

The path around High Peak is well marked but it does not unfortunately go over the top as you, and many others in the past, obviously expected. If you do battle your way to the top you will certainly not be disappointed with the views. The path on the top of Peak Hill immediately west of Sidmouth has been improved to give better seaward views.

The descent from Peak Hill towards Sidmouth takes you down through a wood and out on to the road. Turn right and keep to the right hand side of the road to pass through two kissing gates, then bear right through a gap in the hedge on to parkland for the descent into Sidmouth. Later, flower lovers will prefer the longer route through the Connaught Gardens, but you have to come back to the road in the end.

69 | Sidmouth to Seaton   OS E30 (115 on reprint) and E29 (116 on reprint) (T) Sidmouth

Grading: Strenuous   Distance -   **15**   **856**   **9**   **534**

See also our Sidmouth to Lyme Regis Path Description.

Please note that there are a number of quite considerable ascents and descents on this section. Do not judge the effort required purely on the mileage. There are one or two places in this stretch where it is easy to come off the route but one is not likely to come to any severe harm.

On leaving Sidmouth dramatic cliff falls are the cause of a diversion. It is well marked.

After Branscombe Mouth there are alternative paths. The one over Hooken Cliffs gives superb views and is probably easier to walk. The underdiff path, apart from the beginning among the caravans is scenically better and we would recommend this if the weather is good. You have the interesting underdiff itself, the massive cliffs to the left, interesting rock formations ahead, and good views to seaward. At most states of the tide it is possible to walk along the beach from Seaton Hole to Seaton, avoiding some road work.

WATCH THE TIDE - YOU CAN GET CUT OFF

CP - The path is nearer the coast than the map suggests between Weston Cliff and Branscombe Mouth.

NTG - From Branscombe Mouth to Beer Head the map does not show the path along the top of Hooken Cliffs only through Under Hooken. It is mentioned in the text. Both routes are official.

BMG - The old route is shown east of Littlecombe Shoot.

70 | Seaton to Lyme Regis

OS E29 (116 on reprint) (T) Seaton

| Grading: Moderate | Distance - | 12 | 868 | 8 | 542 |

See also our Sidmouth to Lyme Regis Path Description.

You leave Seaton across its concrete bridge over the River Axe and have to turn inland. Then, go up the road to the golf course then walk due East across the fairway into a lane, along it and in less than $1/_4$ mile turn to the coast.

The section through the Landslip is in a National Nature Reserve and can be very rewarding to some but extremely frustrating to others. Views are extremely limited and the path in places puts on a fair imitation of a corkscrew or helter-skelter; you are unlikely to get lost but most unlikely to know where you are. Suggested times to walk the Landslip range from $1^1/_2$ hours to 4 hours, but we are told that the standard time is about 3 hours.

The path into Lyme Regis has now been improved and you can take a path directly down to The Cobb without having to come into the car park and then down the road.

BMG - Page 70. The path does not enter a car park above Lyme Regis. It is through fields direct to The Cobb.

71 | Lyme Regis to Charmouth

OS E29 (116 on reprint) (T) Lyme Regis

| Grading: Moderate | Distance - | 4 | 872 | 2 | 544 |

See also our Lyme Regis to Abbotsbury Path Description.

This is a difficult section owing to the very insecure nature of the cliffs. Dorset County Council have worked to provide a series of routes here but they are up against a continual problem of slipping cliffs. There have had to be necessary diversions. We think we ought to tell you that having entered Dorset now that it also has a piece of so-called coastal path furthest away from the coast. Having said that, it does have many sections of extremely good walking if only the county would establish a true coast path which is, after all, what it is supposed to be.

From Lyme Regis town centre take Church Street and Charmouth Road (A3052) until you reach Lyme Regis Football Club on the right, beyond which you will find a stile at the corner of a lane and take the footpath across fields to a lane where you turn left (yes west!) for 50 yds. At a finger post sign turn right up through the wood and near the top turn onto the path that runs between the cliff edge and the golf course. On the approach to Charmouth follow the Coast Path sign, ignoring the recommended diversion.

We recommend a low tide diversion along the beach between Lyme Regis and Charmouth especially if the tide is well out because the sand is very firm here. On no account should attempts be made to walk upon the surface of the huge grey mud slide. When the tide permits, keep to seaward on firm sand.

We think we should acknowledge and thank Dorset County Council, The Heritage Coast Service and the Countryside Commission for their efforts in reinstating a coast path along this section.

72 | Charmouth to West Bay

OS E29 (116 on reprint) 1 mile to (V) Charmouth

| Grading: Strenuous | Distance - | 11 | 883 | 7 | 551 |

See also our Lyme regis to Abbotsbury Path Description.

Interesting walking with spectacular views from Golden Cap, the highest mainland point on the south coast of England and later from Thorncombe Beacon. However, be warned, your good views are not obtained without effort!

When you get to what looks like the top of Golden Cap you have to turn left and go a little higher to the trig. point to find your way down, which starts at the north end before later bearing east again.

73 | West Bay to Abbotsbury (Swannery Car Park)   OS OL15

Grading: Moderate   Distance -   15   898   9   560

See also our Lyme regis to Abbotsbury Path Description.

SEE SECTION 80 FOR DETAILS OF THE ALTERNATIVE INLAND COAST PATH FROM WEST BEXINGTON TO OSMINGTON MILLS.

Leaving West Bay do not go seaward again immediately after you have walked round the back of the harbour. Pass to the right of St. John's Church and carry forward to the West Bay Hotel ahead, opposite which is the coast path sign pointing at an angle across a gravel area to the foot of surprisingly steep cliffs. If you go seaward in West Bay too soon you will give yourself a hard stretch along coarse shingle.

Watch for the inland diversion at Burton Freshwater. When the river is low you can 'cut the corner' across the beach but this is not at all possible when the river is flowing strongly; do not try it, you will surely drown. As you start to descend to the caravan park you can look across and see if the river is not reaching the sea, then it is up to you.

At Burton Bradstock Beach just after the hotel there is a seasonal cafe.

At Burton Mere, unless you are particularly interested in maritime flowers, the definitive route goes inland of the Mere, rather than go along the seaward side. You will get quite enough pebbles later.

There is a seasonal cafe at West Bexington, and seasonal snack wagons in the car park where the road turns inland past Abbotsbury Gardens. Walkers, however, should continue along for another couple of hundred yards.

Refreshments, shops and B & B's in Abbotsbury. If you have time the climb up to St Catherine's Chapel is worth the effort.

A permissive path runs to the Swannery from the coast path that contours to the seaward side of Chapel Hill.

74 | Abbotsbury (Swannery Car Park) to Weymouth   OS OL15

Grading: Easy Chesil Beach: Strenuous   Distance -   23   921   14   574

See also our Abbotsbury to Weymouth Path Description.

Presumably you must have wanted to go into Abbotsbury if you did visit the village, but it is worth mentioning that the path does not really go there at all, but only close to it. Therefore, the correct, and sometimes quieter, way out is by the footpath going south to Nunnery Grove, and not the road by Mill Farm.

The path unfortunately now goes over a mile inland, despite our efforts. The inland path is well marked and enjoyable to walk, part of it along a ridge and with some good views. You do not get back to the shores of the Fleet until Rodden Hive.

On the outskirts of Abbotsbury after Horsepool Farm keep going up the ridge, beguiling, much better tracks go round the hill to the right, but they will not bring you to the stile you need at the top. In about 1 mile turn south off to the ridge and turn sharp left after Hodder's Coppice. A track goes forward, but this is NOT the one you want. After you have crossed a minor road, the official path follows the field headland east and then south to the north east corner of Wyke Wood as signposted, and not in a direct line as shown on some maps. Take particular care as you approach Rodden Hive - the path suddenly dives through a hedge on your left. There is an apparent track and even a marker post which might make you think that the path goes to the right of the stream, but it does not.

At Tidmoor Point, follow the red and white posts unless one has to divert as firing on the range is in progress across the definitive right of way. A diversion has been made inland at Wyke Regis for a Service Establishment.

At Ferry Bridge you have the opportunity to extend your walk by including a coastal circuit of the Isle of Portland. The route is outlined in Section 75.

A footpath sign has now been erected to show you where to continue on to Weymouth, but not where to leave the old railway line (at the north end of the shallow cutting) to get back to the coast path. Signs are very sparse in Weymouth to encourage you - we have asked for improvements.

Pass the sailing centre and continue into Old Castle Road; opposite Castle Cove Sailing Club bear right onto a tarmac footpath. Continue on paths close to the coast to Nothe Fort and bear sharp left down to the harbourside which is followed to the Town Bridge, which is crossed and the opposite side of the harbour is followed back to the Pavilion Complex. Here bear left to join The Esplanade. In summer a little ferry may run across the harbour to shorten the route.

An alternative for the tough walker who wishes to stay on the coast is to use the Chesil Beach; this is, of course, much more attractive since the inland route has been worsened. You can do this by going onto the beach where the path turns inland at Abbotsbury but note you cannot `get off' again until you reach the causeway from Wyke Regis to Portland. This is only a walk for the fit and not one to be attempted at times of severe gale! Please note that the Chesil Bank is closed to visitors from 1st May-31st August for the Schedule 1 bird nesting season. During the nesting season please keep to the seaward side of the beach so as not to interfere with nesting birds.

Weymouth Harbour
Weymouth & Portland Borough Council,
Harbour Master's Office,
Municipal Offices, North Quay,
Weymouth, DT4 8TA
(01305-206423 or 01305 206278) Ask for Dep. Borough Engineer.

Seasonal. April - October Daily.
Continuous if passengers are waiting
and weather permits.

---

75 | Optional extra route around the Isle of Portland   OS OL15

Grading: Moderate   **Distance (from Ferry Bridge) -**   **22**   **14**

See also our Isle of Portland Path Description.

As this section is not yet part of the official coast path the distance quoted is not included within our cumulative total.

If you have time to spare a circuit of the Isle of Portland, although at present not part of the definitive route of the South West Coast Path, is well worth the extra effort. While it lacks the beauty of other parts of the coast path in Dorset, it is still a fine walk with much of interest as well as the rugged grandeur of the coast, which can be very spectacular in rough weather. To use its full name, The Island and Royal Manor of Portland, the `island' is heavily occupied (at present) by the Ministry of Defence, and HM Prison Services, and shows the scars of extensive quarrying for its famous limestone.

From Ferry Bridge you have a number of choices, none of them of much merit, for the first two miles: Using the footway beside the busy A354 road; crossing over the car park beyond the Chesil Beach Centre to slog along the pebbles of Chesil Beach, or catching a bus to the roundabout at the south end of the causeway to alight at the Royal Victoria Lodge. This is Fortuneswell where you need to cross the road and follow signs for the Chesil Beach Gallery, turning left before the public toilets. Continue past the Cove House Inn and bear right up onto the promenade. Towards the end of this and just before the `grassy walls', bear left and immediately left again up a zig zag path; then right past the school and up the steep path in the grass incline to the final steps to the road.

Briefly rejoin the main road (A354 - New Road) and bear off right at the hairpin bend onto the coast path running between old quarry banks and the shear cliff face.Three miles of spectacular and airy cliff top walking brings you to Portland Bill with the Pulpit Rock and lighthouse. Continue around the end of the low headland and pass to the seaward of wooden chalets to follow a winding path along the top of low cliffs to join a road above Freshwater Bay after about $1\frac{1}{2}$ miles.

Turn right up the road for 600 yards, past Cheyne Weares Car Park to a finger post on the right. Follow the zig zag path down into the rugged underdiff area, and follow the waymarks through the disused quarry workings down to Church Ope Cove.

Before the 'West Cliff' and 'Coast Path' signs turn right through a gap in the hedge with 'Crown Estate' sign on to the underdiff path. Continue to seaward along the rugged path to Durdle Pier and bear up left to turn right onto a wide firm path (old track bed of the former Weymouth to Easton railway line). Continue along the track to just before a "rock fall" sign where it is necessary to turn left over a bank to follow a rocky path that climbs up the cliffs to an isolated chimney seen above on the skyline. A word of warning here - although the track continues northwards and appears to be well used do not be tempted to continue as the way forward is eventually blocked by the perimeter security fence of the MOD Establishments and there is no other route up the high cliffs.

At the chimney turn sharp right along a prison road, and follow a tarmac road northwards through a gap in a high wall. At the next road turn right and bear down hill toward the gates of the MOD establishment, but shortly go left at a fork through a barrier gate. Continue forward to a left hand bend, and carry on ahead on a grassy path towards a large pinnacle of rock after which, at the 'rock falls' sign, bear left steeply up on to the higher escarpment heading for a large communications mast. At the high wire perimeter fence turn left and follow the fence along and then around to the north to the entrance of Verne Prison. Take a path through a little gap to the left of the entrance, passing beside railings and down steep steps. Bear right along a path that traverses under the grassy banks and emerge onto a hairpin bend.

Turn left and past house number 90 to take a footpath down left. Emerging onto a road bear left, and take path beside a 'No Entry' sign to Ventnor Road. Walk down to Fortuneswell Road, and cross road to a path through a play park and turn right onto the road to the roundabout by the Royal Victoria Lodge. From here retrace your steps for the two miles to Ferry Bridge.

76   Weymouth to Lulworth Cove   OS OL15 (T) Weymouth (Trains)

Grading: This section runs the gamut from easy to moderate to strenuous. Distance - 19   940   12   586

See also our Weymouth to Lulworth Cove Path Description.

SEE SECTION 80 FOR DETAILS OF THE ALTERNATIVE INLAND COAST PATH FROM WEST BEXINGTON TO OSMINGTON MILLS.

The start along the seafront at Weymouth has been called uninteresting but at least you are in sight of the sea all the way. A new sea wall and promenade has been constructed. At Overcombe there is no proper route slgnposted at the time of writing; the official route should go up the minor road to Bowleaze Cove. However, after passing the Spyglass Inn it is best to cross the grass public open space and follow the cliff edge to the Beachside Centre. After Pontin's Riviera Holiday Centre the cliff is sliding away and the path with it. However, a slight diversion on stable ground is possible.

At the stile at the eastern end of the Pontin's Holiday Camp, this is the second Pontin's establishment and is shown as Short Lake House on maps, it is important that you follow the sign. It does in fact point in the right direction; compass carriers check it - it's about 72°. You go up over the hill apparently going inland - you do not follow the cliff edge.

On the downhill approach to Osmington Mills the new route avoiding the landslide bears away from the cliff edge over a stile and down the right hand side of a field. At the bottom it joins the Alternative Inland Route just before it crosses two stiles to meet the narrow road that is followed down to the coast. The new route is signposted.

At Ringstead one is taken slightly inland, although the official path should go along the seafront. At the old coastguard cottages at White Nothe, be careful to take the left fork of the two yellow arrows, that being the correct route. From White Nothe onwards you will find that there are some quite severe gradients to be traversed before you reach Lulworth.

There is an unfortunate diversion slightly inland on the last stretch down to Lulworth Cove, however, some people turn even further inland than they need. Some new signposts have been erected in the Lulworth Cove area indicating `Youth Hostel-Coast Path' and contain the acorn emblem. These signs are intended to indicate the route to the Youth Hostel at East Lulworth and are not the continuation of the coast path.

The wide chalk path leads down through the car park and past the Heritage Centre and on, down a tarmac road, to the cove.

Those who wish to arrive at Lulworth by a quieter; non-car-park route, should, on Hambury Tout, turn right and take the old track down on the right-hand side of the fence. This links with the beach path to St Oswald's Bay. On reaching this turn left. Presently, it comes to a tarmac road which you can follow into Lulworth.

77 | Lulworth Cove to Kimmeridge, Gaulter Gap   OS OL15 and 195 (V) Lulworth

Grading: Severe   Distance -   11   951   7   593

See also our Lulworth to Kimmeridge Path Description.

The path at the start of this section behind the beach cafe has been closed because of a cliff fall. Look out for the signed diversion. T)de permitting the beach route is, by far, the better option.

The coastal path through the Army Ranges is now open again at certain times, see opposite. It is a very fine walk indeed but a tough one. If closed, we now include the walk around, see opposite.

At most states of the tide, it is perfectly possible to walk along the pebble beach at Lulworth Cove, going up the path which rises diagonally on the far side of the beach. At the top of the steep ascent off the beach, the best route proceeds seawards and there the path turns eastwards along the coast to the beginning of the Army Ranges, just by the Fossil Forest.

If, unfortunately, time should be of the essence, when you have crossed the beach and gone up the path, do not turn right but go straight ahead. This way you will come to the Bindon Gate into the range, and you can go ahead here coming out on the coast again at Mupe Bay. It is a little shorter but far less scenic. At Gaulter Gap keep to the seaward side of the cottage unless you want the toilets which are situated beyond the north end.

RAC Gunnery School Lulworth Ranges: No Firing and Firing Periods

1. *NON FIRING PERIOD.* The Range Walks will be open to the public during the following holiday periods, all dates are inclusive.:

EASTER 1998	10 APR - 19 APR 98
SPRING 1998	2 MAY - 4 MAY 98, 23 MAY - 31 MAY 98
SUMMER 1998	25 JULY - 1 SEPT 98
CHRISTMAS/NEW YEAR 1998/99	19 DEC 98- 3 JAN 99

2. *FIRING PERIODS.* The Range Walks are normally open to the public every Saturday and Sunday except for some weekends in the year. For 1998 they have reserved the following 6 weekends for firing:

FIRST WEEKEND	23 - 25 JAN 98
SECOND	13 - 15 MAR 98
THIRD	15 - 17 MAY 98
FOURTH	20 - 21 JUN 98
FIFTH	16 - 18 OCT 98
SIXTH	27 - 29 NOV 98

3. Experience has shown that it is sometimes possible to avoid firing on some of these reserved weekends and if this is the case the Range Walks will be opened. Should this occur in 1998 we will make every effort to publicise the fact.

4. Tyneham Church and the School are normally open for viewing 0900 hrs-1500 hrs when the walks are open.

5. Information is also available from:

    a. The Range Control Office (0900-1630 hrs Mon-Fri and during the six weekend firing periods). Telephone: Bindon Abbey 01929-462721 Ext 4859 or 4700.

    b. The Guardroom (at any time). Telephone: Bindon Abbey 01929 462721 Ext 4859 or 4700.

Unfortunately, there are no permanent staff on duty in the Guardroom. Soldiers posted to or on a course at Lulworth find themselves on Guard Duty from time to time. They have much to do and whether or not the Range Walks are open does not come to the top of the list. Every effort is made to ensure that up to date information is at hand at the Guardroom.

Alternative Route when Lulwolth Range Coast Path is unavailable: Lulwolth Cove to Kimmeridge, Gaulter Gap.

Option 1 - 13^1/2 miles on safer, quieter but more strenuous route using mainly rights of way, and permissive paths through Lulworth Park (pre-plotting of given grid refs. onto map will assist navigation).

Leave the Cove and take 2nd road left (825807).100 yds on right, a footpath leads north for 3/4 mile; turn right (east) and after 100 yds left (north) to pass Belhuish Coppice and Belhuish Farm, and then across B3071 at 835832.

At 844(5)828 eastern boundary of Burngate Wood, use permissive (blue) path north-east past Park Lodge, and across road (855832) onto bridleway.

(The permissive red path across the stile, just up on the left, loops around the lake - if you're ready for a peaceful stop - and meets this bridleway further up at 861(5)834.)

Continue NE along bridleway to 865839 where it veers north, and later north-east through Highwood to meet road at 872862. Road walk east, fork right (signposted Stoborough) at 88258555; over crossroads at 886855 east for further 1^1/$_2$ miles along Holme Lane to 912855.

(*) Turn right just before a railway bridge onto Dorey Farm bridleway at 912855. After 1^1/$_4$ miles turn right onto Creech Road leading south-southwest towards the Purbeck Ridge. Another 1^1/$_2$ miles road walk up a steep gradient to a viewpoint car park. Beyond the car park 902815 take the left road that turns back and down over the ridge to Corfe. (A short cut bridleway 905817 zig-zags down to meet the same road.) As the road levels out at a left hand bend 907812, take the bridleway ahead that leads out south through Steeple Leaze Farm.

200 yds south of the farm a footpath leads south crossing another ridge bridleway, down a steep path, and across a field to Higher Stonehips, and on to Gaulter Gap, the easterly point of the range walks.

Option 2 - 12 miles of mainly road walking. Care needed on narrow bends.

Leave the Cove to West Lulworth on the B3071, and then turn right to East Lulworth on the B3070. After 3 miles turn right (east) at 886855 along Holme Lane, and then continue from (*) above, at 912855.

78	**Kimmeridge, Gaulter Gap to Swanage**	**OS OL15**

Grading: Severe and then moderate		Distance -	19	970	12	605

See also our Kimmeridge to South Haven Point Path Description.

From Gaulter Gap, Kimmeridge, there is a good path all the way to Chapman's Pool. Because of past landslides between Chapman's Pool and St Albans Head in the underdiff area. There is a high level route, and this has increased the distance by about one mile. The path is well signposted.

There is one place, after you have turned inland where you reach a gate in a field by a cattle grid, where you could go wrong. You must not go over the cattle grid where the signpost says, 'The Beach is Closed' but instead follow the path which bears inland up the valley and when the houses are reached there are plenty of signs to guide you from there on.

The first part of the climb up West Hill is uninteresting and sadly away from shoulder and views. However as you gain height going along Emmets Hill views back along the Dorset Coast are very good indeed. Do not miss the Royal Marines memorial just to the left of the path and be sure to read the inscription.

From St Albans Head there is fine high level waking all the way to Durlston Head. There is not much accommodation along this stretch. There is a poor bus service from Worth Matravers to Swanage, so plan ahead.

There is only minimal signing in the Duriston Country Park. However, you keep on the low level path all the way around Durlston Head but as you come up on the north side of it you take the second turning right, not the first which is a dead end into a quarry.

The section of the coastal path is not very clear in and around Swanage, but you are unlikely to get badly lost. A section of the coast path between Peveril Point and the town runs along the rocky shore, at present this is closed whilst drainage works are being carried out and the alternative is to use the road that runs parallel to the coast.

CP - The map suggests that the coast path enters Worth Matravers. It does not. It turns sharply south through the word 'Farm' of Renscombe Farm.

79 Swanage to Sandbanks (South Haven Point)   OS OL15(T) Swanage. (V) Studland

Grading: Moderate	Distance -	12	982	8	613

See also our Kimmeridge to South Haven Point Path Description.

At Ocean Bay Stores at the north end of Swanage Sea Front, tide permitting, it was usually better to keep along the pedestrian promenade to the end and then walk 200 yards along the beach turning up some steps rather than take the poor Official route. At high tide you have to follow the latter route leave the seafront on the main road (Ulwell Road) and where it bears left into a one-way system continue ahead into Reddliffe Road. At the sub Post Office turn sharp right into Ballard Way and at the end do not be put off by the signs 'Ballard Private Estate'. Carry forward into the quaint little estate of chalets and follow signs for the coast path to emerge on to a grassed area on the cliff edge.

From Ballard Down the path is obvious all the way to Handfast Point and the much photographed rocks of Old Harry and Old Harry's Wife. The path is obvious all the way to Studland.

November 1998 - those walking this month and intending to use the Sandbanks Ferry should, on reaching Studland, make a telephone call to the ferry office. It is intended to withdraw the ferry for two weeks in order to give it a thorough overhaul.

There is no public transport at South Haven Point so if the ferry is not operating you have two choices:-

1.   Walk to South Haven Point thus completing the coast path and walk back to Studland or;

2.   Finish your walk to Studland and return another month for your completion

Signposting is bad in Studland. As you come in you reach a road junction by a public toilet. Here turn right. You will then pass two footpaths to the right, but do not take either of them. Carry forward up the road passing the pub. Eventually, you will come to The Manor House Hotel. It is the track/road down to the beach after this hotel that you require. When you get down to the beach, turn left. When the tide is out this is firm, but when it is in more effort is required. Maybe too we should warn those who do not know, that this is a naturist beach, so you must not be put off if you find on this last lap that you are the only one wearing clothes!

If you do not wish to walk the half mile section of a naturists' beach the National Trust have now provided an alternative route through the dunes and this is marked by yellow topped posts (named - The Heather Walk).

Wainwright at the end of his work on the Pennine Way said it all, and said it better, of a shorter path. Ward & Mason in the old Letts Guide simply say 'That's it'. We will add whether you have been lucky enough to walk the whole way from Minehead at one go, or simply, as most of us have, in bits and pieces over a period, nonetheless you will be glad you walked and have just finished Britain's longest and finest footpath. It's a longer step than most take in their lifetime!

IF YOU WISH TO WALK ON, THE BOURNEMOUTH COAST PATH LINKS THE END OF THE SOUTH WEST WAY WITH THE RECENTLY WAYMARKED SOLENT WAY GIVING A CONTINUOUS PATH FROM MINEHEAD TO EMSWORTH

Studland/Sandbanks (Mouth of Poole Harbour) Bournemouth-Swanage Motor Road & Ferry Company, Shell Bay, Studland. BH19 3BA.
Tel: Studland (01929) 450203.

All year round daily. Every 20 minutes, less during peak periods. First ferry 0700 hrs last ferry 2300 hrs.

80 | Alternative Inland Coast Path: West Bexington to Osmington Mills   OS OL15

Grading: Moderate   Distance -   **29   18**

See also our alternative Inland Route Path Description.

Although this is certainly not a coastal path it is an enjoyable walk along a well-marked path with good views seaward from the ridges. Because it is inland a more detailed route is given. When walking this section bear in mind that we found no place for obtaining refreshments between the start of the walk, where there is a cafe, and the village of Osmington.

At West Bexington car park turn inland up the road signposted 'Inland Route - Coast Path', and where the road turns left, continue forward up a stony track, signposted 'Hardy Monument $5^1/_2$ miles'. At top of the hill the footpath briefly joins the main road but you immediately leave again over the stile on the right through the field, signposted 'Hardy Monument 5 miles'. Take care, the way across this field is not clear and one should, at first, keep parallel to the road and then bear right to a waymarked post. After you have crossed wall, you can start to bear upwards to the left to the further signpost near the road, marked with the acorn symbol and the words 'Inland Route'. After about 300 yards continuing through the field and by the corner of a wall there is a further signpost 'Hardy Monument $4^1/_2$, Osmington Mills 15'. Continue forward, very shortly emerging on to the B3157 road which you cross and leave through a gate, signposted 'Hardy Monument $4^1/_2$'.

You now approach Abbotsbury Castle and where the path in front divides. Take the upper right-hand fork along the top of the south side of the Fort past the trig point, from where you can get superb views in all directions, and you should be able to see clearly Hardy Monument in the distance. Proceed eastwards and cross the minor road now and go forward, signpost 'Hardy Monument 4'. Proceed in an approximate easterly direction along the ridge of Wears Hill and the crest of White Hill for about two miles following the signposts and waymarks. However be careful not to follow signs with the acorn symbol incorrectly shown that indicate routes down to the village of Abbotsbury lying in the valley below, with the old chapel clearly visible. At the east end of White Hill bear north east as signposted and leave in the inland corner through a gate on to a minor road. Turn left along the road for approximately 50 yards and then turn right, signposted 'Inland Route - Hardy Monument 2'.

Follow the bridleway marked with blue arrows along the wire fence above the scrub to a path junction where the bridleway carries on forward take the yellow waymarked footpath to the left and cross a stile. At the far side of the field the track then leads approximately 50 yards to a further gate with stile and waymark. Immediately adjacent to this gate is a stone circle which is an ancient monument and there is a sign to this effect. One now continues forward, leaving a small wood to the left, to reach the road from Portisham to Winterbourne Steepleton. Turn left along the road for approximately 60 yards and then turn right into a field over a stile, signposted 'Hardy Monument $1^1/_2$ - Osmington Mills 13'. On the far side of the field proceed forward, signpost 'Hardy Monument 1'. At this point there is a signpost forking right to Hellstone only with a return possible on a different path.

At Blackdown Barn turn left to climb up through the woods, signpost 'Hardy Monument $^1/_2$'. At the monument you will find a small signpost 'Inland Route - Osmington Mills 11 miles' with a blue arrow indicating the way forward. Cross the road to a further signpost with acorn symbol and now descend through the bracken. One shortly reaches the road again, turn left and in a few yards ignore the signpost on the right, cutting back indicating 'Bridleway to Coast Path' and continue forward, (signpost 'Coast Path East') and in another 100 yards turn right, signpost `Inland Route to Courton Hill' on one side of the sign and `Osmington 12 - Courton Hill 2' on the other. Now there is a good ridgeway path without navigational problems for some 3 miles and good views to the seaward in the distance. After passing the radio mast you come to the B3159 marked by the Borough of Weymouth boundary stone, continue across the road, signposted `Inland Route East'.

On reaching the A354 turn right immediately before the main road down the signposted track and after just over $\frac{1}{4}$ mile you will find a stile in the hedge on your left. The path leads across a narrow field to cross the busy A354. Before the farm with its adjacent radio mast take care to go through the gate on the right, marked with a blue arrow. After crossing the field, leaving two tumuli to your left, you reach a metalled road. Turn right and at the next junction there is a signpost surmounted by a symbol 'Dorset - Came Wood' which, unusually, carries the six-figure map reference of the locality (687857). Here you turn right at the signpost `Bridleway to Bincombe'. At the end of the path join a metalled lane and at the junction turn left, signposted 'Inland Route East'.

Drop down the road into the village of Bincombe and where the road turns right take the track forward leaving a small church on your right. Where the path splits take the left-hand fork signposted again with a blue arrow and the acorn symbol. After the overhead high-voltage power lines pass through a small signposted wooden gate and then proceed forward through one field into the next to the footpath sign. Here turn left, following the line of the old indistinct curving grassy track until it meets the road at the bottom of Combe Valley. Turn left here and follow the road until you reach the Combe Valley road sign to `Sutton Poyntz' and take this turn to the right. After 70 yards turn left through a gate, signposted `White Horse Hill - Osmington Mills'. The path now is easy to follow with extensive views to seaward over Weymouth and Portland. On passing a ruined building on your left you reach a broad track and turn right, signposted `Osmington $1\frac{1}{2}$' and after about 200 yards go through a gate, signposted `Inland Route Osmington'. You will shortly pass the trig point on your right and at the next field gate bear left and follow the field boundary along White Horse Hill. Just beyond the next gate fork right, signpost 'Osmington 1, Lulworth 8'.

Descend to the village of Osmington and follow the signs through the village. When you reach the main Weymouth road at the Sun Ray Inn turn left and in about 250 yards turn right at a signpost, over a stile and footbridge, and follow the field boundary on the left through two fields and at the top look back to see Hardy Monument in the distance and also the white horse on the hillside. Go over the stile to the footpath sign, turn half right to cross the field at an angle to a further stile. Cross it and turn left along the hedge side to the bottom. At the end of the field there is a very short length of enclosed footpath to the road, turn right along it descending to Osmington Mills.

ACCOMMODATION

This list of accommodation has been prepared in path order anti-clockwise.

The following letter code is used.

PL	= Packed lunches available.	EM	= Evening meal available.
O	= Open all the year.	CP	= Overnight car parking.
D	= Drying facilities for wet clothes.	LSP	= Long stay parking.
MR	= Map reference.	DW	= Dogs welcome.
S	= Single room.	DR	= Double room.
F	= Family room.	T	= Twin room.
ES	= En suite facilities.		

The part of the address in CAPITALS is an aid to location. It does not signify the postal town. The extreme left hand column refers to the appropriate section in the "Trail Description" part. We think it might help walkers find addresses quickly. The amount after the address gives an indication of the starting price for bed and breakfast. If working on a tight budget it is best to ask first.

In respect of the hostels listed, greater details will be found in the Hostel Handbook, available from Youth Hostels Association (England & Wales), St Albans, Herts. ALl 2DY. In particular watch the closed periods of the hostels.

The majority of our B & B address have been submitted by members. The fact that they are included in this book does not indicate a recommendation by The South West Way Association. Their inclusion is merely for information purposes, there they are, if you want them. We cannot, for financial and practical reasons, introduce vetting, inspection or any form of 'Star' rating. We do have a system whereby addresses can be removed from the list.

We wish to develop this list especially for many 'sparse' areas. Suggestions for inclusion in our next list will be welcome. Details of any new accommodation should be addressed to the Membership Secretary. Our list is not comprehensive, walkers will find many B&B's in towns and villages along the coast path that are not recorded in this book.

It would not be out of place here to add a word of thanks from those who walk to those who kindly board. How many times have we been thankful for a friendly welcome and good 'digs'? Maybe a note we had from one of our accommodation addresses puts it well. "We have had quite a lot of walkers this year and we have usually managed to dry them out - and feed them up."

Although there are a lot of addresses that state they are 'open all the year', some of these close for the Christmas period. Walkers should remember that during the holiday season many of our accommodation addresses could be fully booked up in advance by holidaymakers staying for a week or two. Conversely a walker could book up for one night only in good time thus preventing a guest house proprietor from taking a week or more booking later on. Accommodation problems can be frustrating to all parties concerned so bear these facts in mind when bed hunting.

During your initial contact with your selected host you could ask - 'Do you pick up and return to the coast path?' 'Do you provide early breakfasts?'And, if it should bother you that much, 'are there smokers in the house?'

TOURIST INFORMATION CENTRES can be a source of B & B addresses. If you have difficulties in booking accommodation then they should be approached. To help we have included details of TIC's in the appropriate path order in this accommodation section.

Important If having booked ahead, and for some reason or other you are unable to get to your accommodation address please telephone and explain your absence to your intended host. We have known instances where the host has become so worried about the non-appearance of walkers that they have informed the emergency services. The last thing we want is Police, Coastguards and Royal Navy helicopters out on a wild goose chase.

Section	Name and Address	Phone No./ Map reference/ Starting Price	Facilities Offered
	SOMERSET		
	YOUTH HOSTEL MINEHEAD - **SEE YHA SECTION PAGE**		
1	Tourist Information Centre, 17 Friday Street, MINEHEAD, Somerset.	01643 702624	
1	Mrs H Morris 11 Glenmore Road, MINEHEAD, Somerset, TA24 5BQ	01643 705253 £16.00	O D PL CP 2DR 1T 1S 1F
1	Mr & Mrs Mason 1 Glenmore Road, MINEHEAD, Somerset, TA24 5BQ	01643 706225 £15.00	D PL CP LSP 5DR 5T 2S 5F 2ES
1	Mrs D Morris Badgers, 38 Summerland Road, MINEHEAD, Somerset, TA19 0BJ	01643 704583 £15.00	O D EM PL CP 2DR 1T 1S 1F
1	Mrs S Phillips The Old Ship Aground, Quay Street, MINEHEAD, Somerset, TA24 5UL	01643 702087 £18.50	O D EM PL CP LSP 1DR 2T 1S 3F 7ES
1	Mrs H Marris 11 Glenmore Road, MINEHEAD, Somerset, TA24 5BQ	01643 705253 £15.00	O D PL CP DW 2DR 2T 1S 1F
1	Mr & Mrs J Segenhout Mayfair Hotel, The Avenue, MINEHEAD, Somerset, TA24 5AY	01643 702719 £24.00	D EM PL CP 4DR 1T 2S 6F 13ES
1	Mr E Bower Countrywide Holidays, Doverhay Place, PORLOCK, Somerset, TA24 8EX	01643 862398 891 468 £23.50	O D EM PL CP LSP 6DR 12T 9S 20ES
1	Mrs S Coombe Hurlstone, Sparkhayes Lane, PORLOCK, Somerset, TA24 8NE	01643 862650 887 469 £16.00	O D PL CP DW 1DR 1T
1	Mrs J Robinson The Ship Inn, High Street, PORLOCK, Somerset, TA24 8QD	01643 862507 £19.50	O D EM PL CP LSP 6DR 3T 2F 11ES
1	Mrs J Stiles-Cox Leys, The Ridge, Off Bossington Lane, PORLOCK, Somerset, TA24 8HA	01643 862477 £17.00	O D PL CP LSP 1DR 1T 2S
1	Mr & Mrs R Thornton Lorna Doone Hotel, High Street, PORLOCK, Somerset, TA24 8PS	01643 862404 £22.50	O D EM PL CP DW 6DR 4T 2S 2F 14ES
1	Mrs B Starr Sea View Cottage, PORLOCK WEIR, Somerset, TA24 8PE	01643 862523 864 478 £17.00	O D PL CP DW 1T 1S 1ES
1	Mrs E Richards Silicombe Farm, PORLOCK, Somerset, TA24 8JN	01643 862248 £16.00	O D EM PL CP DW 1DR 2T 1S 2ES
	NORTH DEVON		
	YOUTH HOSTEL - LYNTON, ILFRACOMBE - **SEE YHA PAGE**		
2	Mr & Mrs Irlam North Cliff Hotel, North Walk, LYNMOUTH, North Devon, EX35 6HJ	01598 752357 £25.00	D EM PL CP 9DR 2T 2S 1F 14ES
2	Mr & Mrs C Parker-Clifford Tregonwell, Riverside G.H., 1 Tors Road, LYNMOUTH, Devon, EX25 6ET	01598 753369 £19.50	O D EM PL CP LSP 7DR 2T 1S 1F 4ES
2	Mrs J Pile Oakleigh, 4 Tors Road, LYNMOUTH, North Devon, EX35 6ET	01598 75220 £17.50	O D EM PL CP LSP 5DR 2T 2S
2	Mr & Mrs Price East Lyn House Hotel, Watersmeet Road, LYNMOUTH, Devon, EX35 6EP	01598 752540 £27.00	D EM PL CP LSP DW 7DR 1T 8ES

Section	Name and Address	Phone No./ Map reference/ Starting Price	Facilities Offered
2	The Bath Hotel LYNMOUTH, Devon, EX35 6EL	01598 752238 £28.50	D EM PL CP DW 12DR 7T 1S 4F 24ES
2	Mr & Mrs J Kuczer Woodlands, Lynbridge Road, LYNTON, Devon, EX35 6AX	01598 752324 £17.00	D EM PL CP LSP 5DR 1T 1S 5ES
2	Mrs N Hill The Denes, Longmead, LYNTON, Devon, EX35 6DQ	01598 753573 £15.00	O D PL CP 2DR 1S 3F 1ES
2	Mrs M Kirk 12 Crossmead, LYNTON, Devon, EX35 6DG	01598 753288 £14.50	O D EM PL CP LSP 1DR 1T 2S
2	Mrs P Morgan Kingford House, Longmead, LYNTON, Devon, EX35 6DQ	01598 752361 £20.50	O D EM PL CP 3DR 1T 2S 4ES
2	Mr & Mrs J Oborne The Retreat, No 1 Park Gardens, Lydiate Lane, LYNTON, Devon	01598 753526 £15.00	D PL CP DW 2DR 2T 1F
2	Tourist Information Centre Town Hall, Lee Road, LYNTON, Devon, EX35 6BT	01598 752225	
2	Mrs Dallyn Mannacott Farm, Nr Hunters Inn, MARTINHOE, Devon, EX31 4QS	01598 763227 £14.00	D PL CP LSP 1DR 1T
3	Mr & Mrs F Barry Glendower, King Street, COMBE MARTIN, Devon, EX34 0AL	01271 883449 £12.00	O D PL CP LSP DW 2DR 1T 2ES
3	Mr & Mrs L Pallatt Autumn Lodge, Victoria Street, COMBE MARTIN, Devon, EX34 0JS	01271 883558 £15.00	O D EM PL CP DW 4F 2ES
3	Mrs J Bosley Hillview Guest House, The Woodlands, COMBE MARTIN, Devon, EX34 0AT	01271 882331 575 469 £15.00	D PL CP LSP 4DR 1T 2ES
3	Mrs M Mangnall Moorlands, Holstone Down, COMBE MARTIN, Devon, EX34 0PF	01271 883463 £16.00	O D EM PL CP 1DR 1T 2ES
3	Saffron House Hotel King Street, COMBE MARTIN, Devon, EX34 0BX	01271 883521 581 469 £19.00	D EM PL CP DW 4DR 1T 4F 7ES
3	Mrs A Waldon Idlehour, Borough Road, COMBE MARTIN, Devon, EX34 0AN	01271 883217 £12.00	D PL CP DW 2DR 2T 2S
3	Tourist Information Centre Sea Cottage, Cross Street, COMBE MARTIN, Devon, EX34 9EH	01271 883319	
4	Mr & Mrs T White Trafalgar Hotel, Larkstone Terrace, Hillsborough Road, ILFRACOMBE, Devon, EX34 9NU	01271 862145 £21.00	O D EM PL CP DW 9DR 9T 4S 3F 25ES
4	Mr & Mrs A Furber Slipway Cottage, 2 Hierns Lane, The Harbour, ILFRACOMBE, Devon, EX34 9EH	01271 863035 £15.00	O D EM PL CP LSP 4DR 1T 4S 2ES
4	Mrs M Howard 2 Capstone Place, ILFRACOMBE, Devon, EX34 9TQ	01271 865201 £14.00	D EM PL DW 1DR 1T
4	Mrs & Mrs Millington Sherbourne Lodge Hotel, Torrs Park, ILFRACOMBE, Devon, EX34 8AY	01271 862297 £15.50	O D EM PL CP LSP 7DR 3T 1S 1F 6ES
4	Tourist Information Centre The Promenade, ILFRACOMBE, Devon, EX34 9BX	01271 863001	

Section	Name and Address	Phone No./ Map reference/ Starting Price	Facilities Offered
5	Mrs M Newcombe Sunnyside, LEE, Nr Ilfracombe, Devon, EX34 8LW	01271 863189 £15.00	O D CP LSP 1DR 1T
5	Mrs F Nustedt The Grampus Inn, LEE, Nr Ilfracombe, Devon	01271 862906 £17.50	O D EM PL CP LSP 1DR 1T 1F 3ES
5	Lundy House Hotel Chapel Hill, MORTEHOE, Devon, EX34 7DZ	01271 870372 £17.50	D EM PL CP DW 3DR 1S 4F 6ES
6	Mrs A Braund Clyst House, Rockfield Road, WOOLACOMBE, Devon, EX34 7DH	01271 870220 £18.00	D EM CP 3DR 2T 1S 2F
6	Mrs T Gyles Ocean View, The Esplanade, WOOLACOMBE, Devon, EX34 7DJ	01271 870359 £16.00	O D PL CP LSP 8DR 2T 2S 4F 16ES
6	Mr & Mrs H Riley Camberley, Beach Road, WOOLACOMBE, Devon, EX34 7AA	01271 870231 465 438 £16.00	O D PL CP 3DR 2T 1F 6ES
6	Tourist Information Centre Bed Barn Cafe Car Park, Barton Road, WOOLACOMBE, Devon	01271 870553	
7	Mr & Mrs C Gedling West Winds Guest House, Moor Lane, CROYDE BAY, Devon, EX33 1PA	01271 890489 £23.00	D EM PL CP LSP DW 3DR 2T 1S 5ES
7	Mrs Windsor Chapel Farm, Hobbs Hill, CROYDE, Devon, EX33 1NE	01271 890429 £17.00	D PL CP 3DR 1T 1S 2ES
7	Mr & Mrs S Butler Shuna Guest House, Downend, CROYDE, Devon, EX33 1QE	01271 890537 437 387 £20.00	O D CP 4DR 1T 2F 7ES
8	Mrs E Dale 2 Links View, SAUNTON, Devon, EX33 1LL	01271 812233 £14.00	O D EM PL CP LSP 2DR 1T 1S 1F
8	Mrs R Saunders Stockwell Lodge, 66 South Street, BRAUNTON, Devon	01271 814338 £15.00	O D PL CP LSP DW 1DR 2T 1S 2F 2ES
8	Mrs J Watkins North Cottage, 14 North Street, BRAUNTON, Devon, EX33 1AJ	01271 812703 485 367 £13.50	O D EM PL CP DW 3DR 1T 2S 1ES
8	Tourist Information Centre Caen Street Car Park, BRAUNTON, Devon, EX33 1AA	01271 816400	
8	Mr & Mrs B Capp Crossways, Braunton Road, BARNSTAPLE, Devon, EX31 1JY	01271 379120 553 336 £14.50	O D PL CP LSP 2DR 2T 1F 2ES
8	Mr & Mrs J Harrison Cresta Guest House, Sticklepath Hill, BARNSTAPLE, Devon	01271 374022 £16.00	O D PL LSP 1DR 2T 2F 2S 3ES
8	Mrs L Tucker Enfield, Top of Sticklepath Hill, BARNSTAPLE, Devon, EX31 2DW	01271 22949 £16.00	O D CP LSP 1DR 2T 1S
8	Tourist Information Centre Devon Library, Boutport Street, BARNSTAPLE, Devon, EX31 1TY	01271 47177	
8	Mrs D George Oakwood, 34 Yelland Road, FREMINGTON, Barnstaple, Devon, EX31 3DS	01271 73884 £12.50	O D EM PL CP 3DR 1T 1S 2F
9	Mrs Garnsey Ellerton, Glenburnie Road, BIDEFORD, Devon, EX39 2LW	01237 473352 £15.00	O D PL CP LSP DW 1DR 2T

Section	Name and Address	Phone No./ Map reference/ Starting Price	Facilities Offered
9	Mount Hotel Northdown Road, BIDEFORD, Devon, EX39 3LP	01237 473748 £20.00	O D EM PL CP 3DR 2T 2S 1F 7ES
9	Tourist Information Centre Victoria Car Park, The Quay, BIDEFORD, Devon, EX39 2QQ	01237 477676	
9	Mrs Clegg Mayfield, Avon Lane, WESTWARD HO!, Devon, EX39 1LR	01237 477128 £13.00	O D Pl CP LSP 3DR 1T 1S
9	Mr & Mrs Wise Buckleigh Lodge, Bay View Road, WESTWARD HO!, Devon, EX39 1BJ	01237 475988 £19.00	O D EM PL CP LSP 2DR 2T 1S 1F 6ES
9	Mr & Mrs P Snowball Brockenhurst, 11 Atlantic Way, WESTWARD HO!, Devon, EX39 1HX	01237 423346 432 290 £20.50	O D PL CP LSP DW 2DR 1T 3ES
10	Mrs C Powell Laburnum Cottage, BUCKS MILL, Nr Bideford, Devon, EX39 5DY	01237 431582 £14.00	O D PL CP LSP DW 3DR 2T 1S 2F 1ES
10	Mrs Curtis Fuchsia Cottage, Burscott Lane, Burscott Lane, HIGHER CLOVELLY, Devon, EX39 5RR	01237 431398 £15.00	O D PL CP LSP DW 1DR 1S 1F 2ES
10	Mrs B May The Boat House, 148 Slerra Hill, HIGHER CLOVELLY, Devon, EX39 5ST	01237 431209 £15.00	O D EM PL CP LSP 2DR 1T 1S 1F
10	Mrs P Vanstone The Old Smithy, Slerra, HIGHER CLOVELLY, Devon, EX39 5ST	01237 431202 £15.00	O D PL CP LSP DW 2DR 2T 2ES
10	Mrs M Dunn 55 The Quay, CLOVELLY, Devon, EX39 5TF	01237 431436 £17.50	O D PL CP LSP DW 1DR 1F
10	Mrs C Giddy Temple Bar, CLOVELLY, Devon, EX39 5TE	01237 431438 £17.50	O D CP LSP 1DR 1T
11	The New Inn High Street, CLOVELLY, Bideford, Devon, EX39 5TQ	01237 431303 £17.50	O D EM PL CP LSP 13DR 5T 2S 3F 8ES
11	Mrs Y Heard West Titchberry Farm, HARTLAND POINT, Devon, EX39 6AU	01237 441287 242 271 £15.00	O D EM PL CP LSP 1DR 1T 1F
11	Mrs H Davey Stoke Barton Farm, Stoke, HARTLAND, Devon, EX39 6DU	01237 441238 237 246 £17.00	D PL CP LSP DW 1DR 1T 2ES
11	Mr & Mrs D Mace Lower Hardisworthy, Hardisworthy, HARTLAND, Devon, EX39 6ER	01237 441850 £16.50	O D EM PL CP LSP 1DR 1T 1ES
11	Mr & Mrs J George Gawlish Farm, HARTLAND, Devon, EX39 6AT	01237 441320 £15.00	O D EM PL CP LSP 1DR 2T 1ES
11	Mr & Mrs Johns Hartland Quay Hotel, HARTLAND, Devon, EX39 6DU	01237 441371 £20.00	D EM PL CP LSP DW 6DR 6T 3S 2F 10ES
11	Mrs B Slee Homeleigh, Stoke, HARTLAND, Devon, EX39 6DU	01237 441465 235 247 £15.00	D PL CP LSP 1DR 1T

Section	Name and Address	Phone No./ Map reference/ Starting Price	Facilities Offered
	NORTH CORNWALL		
	YOUTH HOSTELS, BOSCASTLE, TINTAGEL, PADSTOW, NEWQUAY, PERRANPORTH SEE YHA SECTION PAGE		
12	Mrs Heywood Cornakey Farm, MORWENSTOW, Cornwall, EX23 9SL	01288 331260 £16.00	O D EM PL CP LSP 3DR 1F 1ES
12	Mrs I Heard Dene Farm, MORWENSTOW, Cornwall, EX23 9SL	01288 331330 £17.00	O D EM PL CP LSP 2DR 1F 1ES
12	Mrs D Hobbs Meadow Park, MORWENSTOW, Cornwall, EX23 9ST	01288 331499 £16.00	D EM PL CP LSP 1S 1T 1F
12	Mrs Cholwill Darzle Farm, Woodford, MORWENSTOW, Cornwall	01288 331222 £17.00	O D EM PL CP LSP 3T 2F 4ES
12	Mrs S Trewin Lower Northcott Farm, POUGHILL, Bude, Cornwall, EX23 7EQ	01288 352350 £17.00	O D EM PL CP LSP 2DR 1T 1S 2F 5ES
12	Mrs B Dunstan Strands, Stibb, BUDE, Cornwall, EX23 9HW	01288 353514 £14.00	O D EM CP 2DR 1F 2ES
12	Mrs Y Hanns Dol Amroth, 23 Downs View, BUDE, Cornwall, EX23 8RG	01288 352202 £14.00	O D PL CP 3DR 1T 2S 2F 5ES
12	Mr & Mrs E Hatch Seaview, 51 Killerton Road, BUDE, Cornwall, EX23 8EN	01288 352665 £16.00	O D PL CP LSP 2DR 1F
12	Mrs J Rouse Corisande Hotel, 24 Downs View, BUDE, Cornwall, EX23 8RG	01288 353474 £15.00	O D EM PL CP LSP 5DR 2F 5ES
12	Mr & Mrs P Kimpton Kisauni, 4 Downs View, BUDE, Cornwall, EX23 8RF	01288 352653 £14.00	O D EM PL CP LSP 4DR 1T 1S 2F 3ES
12	Mr & Mrs H Laurence Treriven, 24 Ocean Road, BUDE, Cornwall, EX23 8NN	01288 353177 £14.00	D CP 1DR 1T 1S 2ES
12	Mrs E Luxton Wyvern House, 7 Downs View, BUDE, Cornwall, EX23 8BF	01288 352205 £14.00	O D EM PL CP LSP 2DR 1T 2S 1F 3ES
12	The Meva-Gwin Hotel Upton, BUDE, Cornwall, EX23 0LY	01288 352347 102 049 £22.00	D EM PL CP LSP 5DR 3T 3S 2F 11ES
12	Mornish Hotel Summerleaze Crescent, BUDE, Cornwall, EX23 8HJ	01288 352972 £18.95	D EM PL CP LSP DW 5DR 2T 3F 10ES
12	Seabreeze 5 Hartland Terrace, BUDE, Cornwall, EX23 8JT	01288 355922 £15.00	O D 1DR 2T 1ES
12	Mr M Payne Pencarrol Guest House, 21 Downs View, BUDE, Cornwall, EX23 9RF	01288 352478 £14.50	D EM PL CP LSP 4DR 1T 1S 1F
12	Mr & Mrs M Fly 8 Downs View, BUDE, Cornwall, EX23 8RF	01288 355059 £14.50	O D EM PL CP DW 3DR 2T 1S 1F 4ES
12	Mr & Mrs J Thorne The Farthings, 4 Killerton Road, BUDE, Cornwall, EX23 8EL	01288 355310 £13.50	O D PL CP DW 1DR 1T 1S
12	Tourist Information Centre Crescent Car Park, BUDE, Cornwall, EX23 8LE	01288 352240	
13	Bay View Inn Marine Drive, WIDEMOUTH BAY, Cornwall, EX23 0AW	01288 361273 201 022 £13.00	O D EM PL CP LSP 3DR 1T 2S 3F 4ES

Section	Name and Address	Phone No./ Map reference/ Starting Price	Facilities Offered
13	Mr & Mrs Marks Penhalt Farm, WIDEMOUTH BAY, Cornwall, EX23 0DG	01288 361210 £13.00	D PL CP LSP DW 1DR 1T 1F 1ES
13	Mr & Mrs J Cooper Coombe Barton Inn, CRACKINGTON HAVEN, Cornwall, EX23 0JG	01840 230345 £18.50	D EM PL CP LDP DW 5DR 1T 1S 3ES
13	Mrs R Crocker Lower Tremorn Farm, CRACKINGTON HAVEN, Cornwall, EX23 0NU	01840 230667 £18.00	O D EM PL CP LSP 3DR 2ES
14	G Crown Tolcarne House Hotel, Tintagel Road, BOSCASTLE, Cornwall, PL35 0AS	01840 250654 £23.00	D EM PL CP LSP DW 5DR 2T 1S 8ES
14	Mrs J Horwell Higher Pennycrocker Farm, St Juliot, BOSCASTLE, Cornwall, PL35 0BY	01840 250488 127 927 £15.00	O D PL CP LSP 1DR 1T 1F 2ES
14	Lower Meadow House Penally Hill, BOSCASTLE, Cornwall, PL35 0HF	01840 250570 102 913 £17.00	O D PL CP 2DR 1T 2F 6ES
14	Mr & Mrs M Lovell Rivendell Court, BOSCASTLE, Cornwall, PL35 0BN	01840 250130 £19.00	O D EM PL CP LSP 2DR 1T 3ES
14	Mr & Mrs G Mee Bottrraux House Hotel, BOSCASTLE, Cornwall, PL35 0BG	01840 250231 £20.00	O D EM PL CP LSP 4DR 2T 1S 1F 7EN
14	Mrs C Nicholls Trerosewill Farm, Paradise, BOSCASTLE, Cornwall, PL35 0DL	01840 250545 £19.00	O D EM PL CP LSP 2DR 2T 1S 1F 6ES
15	Mrs A Jones Grange Cottage, BOSSINEY, Tintagel, Cornwall, PL34 0AX	01840 770487 £16.00	D PL CP 1DR 1T 1S 1F
15	L Leeds Willapark Manor Hotel, BOSSINEY, Tintagel, Cornwall, PL34 0BA	01840 770782 £30.00	O D EM PL CP DW 6DR 2T 3S 3F 14ES
15	Mrs P Tinney Bossiney Cottage, BOSSINEY, Cornwall, PL34 0AY	01840 770327 066 888 £15.00	O DW EM PL CP 1DR 1S 1F
15	Bosayne Guest House Atlantic Road, TINTAGEL, Cornwall, PL34 0DE	01840 770514 £14.00	O D PL CP LSP DW 3DR 1T 3S 2F 1ES
15	Mrs A Townsend 'Kilmorie Guest House', Bossiney Road, TINTAGEL, Cornwall PL34 0AH	01840 770140 £14.00	O D PL CP DW 3DR 2T 2F
16	Mr & Mrs D Willcocks Sgitheath Cottage, 6 Trecarne Gardens, Trebarwith Road, TREBARWITH, Cornwall, PL33 9DB	01840 212546 073 848 will collect £15.00	O D EM PL CP LSP 1DR 1S
16	Mr & Mrs J Andrews Bay Hotel, 1 The Terrace, PORT ISAAC, Cornwall, PL29 3SG	01206 880380	D EM PL CP LSP DW 3DR 1T 2S 4F 4ES
16	Mr & Mrs J Andrews Hathaway Bed & Breakfast, Roscarrock Hill, PORT ISAAC, Cornwall, PL29 3RG	01208 880416 £16.00	D CP LSP DW 2DR 2T 1S 1ES
16	Mrs J Corrigan The Homestead, Tintagel Terrace, PORT ISAAC, Cornwall, PL29 3SE	01208 880064 £15.00	O D PL CP LSP DW 2DR 1T
16	Ms J Mann The Castle Rock Hotel, 4 New Road, PORT ISAAC, Cornwall, PL29 3SB	01208 880300 £32.00	O D EM PL CP LSP 10DR 5T 2S 1F 18ES
16	St Andrews Hotel 18 The Terrace, PORT ISAAC, Cornwall, PL29 3SG	01208 880240 £19.00	O D PL CP LSP DW 4DR 2T 2S 1F 9ES

Section	Name and Address	Phone No./ Map reference/ Starting Price	Facilities Offered
16	Mrs L Von Lintzgy Fairholme, 30 Trewetha Lane, PORT ISAAC, Cornwall, PL29 3RW	01208 880397 001 805 £16.00	O D EM PL CP LSP 3DR 2T 2F 2ES
17	Mrs M Pashley Pentire View Guest House, POLZEATH, Cornwall, PL27 6TB	01208 862484 £15.00	O D EM PL CP LSP 2DR 2T 2S 1F
17	Mrs P White Seaways, POLZEATH, Cornwall, PL27 6SU	01208 862382 £17.50	O D EM CP LSP 2DR 2T 1S 1F 3ES
18	Mr M Martin Silvermead, ROCK, Wadebridge, Cornwall, PL27 6LB	01208 862425 935 758 £17.50	O D EM PL CP LSP 2DR 2T 2S 3F 5ES
18	Roskarnon House Hotel ROCK, Nr Wadebridge, Cornwall, PL27 6LD	01208 862785 £20	D EM PL CP LSP 4DR 6T 2F 10ES
18	Mrs J Marshall Skyber, Higher Treworder, Egloshayle, WADEBRIDGE, Cornwall, PL27 6HX	01208 816042 £15.00	D EM PL CP LSP 1DR 1T 1F 1ES
18	Mrs E Champion Estuary Views, 8 Treverbyn Road, PADSTOW, Cornwall, PL28 8DW	01841 532551 £18.00	O D PL CP DW 3DR 1T 1S 2ES
18	Mrs M Romer 23 Barry's Lane, PADSTOW, Cornwall, PL28 8AU	01841 532178 917 754 £16.00	D 1DR 1S
18	Mrs M Meyer Rosehill House, High Street, PADSTOW, Cornwall, PL28 8BB	01841 532761 £16.00	O D DW 1DR 1T 1S 1F
18	Mr & Mrs J Stock Woodlands Close, Treator, PADSTOW, Cornwall, PL28 8RU	01841 533109 £15.00	O D PL CP LSP 1DR 1T 1S
18	Tourist Information Centre North Quay, PADSTOW, Cornwall, PL28 8AF	01841 533449	
19	Mrs J Ball Gwel-an-Nans, Homer Park Road, TREVONE, Cornwall, PL28 8QU	01841 520769 £18.00	O D PL CP LSP 1DR 1T 2F 2ES
19	Mrs S Hamilton Trevone Bay Hotel, TREVONE, Padstow, Cornwall, PL28 8QS	01841 520243 892 755 £25.00	D EM PL CP DW 4DR 3T 3S 2F 12ES
20	Mr & Mrs J Shadbolt Trelooan, Treporth, PORTHCOTHAN BAY, Cornwall, PL28 8LS	01841 521158 £15.00	O D PL CP LSP 1DR 1T
21	Miss A Allbutt Trevarrian Lodge, Trevarrian, MAWGAN PORTH, Cornwall, TR8 4AQ	01637 860422 £20.00	O D EM PL CP LSP 3DR 2T 1S 3F 5ES
21	Mrs L Bennett The Merrymoor Inn, MAWGAN PORTH, Cornwall, TR8 4BA	01637 860258 £17.50	EM PL CP LSP DW 4DR 2T 1S 2F
21	Mr & Mrs C Robinson Sea Vista Hotel, MAWGAN PORTH, Cornwall, TR8 4AL	01637 860276 £20.00	O D EM PL CP DW 5DR 3S 1F 4ES
21	Mr & Mrs J Parry White Lodge Hotel, MAWGAN PORTH, Cornwall, TR8 4BN	01637 860512 £20.00	D EM PL CP LSP DW 8DR 8T 2S 8F 13ES
21	D Molloy Tregurrian Hotel, Watergate Bay, NEWQUAY, Cornwall, TR8 4AB	01637 860280 842 649 £21.00	D EM PL CP LSP DW 11DR 5T 4S 7F 22ES
21	Mrs M Atkinson Springvale Guest House, 112 Henver Road, NEWQUAY, Cornwall TR7 3EQ	01638 873857 829 621 £13.00	O D EM PL CP LSP 3DR 1T 1F 4ES
21	Corisande Manor Hotel Riverside Avenue, Pentire, NEWQUAY, Cornwall, TR7 1PL	01637 872042 £29.00	O D EM PL CP LSP 10DR 3T 3S 16ES

Section	Name and Address	Phone No./ Map reference/ Starting Price	Facilities Offered
21	Mrs S Harper Chichester, 14 Bay View, NEWQUAY, Cornwall, TR7 1LR	01637 874216 813 614 £14.00	D EM PL OP 2DR 1T 2S 2F 5ES
21	Mrs S Schofield Hemick Lodge, 33 Pentire Avenue, NEWQUAY, Cornwall, TR7 2PB	01637 872592 £13.50	D EM CP 2DR 1T 1S 2F
21	St Mawes Hotel Springfield Road, NEWQUAY, Cornwall, TR7 1RT	01637 872754 £15.00	O D PL CP 3DR 2T 3S 2F 7ES
21	Mr G Stevenson Trevalsa Hotel, Watergate Road, Porth NEWQUAY, Cornwall, TR7 3LX	01637 873336 £22.00	D EM PL CP LSP DW 12DR 4T 4S 4F 21ES
21	Tourist Information Centre Municipal Offices, Marcus Hill, NEWQUAY, Cornwall, TR7 1BD	01637 871345	
22	Mr & Mrs D Eyles Crantock Bay Hotel, West Pentire, CRANTOCK, Cornwall, TR8 5SE	01637 830229 777 607 £35.00	D EM PL CP LSP DW 8DR 13T 9S 3F 33ES
22	Mr & Mrs J Somerville The Goose Rock Hotel, West Pentire, CRANTOCK, Cornwall	01637 830755 £19.00	EM CP LSP DW 3DR 1T 1S 4F 9ES
22	S Wrigley Tregenna House, West Pentire Road, CRANTOCK, Cornwall, TR8 5RZ	01637 830222 605 788 £16.00	O D EM PL CP LSP 6DR 6T 1S 4F 5ES
23	Kerensa Cliff Road, PERRANPORTH, Cornwall, TR6 0DR	01872 572470 755 543 £16.00	O D PL CP DW 6DR 4T 3S 3F 4ES
23	Mrs M Crofts Tremore, Liskey Hill Crescent, PERRANPORTH, Cornwall, TR6 0HP	01872 573537 £18.00	D PL CP LSP 3DR 1T 1S 2ES
23	Mrs S Wells 44 Tywarnhayle Road, PERRANPORTH, Cornwall, TR6 0DX	01872 572380 £12.50	O D EM PL CP 4DR 3S 4S 3F
23	Tourist Information Centre Beiners Arms Hotel, PERRANPORTH, Cornwall	01872 573368	
24	Mrs Gill-Carey Penkerris, Penwinnick Road, ST AGNES, Cornwall	01872 552262 £15.00	O D EM PL CP LSP 3DR 2T 1S 2F 3ES
24	Mrs P Harding Trewarren, Mithian Downs, ST AGNES, Cornwall, TR5 0PY	01872 553851 742 498 £16.00	D PL CP LSP 2DR 2T 1S 1F 1ES
24	Ms F Appleton Glen Cottage, Quay Road, ST AGNES, Cornwall, TR5 0RP	01872 553546 £15.00	O D EM PL CP DW 2DR 1T 1S
24	Mrs Glover Beach Cottage, Quay Road, ST AGNES, Cornwall, TR5 0RS	01872 553802 £15.00	O D PL CP 3DR 1T 1F 1ES
24	Mrs Treleaven Driftwood Spars Hotel, Trevaunance Cove, ST AGNES, Cornwall, TR5 0RT	01872 552428 £29.00	O D EM PL CP LSP 7DR 1T 1F 9ES
25	Ms V Parkinson Buzby View, Forthvean Road, PORTHTOWAN, Cornwall, TR4 8AY	01209 891178 691 473 £16.00	D PL CP 2DR 1T 1S
26	Mr & Mrs P Allen Sycamore Lodge, Primrose Terrace, PORTREATH, Cornwall, TR16 4JS	01209 842784 £16.00	D EM PL CP LSP 2DR 1T 1S
26	Fountain Springs Glenfeadon House, PORTREATH, Cornwall, TR16 4JU	01209 842650 £18.50	O D EM PL CP 1DR 4T 1S 2F 3ES

Section	Name and Address	Phone No./ Map reference/ Starting Price	Facilities Offered
26	C Healan Cliff House, The Square, PORTREATH, Cornwall, TR16 4LB	01209 842008 £17.50	O D EM PL CP 1DR 1T 2S 2ES
26	Victoria Cole-Porter Portreath Arms Hotel, The Square, PORTREATH, Cornwall, TR16 4LA	01209 842259 £18.00	O D EM PL CP LSP 4DR 3T 1F 5ES
26	Mr & Mrs P Smythe Benson's, 1 The Hillside, PORTREATH, Cornwall, TR16 4LL	01209 845324 £25.00	O D PL CP LSP 2DR 2S 4ES
26	Mrs M Symonds Suhaili, 14 Forth-an-Nance, PORTREATH, Cornwall, TR16 4NQ	01209 842110 £14.00	O D PL CP LSP DW 1DR 1T 1F 3ES
26	Mrs A Ellis Vellynsaundry, Pendarves, CAMBORNE, Cornwall, TR14 0RS	01209 712983 Collection Service £13.00	D PL CP LSP 1DR 1T 2S
27	Mrs P Bailey Calize Country House, Prosper Hill, GWITHIAN, Cornwall, TR27 5BW	01736 753268 £15.00	O D PL CP LSP DW 2DR 3T 2S 4ES
27	Mrs L Davies Nanterrow Farm, GWITHIAN, Cornwall, TR27 5BP	01209 712282 £16.00	O D PL CP LSP 1DR 1T 1S 1F
27	Mrs D Eddy Orchard Close, 3 Church Town Road, GWITHIAN, Cornwall, TR27 5BX	01736 753077 £14.00	O D PL CP LSP DW 1DR 1T
27	Mrs A Cooper 54 Penpol Terrace, HAYLE, Cornwall, TR27 4BQ	01736 752855 £16.00	O D PL CP LSP 1DR 1T 1S
27	Mrs R Hosking 34 Penpol Terrace, HAYLE, Cornwall, TR27 4BQ	01736 754484 551 367 £13.50	O D CP DW 1DR 1T
27	White Hart Hotel 10 Foundry Square, HAYLE, Cornwall, TR27 4HQ	01736 752322 £29.50	O D EM PL CP LSP 5DR 6T 3S 1F 15ES
28	Mr & Mrs D O'Sullivan Hindon Hall, LELANT, St Ives, Cornwall, TR26 3EN	01736 753046 £18.00	O D PL CP LSP 3DR 1T 4ES
28	Mr & Mrs Batty The Grey Mullet, 2 Bunkers Hill, ST IVES, Cornwall	01736 796635 517 408 £21.00	O D CP LSP 5DR 1T 1S 6ES
28	Mrs Bowden Carhill, 9 Porthminster Terrace, ST IVES, Cornwall, TR26 2DQ	01736 796738 £15.00	O EM PL CP LSP DW 3DR 2T 1S 2F 1ES
28	Mr & Mrs D Mason Kandahar, 11 The Warren, ST IVES, Cornwall, TR26 2EA	01736 796183 519 403 £19.00	D PL CP LSP 3DR 1T 1S 2F 4ES
28	Mrs Hart Chy-an-Gwedhen, St Ives Road, Carbis Bay, ST IVES, Cornwall, TR26 2PN	01736 798684 £18.00	O D EM PL CP 3DR 2T 1S 2F 8ES
29	Tourist Information Centre The Guildhall, Street an Pol, ST IVES, Cornwall, TR26 2DT	01736 796297	
29	The Old Chapel Backpackers Hostel, ZENNOR, St Ives, Cornwall	01736 798307 455 385 £8.00	O D EM CP LSP Bunkhouse
29	Mrs N Mann Trewey Farm, ZENNOR, St Ives, Cornwall, TR26 3DA	01736 796936 454 384 £16.00	D PL CP DW 2DR 1T 1S 2F
29	Dr Gynn Boswednack Manor, ZENNOR, St Ives, Cornwall, TR26 3DD	01736 794183 442 378 £17.00	O EM PL CP LSP 2DR 1T 1S 1F 2ES

Section	Name and Address	Phone No./ Map reference/ Starting Price	Facilities Offered
29	Mrs A Prowse Trewey Vean Farm, ZENNOR, St Ives, Cornwall, TR26 3DA	01736 766919 £15.00	D PL CP LSP DW 1S 3F
29	Mrs Berryman Treen Farm, Gurnards Head, ZENNOR, St Ives, Cornwall, TR26 3DE	01736 796932 436 377 £14.00	D PL CP LSP DW 1DR 1T 1S
29	Mrs Andrews Quiddles, PENDEEN, Cornwall, TR19 7DW	01736 787278 £14.00	PL CP LSP DW 2DR 1T 1S 1ES
29	Mrs Bailey Trewellard Manor Farm, PENDEEN, Cornwall, TR19 7SU	01736 788526 £17.00	O D CP 2DR 1T 1ES
29	Mrs J Davey Pendeen Manor, PENDEEN, Cornwall, TR19 7ED	01736 788753 £17.00	O D PL CP LSP DW 2DR 1T 1S 2F 2ES
29	Mr & Mrs T Dymond The Old Count House, Boscaswell Down, PENDEEN, Nr Penzance, Cornwall, TR19 7ED	01736 788058 383 344 £15.00	D PL CP LSP 2DR
29	The Radjel Inn PENDEEN, Cornwall, TR19 7DS	01736 788446 385 344 £16.00	O D EM PL CP LSP 1DR 1T 1S 1F
30	Miss C Bailey Field House, 8 Trewellard Road, PENDEEN, Cornwall, TR19 7ST	01736 788097 3770337 £16.00	O D PL 1DR 2T
30	Mrs J Cargeeg Manor Farm, BOTALLACK, Cornwall, TR19 7QG	01736 788525 £48.00	O D CP LSP 2DR 1T 3ES
30	Mrs E Lawry Llawnroc, 1 Truthwall Villa, ST JUST, Penzance, Cornwall, TR19 7QL	01736 788814 £14.00	O D EM PL CP 3DR 2T 1S 1F
30	Boswedden House Hotel Cape Cornwall, ST JUST, Penzance, Cornwall TR19 7NJ	01736 788733 £23.00	D PL CP LSP DW 2DR 3T 2S 1F 8ES
30	Mr & Mrs B Collins Cape House, Cape Cornwall, ST JUST, Penzance, Cornwall, TR19 7NN	01736 787112 £18.00	D CP LSP DW 1T 1S
30	Mrs A Eddy Trethewes, Carrallack Terrace, ST JUST, Penzance, Cornwall, TR19 7LP	01736 788528 £14.00	D PL CP LSP 2DR 1S 1F
30	Mr & Mrs C Lilley Bosavern House, St JUST, Penzance, Cornwall, TR19 7RD	01736 788301 371 305 £16.50	O D PL CP LSP DW 6DR 3T 1S 3F 8ES
31	Mr & Mrs D Gallie Polwyn Cottage, Old Coastguard Row, SENNEN COVE, Cornwall, TR19 7DA	01736 871349 350 264 £14.50	O D CP LSP DW 1DR 1T 1ES
31	Mrs S Adams Homefields, Mayon, SENNEN, Cornwall, TR19 7AD	01736 871418 £12.50	O D EM PL CP LSP 3DR 2T 1F 1ES
31	Mrs Harrison Lyonesse Guest House, Land's End, SENNEN, Cornwall, TR19 7AD	01736 871207 £15.00	O D EM PL CP LSP 2DR 2T 1S 3F 3ES
31	Mr T Ellison Whitesands Lodge, SENNEN, Cornwall, TR19 7AR	01736 871776 366 264 £17.50	O D EM PL CP LSP 2DR 1T 28S 1F 2DR

Section	Name and Address	Phone No./ Map reference/ Starting Price	Facilities Offered

SOUTH CORNWALL

YOUTH HOSTELS - PENZANCE, HELSTON, FALMOUTH, ST AUSTELL SEE YHA SECTION PAGE

Section	Name and Address	Phone No./ Map reference/ Starting Price	Facilities Offered
32	Mrs P Armitage Nanjizal Guest House, Higher Bosistow, Higher Bosistow, ST LEVAN, Cornwall, TR19 6JJ	01736 871269 366 234 £17.00	O D EM PL CP LSP 2DR 1T 3ES
32	Mr & Mrs P Christ Sea View House, The Valley, PORTHCURNO, Penzance, Cornwall, TR19 6JX	01736 810638 £16.00	D EM PL CP DW 3DR 2T 1S 1F 1ES
32	Mr & Mrs J Ring 'Corniche' Guest House, Trebehor, PORTHCURNO, Cornwall, TR19 6LX	01736 871685 375 243 £14.00	O D EM PL CP 3DR 1T 1S 1F
32	Al Singer & Richard Sweet The Porthcurno Hotel, The Valley, PORTHCURNO, Cornwall, TR19 6JX	01736 810119 £16.00	O D CP LSP DW 5DR 6T 2S 2ES
32	Mrs B Thomas Grey Gables, PORTHCURNO, Cornwall, TR19 6JT	01736 810421 £16.50	D EM PL CP LSP 3DR 3T 5ES
32	Mrs A Jilbert Penver House Farm, TREEN, Nr Porthcurno, Penzance, Cornwall, TR19 6LG	01736 810778 £16.00	O D PL CP LSP DW 1DR 1T 1S 1ES
33	Mr & Mrs B Richards Tremeneth Hotel, LAMORNA, Nr Penzance, Cornwall, TR19 6XL	01736 731367 £15.00	O D EM PL CP DW 6DR 2T 2S 2F 5ES
34	Mrs G Ash Torre Vene, Lescudjack Terrace, PENZANCE, Cornwall, TR18 3AE	01736 64103 £17.00	O D EM PL CP LSP 4DR 2T 2S 2F
34	Tarbert Hotel Clarence Street, PENZANCE, Cornwall, TR18 2NU	01736 63758 £26.00	D EM PL CP 6DR 4T 2S 12ES
34	Mrs Buswell Penalva, Alexandra Road, PENZANCE, Cornwall, TR18 4LZ	01736 69060 £13.00	O D PL CP LSP 2DR 2T 1S 4ES
34	Mrs P Schofield Chy-an-Gof, 10 Regent Terrace, PENZANCE, Cornwall, TR18 4DW	01726 332361 £18.00	O D PL CP LSP 2T 2S 1ES
34	Mr & Mrs D Glenn Trewella Guest House, 18 Mennaye Road, PENZANCE, Cornwall, TR18 4NG	01736 63818 £14.00	EM CP 4DR 2T 2S 5ES
34	Mr & Mrs J Hopkins Woodstock Guest House, 29 Morrab Road, PENZANCE, Cornwall, TR18 4EZ	01736 69049 472 300 £11.00	O D PL DW 3DR 2T 2S 1F 5ES
34	Mr & Mrs J Leggatt Cornerways, 5 Leskinnick Street, PENZANCE, Cornwall, TR18 2HA	01736 64645 £15.00	O D EM PL CP LSP 1DR 3S 1ES
34	Mr & Mrs J Murphy Greenbury Cottage, Rosudgeon, PENZANCE, Cornwall, TR20 9QG	01736 763785 £17.50	O D PL CP LSP 2DR 1ES
34	Mrs T Stacey Lynwood Guest House, 41 Morrab Road, PENZANCE, Cornwall, TR18 4EX	01736 65871 £11.50	O D PL CP DW 2DR 1T 1S 2F 2ES
34	Tourist Information Centre Station Road, PENZANCE, Cornwall, TR18 2NF	01736 62207	
35	Mrs S Stevens Marazion Hotel, MARAZION, Cornwall, TR17 0AP	01736 710334 £20.00	O D EM PL CP LSP 4DR 4T 1S 2F 8ES
35	Mr I Glover Anneth Lowen, Leys Lane, MARAZION, Cornwall, TR17 0AQ	01736 710211 £12.50	O D PL CP DW 2DR 2T

Section	Name and Address	Phone No./ Map reference/ Starting Price	Facilities Offered
35	Mr & Mrs S Lugg The Ferryboat, Kings Road, MARAZION, Cornwall, TR17 0EJ	01736 710569 £15.00	O D PL EM CP LSP 2DR 2ES
36	Mrs M Foy Mzima, Penlee Close, PRAA SANDS, Nr Penzance, Cornwall, TR20 9SR	01736 763856 582 287 £15.00	O D PL CP 1T 2F
36	Mrs G Garragham Bodeeve, PRAA SANDS, Cornwall, TR20 9TQ	01736 763246 £12.50	O D PL CP LSP 2T 1S
36	Mrs Jennings Boslowen-Mor, Castle Drive, PRAA SANDS, Cornwall, TR20 9TF	01736 76223 £12.50	D PL CP 2DR 1T 1ES
36	Mrs P Williams 2 Penlee Close, PRAA SANDS, Cornwall, TR20 9SR	01736 762785 578 288 £13.00	O D CP LSP 2DR 1S
36	Mr & Mrs Sharp 'Gurynoon', Chy-An-Dour Road, PRAA SANDS, Penzance, Cornwall, TR20 4D6	01736 763426 £18.00	O D PL CP LSP DW 4DR 4T 4S 2F 4ES
37	Mrs C Cookson Pentre, Peverell Terrace, PORTHLEVEN, Cornwall, TR13 9DZ	01326 574493 630 255 £16.50	D PL CP LSP DW 1DR 1T 2S
37	Mr Hallam Seefar, Peverell Terrace, PORTHLEVEN, Cornwall, TR13 9D2	01326 573778 £15.00	O D EM PL CP LSP 3DR 1T 2S
37	Tye Rock Hotel Loe Bar Road, PORTHLEVEN, Cornwall, TR13 9EW	01326 572695 £30.00	O D EM PL 5DR 2T 7ES
37	Mr & Mrs P Ingham Anchor Cottage, Cliff Road, PORTHLEVEN, Cornwall	01326 574391 629 257 £15.00	O D PL 1DR 1T
37	Ms M Kelymack An Mordos Hotel, Peverell Terrace, PORTHLEVEN, Cornwall, TR13 9BZ	01326 562236 £17.00	O D EM PL 4DR 6T 2S 3F 4ES
38	Mrs J Lugg Tregaddra Farm, Cury Cross Lanes, HELSTON, Cornwall, TR12 7BB	01326 240235 701 219 £19.50	O D EM PL CP LSP 3DR 1T 1F 5ES
38	Mr B Griffin Riverside Guest House, Nantithet, HELSTON, Cornwall, TR12 7RB	01326 241027 682 226 £17.50	O D PL EM CP LSP 3DR 1T 2ES
38	Mr Tucker Lyndale Guest House, 4 Greenbank, Meneage Road, HELSTON, Cornwall, TR13 8JA	01326 561082 £15.50	O D EM PL CP LSP 5DR 2T 1F 3ES
38	S Archer Redannack Bungalow, Lender Lane, MULLION, Cornwall, TR12 7HS	01326 240936 £15.00	D PL CP CP LSP 1DR 1T 1F
38	Mr M Bolton Croggan Mill, MULLION COVE, Cornwall, TR12 7EU	01326 240496 667 180 £16.00	O D EM PL CP LSP 21DR 18T 15S 15F 69ES
38	Mrs J Tyler-Street Trenance Farmhouse, MULLION, Cornwall, TR12 7HB	01326 240639 673 185 £16.50	D PL CP LSP 3DR 1T 4EN
38	Mr & Mrs T Valender The Old Vicarage, Nansmellyon Road, HELSTON, Cornwall, TR12 7DQ	01326 240898 £18.50	O D CP LSP 1DR 2T 2F 3ES
38	Mr & Mrs M Wood Trenance Barton, MULLION, Cornwall, TR12 7HB	01326 240893 £16.00	O D PL CP LSP DW 1DR 1T 1ES
39	Mr & Mrs J Barlow The Lizard Hotel, Penmenner Road, THE LIZARD, Cornwall, TR12 7NP	01326 290305 £20.00	O D EM PL CP LSP 5DR 1T 1S 1F 2ES

Section	Name and Address	Phone No./ Map reference/ Starting Price	Facilities Offered
39	Mrs P Hocking Bayview, Cross Common, THE LIZARD, Helston, Cornwall, TR12 7PD	01326 290369 £13.00	D CP DW 1DR 1T
39	Mr & Mrs S Kilmister Parc Brawse House, Penmenner Road, THE LIZARD, Helston, Cornwall, TR12 7NR	01326 290466 £15.00	O D EM PL CP DW 3DR 2T 1S 1F 4ES
39	Cornish Diving Lodge Treynwyns, THE LIZARD, Cornwall, TR12 7PE	01326 290633 708 218 £15.00	O D EM PL CP LSP 1DR 1T 2S 2F
39	Mr N Palmer The Crowndale Restaurant, The Cellars, THE LIZARD, Cornwall, TR12 7PH	01326 290674 715 127 £15.00	O D EM PL CP DW 1DR 1T
39	Mr & Mrs James Carmelin, Pentreath Lane, THE LIZARD, Helston, Cornwall, TR12 7NY	01326 290677 699 126 £30.00	D PL CP DW 1DR
39	Mrs G Rowe Trethvas Farm, THE LIZARD, Helston, Helston, Cornwall, TR12 7AR	01326 290720 709 136 £15.00	D PL CP LSP 2DR 1T 1ES
39	Mrs K Thirlaway Green Cottage, THE LIZARD, Cornwall, TR12 7NZ	01326 290099 £13.00	O D PL CP LSP DW 2DR
39	Mrs I Sowden The Most Southerly House LIZARD POINT, Cornwall, TR12 7NU	01326 290300 702 115 £18.00	O D PL CP LSP 2DR 1T 1S 1ES
40	Mrs B Rosindale Trewarder Farm, RUAN MINOR, Nr Helston, Cornwall, TR12 7JL	01326 290970 £17.00	D PL CP LSP 1DR 1T 2ES
40	Mrs T Carey Tamarisk Cottage, COVERACK, Helston, Cornwall, TR12 6TG	01326 280638 £15.00	D PL CP DW 1DR 1T 1S
40	Mr P Cheze-Brown The Croft, Lowlands Lane, COVERACK, Cornwall, TR12 6TF	01326 280387 783 187 £18.00	O D EM PL CP LSP 3T 2ES
40	Mrs L Goldsworthy The Bay Hotel, COVERACK, Cornwall, TR12 6TF	01326 280464 £45.00	D EM PL CP DW 8DR 5T 1S 13ES
40	Mrs E Daw Bakery Cottage, Polcoverack Lane, COVERACK, Nr Helston, Cornwall, TR12 6TD	01326 280474 £15.50	O D EM PL CP LSP 1DR 1F
40	Mrs R Whitaker Wych Elm, Ponsongath, COVERACK, Cornwall, TR12 6SQ	01326 280576 756 179 £16.50	O D EM PL CP LSP 1T 1ES
40	White Hart Inn The Square, ST KEVERNE, Cornwall, TR12 6ND	01325 280325 791 212 £20.00	O EM PL CP LSP DW 1DR 1T 2ES
40	Mrs R Kelly Trevinock, PORTHOUSTOCK, Cornwall, TR12 6QP	01326 280498 802 216 £17.00	D EM PL CP LSP DW 2DR 2S 1ES
41	Mrs P Peters Gallen-Treath Guest House, PORTHALLOW, St Kevern, Cornwall, TR12 6PL	01326 280400 £20.50	O D PL CP LSP DW 3DR 1T 4ES
41	Mrs D Lambert Clifton Cottage, PORTHALLOW, Cornwall, TR12 6PP	01326 280916 £15.00	1F
41	Mrs P Julian Landrivick Farm, MANACCAN, Cornwall, TR12 6HX	01326 231249 £18.00	O D EM PL CP LSP 3DR 2T 2S 1F 8ES
41	Mrs J Davies Pengwedhen, HELFORD, Cornwall, TR12 6JZ	01326 231481 755 265 £17.50	O D PL CP LSP DW 1DR 2T 1S 1F

Section	Name and Address	Phone No./ Map reference/ Starting Price	Facilities Offered
42	Mrs Spike Carwinion Vean, Grove Hill, MAWNAN SMITH, Cornwall, TR11 5ER	01326 250513 £18.00	O D PL CP LSP DW 3S 2T 1F 2ES
42	Mr & Mrs Cork Grove Hotel, Grove Place, FALMOUTH, Cornwall, TR11 4AV	01326 319577 £21.00	O D EM PL 5DR 5T 2S 3F 13ES
42	Mr T Soper Rosehill, 38 Kimberley Park Road, FALMOUTH, Cornwall, TR11 2BD	01326 318597 £16.00	O D PL CP LSP DW 2DR 1S 2S
42	Mr J Walker Ambleside, 9 Marlborough Road, FALMOUTH, Cornwall, TR11 3LP	01326 319630 £14.00	O D EM PL CP LSP 4DR 4T 1S 1F
42	Harbour House 1 Harbour Terrace, FALMOUTH, Cornwall,	01326 311344 £15.00	DW PL CP LSP 3DR 1T 1S 1F 3ES
42	Mrs M Appleton Castleton Guest House, 68 Killigrew Street, FALMOUTH, Cornwall, TR11 3PR	01326 311072 £17.00	O D DW 2DR 3F 4ES
42	Mr & Mrs B Watmore Rosemary Hotel, Gyllyngvase Terrace, FALMOUTH, Cornwall, TR11 4DL	01326 314669 810 318 £18.50	D EM PL CP 4DR 2T 2S 2F 10ES
42	Tourist Information Centre 28 Killigrew Street, FALMOUTH, Cornwall	01326 312300	
44	M Davis Harberton House, Churchtown Road, Gerrans, PORTSCATHO, Cornwall, TR2 5DZ	01872 580598 £17.00	D PL CP LSP 1DR 1T
44	Mr & Mrs S Evans Tregerein Guest House, PORTSCATHO, Cornwall, TR2 5HT	01872 580336 877 358 £15.50	O D EM PL CP LSP 3DR 2T 1F 2ES
44	Mrs J Hickley 40 Churchtown Road, Gerrans, PORTSCATHO, Cornwall, TR2 5DY	01872 580389 £17.00	D CP LSP DW 1DR 1T
44	Mrs A Palmer Trenestrall Farm, Ruan High Lanes, PORTHSCATHO, Truro, Cornwall, TR2 5LX	01872 501259 £15.00	O D EM CP LSP DW 1DR 2T 1F
44	Mrs J Smith Maraval, 4 Parc An Dillon, PORTSCATHO, Cornwall, TR2 5DU	01872 580310 £17.00	D CP 1T
45	Mrs C Holdsworth Tregain Tea Room & Restaurant, The Post Office, PORTLOE, Truro, Cornwall, TR2 5QU	01872 501252 937 395 £19.00	O D EM PL CP LSP 1T 1S
45	Mr & Mrs R Foley St Petroc, PORTLOE, Cornwall, TR2 5RA	01872 501143 £17.50	O D CP DW 1DR 1T
47	Mr J Gregory Llawnroc Inn, GORRAN HAVEN, Cornwall, PL26 6NU	01726 843461 £18.00	O D EM PL CP LSP 3S 4T 1F 7ES
47	Ms G Mott Piggy Pantry, The Willows, GORRAN HAVEN, Cornwall	01726 843545 £16.00	O D EM PL CP DW 1T 1F
47	Mr & Mrs R Smith 'Homestead', 34 Chute Lane, GORRAN HAVEN, Cornwall, PL26 6NU	01726 842567 £20.00	O D CP 1DR 1T
48	Mr & Mrs D Youlden Steep House, PORTMELLON COVE, Nr Cornwall, PL26 6PH	01726 843732 £17.50	O D PL CP LSP 5DR 1T 1S 2ES
48	Ms J Connolly Mandalay Hotel, School Hill, MEVAGISSEY, Cornwall, PL26 6TQ	01726 842435 £18.00	O D EM PL CP LSP 5DR 3T 1S 2F 6ES

Section	Name and Address	Phone No./ Map reference/ Starting Price	Facilities Offered
48	Mrs R Mazirel Cawtes Cottage, 37 Cliff Street, MEVAGISSEY, Cornwall, PL26 6QJ	01726 842396 £13.00	O D EM PL DW 3DR 1T 1S 1F 1ES
48	Mrs Harris Polvellan School Hill, MEVAGISSEY, Cornwall, PL26 6TG	01726 842197 £17.00	D PL CP DW 2DR 1T 1F 2ES
48	Mrs A Lawrence Tregorran Guest House, Cliff Street, MEVAGISSEY, Cornwall, PL26 6QW	01726 842319 £16.50	D EM PL CP LSP DW 4DR 1T
38	Mrs M Bainbridge & Mrs Jackson Polrudden Farm, PENTEWAN, Mevagissey, Cornwall, PL26 6BJ	01726 842051 £20.00	D PL CP LSP 1DR 2T 3ES
49	Mrs A Arnold Treveglos, Church Road, CHARLESTOWN, Cornwall, PL25 3NS	01726 61424 £17.50	O D CP DW 1DR 1T 1S
49	Mrs E Kesibart The Beeches, Charlestown Road, CHARLESTOWN, Nr St Austell, Cornwall	01726 75469 £20.00	O PL CP LSP 2DR 1T 3ES
49	Mr & Mrs Callis Ardenconnel, 179 Charlestown Road, CHARLESTOWN, Nr St Austell, Cornwall, PL25 3NN	01726 75469 £16.00	O PL CP LSP 2F 1ES
49	Ms S Mathieson Coastguard House, 11 Coastguard Terrace, CHARLESTOWN, Nr St Austell, Cornwall, PL25 3NJ	01726 72828 039 515 £14.50	O D PL CP LSP DW 1DR 1T
50	Ms K Bailey 25 Chatsworth Way, CARLYON BAY, Cornwall, PL25 3SL	01726 812560 £15.00	O D PL CP LSP 1DR 1ES
50	Cliff Head Hotel Sea Road, CARLYON BAY, Cornwall, PL25 3RB	01726 812125 £35.00	O D EM PL CP LSP 20DR 25T 10S 2F 57ES
50	Mr & Mrs N Perrett Porth Avalen Hotel, Sea Road, CARLYON BAY, Cornwall, PL25 3SG	01726 812802 £40.00	O D EM PL CP LSP 9DR 11T 3S 1F 24ES
50	Mrs M Ball Polbrean House, Woodland Avenue, Tywardreath, PAR, Cornwall PL24 2PL	01726 812530 £20.00	O D PL CP LSP 2DR 1S
50	Mrs B Burgess 55 Polmear Road, PAR, Cornwall, PL24 2AW	01726 812967 086 535 £12.50	O D CP 1T 2S
51	Mr & Mrs R Bullock Trevanion Guest House, 80 Lostwithiel St, FOWEY, Cornwall, PL23 1BQ	01726 832602 124 518 £18.00	D PL CP 1DR 1T 2S 1F 2ES
51	The Ship Inn Trafalgar Square, FOWEY, Cornwall, PL23 1AZ	01726 833751 £19.50	O D EM PL DW 4DR 2T 1ES
51	Mrs J Reid Panorama, Daglands Road, FOWEY, Cornwall, PL23 1JL	01726 833153 £15.00	O D CP 1DR 1T 1S
51	Mr & Mrs D Turner Topsides, Esplanade, FOWEY, Cornwall, PL23 1HZ	01726 833715 £16.00	O D PL DW 2DR
51	Tourist Information Centre The Post Office, 4 Custom House Hill, FOWEY, Cornwall	01726 733616	
52	Mrs B Blamey Holly House, 18 Fore Street, POLRUAN, Cornwall, PL23 1PQ	01726 870478 £13.50	O D PL DW 3T
52	Mrs C Talling Lansallos Barton Farm, Lansallos, POLPERRO, Cornwall, PL13 2PU	01503 272192 £14.00	O D PL CP LSP DW 1DR 1T 1F

Section	Name and Address	Phone No./ Map reference/ Starting Price	Facilities Offered
52	Mrs P Moore Chyavallon, Landaviddy Lane, POLPERRO, Cornwall, PL13 2RT	01503 272788 £16.50	O D PL CP DW 2D 1T 3ES
52	Mr & Mrs M Westcott Penahallow-on-Brent, Talland Hill, POLPERRO, Cornwall, PL13 2RY	01503 272689 £18.00	O CP DW 2T 1S 2ES
52	Mrs P Wilcox The Watchers, The Warren, POLPERRO, Cornwall, PL13 2RD	01503 272296 £17.00	O D PL DW 1D 2T 3ES
52	Mr & Mrs B Spring Allhays Country House, TALLAND BAY, Polperro, Cornwall, PL13 2JB	01503 272434 £30.00	O D EM PL CP LSP 3D 3T 1S 1F 5ES
53	Mr M Neaves Schooner Point, 1 Trelawney Terrace, WEST LOOE, Cornwall, PL13 2AG	01503 262670 £12.00	O D PL CP 4D 2S 1F 2ES
53	Mr & Mrs C Eveleigh Grassmere, St Martins Road, EAST LOOE, Cornwall, PL13 1LP	01503 262556 254 544 £15.00	O D EM PL CP 3D 2F
53	Marwinthy Guest House East Cliff, EAST LOOE, Cornwall, PL13 1DE	01503 264382 256 533 £17.00	O D PL DW 2D 1T 2F 2ES
53	Tourist Information Centre The Guildhall, Fore Street, LOOE, Cornwall, PL13 1AA	01503 262072	
54	Mrs A Harvey The Bungalow, Cliff Road, CRAFTHOLE, Nr Torpoint, Cornwall, PL11 3BY	01503 230334 355 541 £15.00	D PL CP LSP 1D 1T
54	Mrs K Ridpath Fir Cottage, Lower Tregantle, Antony, CRAFTHOLE, Nr Torpoint, Cornwall, PL11 3AL	01752 822626 £15.00	O D EM PL CP LSP 1T 1S 2F
55	C Collins Avon House, Garrett Street, CAWSAND, Cornwall, PL10 1PB	01752 822229 £12.00	O D PL DW 1D 1T 1S 1ES
55	Mr & Mrs A Fidler Rame Barton, Rame, CAWSAND, Cornwall, PL10 1LG	01752 822789 425 492 £18.00	D EM PL CP LSP DW 1D 1ES
55	Mrs D Goodwright Clarendon, Garrett Street, CAWSAND, Cornwall, PL10 1PD	01752 823460 £14.00	O D PL LSP 1D 1T 1S
55	Mrs P Taylor The Haven, Market Street, KINGSAND, Cornwall, PL10 1ND	01752 823860 £16.00	O D PL CP LSP 1D 1T 1S
55	Mr A Ogilvie Algoma, The Green, KINGSAND, Cornwall, PL10 1NH	01752 822706 434 506 £18.50	O D PL CP 1D 1F 2ES

SOUTH DEVON

YOUTH HOSTELS - PLYMOUTH, BRIXHAM, SEATON, SEE YHA SECTION PAGE

Section	Name and Address	Phone No./ Map reference/ Starting Price	Facilities Offered
56	Mrs A Coon Berkeley's of St James, 4 St James Place East, The Hoe, PLYMOUTH, Devon, PL1 3AS	01752 221654 £20.00	O D EM PL CP LSP 2D 2T 1S 1F
56	Mrs M Emery Acorns & Lawns, 171 Citadel Road, The Hoe, PLYMOUTH, Devon, PL1 2HY	01752 229474 £15.00	O D PL 6D 3T 2S 2F 3ES
56	Kynance Hotel 107/113 Citadel Road (West), The Hoe, PLYMOUTH, Devon, PL1 2RN	01752 266821 £23.50	O D EM PL CP LSP 6D 13T 5S 2F 26ES

Section	Name and Address	Phone No./ Map reference/ Starting Price	Facilities Offered
56	Mr & Mrs J Lake Sea Breezes, 28 Grand Parade, West Hoe, PLYMOUTH, Devon, PL1 3DJ	01752 667205 483 538 £16.00	O D EM PL DW 3D 2T 1S 3F 2ES
56	Mrs J Turner Rusty Anchor, 30 Grand Parade, West Hoe, PLYMOUTH, Devon, PL1 3DJ	01752 663924 £12.50	O D EM PL CP LSP 1D 2T 2S 4F 4ES
56	Mr & Mrs D Riggs Plymouth Backpackers Hotel, 172 Citadel Road, The Hoe, PLYMOUTH, Devon PL1 3DB	01752 225158 £7.50	O D 2D 2T 7F 1ES
56	Tourist Information Centre Island House, 9 The Barbican, PLYMOUTH, Devon	01752 264849/51	
57	Mrs J Rayne The Borington Arms, TURNCHAPEL, Nr Plymouth, Devon, PL9 9TQ	01752 402053 495 531 £15.00	O D EM PL CP DW 3D 1T 2F
57	Heybrook Bay Private Hotel Beach Road, HEYBROOK BAY, Nr Plymouth, Devon, PL9 0BS	01752 862345 496 488 £16.00	O D EM PL CP LSP 4D 2T
57	Mrs S Farrington Bay Cottage, 150 Church Road, WEMBURY, Devon, PL9 0HR	01752 862559 520 485 £23.00	O D EM PL CP LSP 2D 2T 1S 3ES
57	Mrs J Mills Willowhayes, Ford Rd, Nr Post Office, WEMBURY, Devon, PL9 0JA	01752 862581 524 494 £12.50	O D PL CP DW 2D 1F 1ES
58	Mrs J Cross Wood Cottage, Bridgend, NEWTON FERRERS, Devon, PL8 1AW	01752 872372 555 487 £17.50	O D EM PL CP DW 1D 1T 1S 1ES
58	River Yealm Hotel Yealm Road, NEWTON FERRERS, Devon, PL8 1BL	01752 872419 £35.00	O D EM PL CP LSP 6D 6T 2S 1F 10ES
58	Mrs A Hill Rowden House, Stoke Road, NOSS MAYO, Plymouth, Devon, PL8 1JG	01752 872153 555 472 £17.50	D PL CP LSP DW 1D 2T
58	Mrs B Sherrell Brookingdale, NOSS MAYO, Devon, PL8 1EJ	01752 872665 547 475 £15.00	O D PL CP LSP 2D 1T
58	Mrs J Rogers Higher Shippen, Worswell Farm, NOSS MAYO, Devon	01752 872977 £16.50	O D PL CP 1D 1F
58	Mrs F Kempt West Hanover Lodge, HOLBETON, Devon, PL8 1JN	01752 830582 617 502 £18.00	D PL CP 1D 1ES
58	Ms J Stockman Bugle Rocks, The Old School, Battsborough, HOLBETON, Devon, PL8 1JX	01752 830422 601 473 £20.00	O D PL CP LSP 2D
58	Mrs L Wallis Windlestraw, Penquit, ERMINGTON, Devon, PL21 0LU	01752 896237 646 544 will pick up/ drop Yealm, Erme,Avon. £17.50	O D PL CP LSP 1T 1S
58	Mr N Kies Torr House, KINGSTON, Kingsbridge, Devon, TQ7 4PT	01548 810723 640 480 £18.00	O D PL CP 2D 1T 1S
58	Mrs P Brunskill Cliff Path, RINGMORE, Kingsbridge, Devon, TQ7 4HR	01548 810654 651 456 £16.00	O D PL CP 1T
58	Mrs I Dodds Ayrmer House, RINGMORE, Nr Kingsbridge, Devon	01548 810391 £20.00	O D PL CP 3D 1T 2ES
59	Mr S Chapman CHALLABOROUGH, Devon, TQ7 4JB	01548 810425	Holiday Bungalows

Section	Name and Address	Phone No./ Map reference/ Starting Price	Facilities Offered
59	Mr & Mrs Walsh Folly Foot, CHALLABOROUGH, Devon, TQ7 4JB	01548 810036 £17.00	O D PL EM CP LSP 1DR 1T 1F 1ES
59	Mr A Farrell Warren Cottage, Marine Drive, BIGBURY ON SEA, Devon, TQ7 4AS	01548 810216 650 444 £21.00	D EM PL CP LSP 1T
59	Mrs J Balkwill Court Barton, AVETON GIFFORD, Nr Kingsbridge, Devon, TQ7 4LE	01548 550312 696 479 £20.00	O D PL CP LSP 2DR 2T 1S 2F 6ES
59	Mrs P Rowland Heron House Hotel, THURLESTONE SANDS, Devon, TQ7 3JY	01548 561600 £20.00	O D EM PL CP LSP 7DR 7T 3S 7F
59	N Upslade La Mer, THURLESTONE SANDS, Devon, TQ7 3JY	01548 561207 £25.00	O D CP LSP DW 3DR 3ES
59	Ms T Wilson 2 Horswell Cottages, SOUTH MILTON, Devon, TQ7 3JU	01548 561328 679 423 £17.00	O D PL CP 2T
59	Mr & Mrs L Clarke Hope Cove Hotel, HOPE COVE, Devon TQ7 3HH	01548 561233 £24.00	D EM PL CP LSP 4DR 2T 1F 7ES
59	Mrs J Guymer Cove Cottage, HOPE COVE, Devon, TQ7 3HG	01548 561446 £13.50	O P CP LSP DW 1DR 1T 1S
60	Mr & Mrs R Petty-Brown Rocarno, Grenville Road, SALCOMBE, Devon, TQ8 8BJ	01548 842732 736 389 £14.50	O D EM PL CP DW 1DR 1T 1S 1F
60	Mr & Mrs Axtell Amalfi, Grenville Road, SALCOMBE, Devon, TQ8 8BJ	01548 842155 736 389 £17.50	O D CP 2DR 2T 2ES
60	Mr & Mrs A Bouttle Torre View Hotel, Devon Road, SALCOMBE, Devon TQ8 8HJ	01548 842633 £24.00	D EM PL CP 4DR 2T 1S 1F 8ES
60	Mrs N Carter Karenza, Grenville Road, SALCOMBE, Devon, TQ8 8BJ	01548 843422 £18.00	O D EM PL CP LSP 1DR 2F
60	Mr & Mrs R Vaughan Trennels Hotel, Herbert Road, SALCOMBE, Devon, TQ8 8HR	01548 842500 £20.00	CP 6DR 1T 1S 5ES
60	Tourist Information Centre Council Hall, Market Street, SALCOMBE, Devon, TQ8 8QL	01548 842736	
61	Mr C Richards The Gara Rock Hotel, EAST PORTLEMOUTH, Devon, TQ8 8PH	01548 842342 753 372 £27.00	D EM PL CP LSP DW 10DR 10T 2S 10F
61	Mr & Mrs M Mitchelmore Sunnyside, EAST PRAWLE, Devon, TQ7 2BY	01548 511387 £15.00	O D PL CP DW 1DR 1T 1S
61	Mrs C Light Hallsands Hotel, HALLSANDS, Kingsbridge, Devon, TQ7 2EY	01548 51124 £20.00	O D EM PL CP LSP 4DR 7T 3F 2ES
61	Mr R Kerswell The Cricket Inn, BEESANDS, Torcross, Devon, TQ7 2EN	01548 580215 879 403 £18.00	O D EM PL CP LSP 2DR 1T 1F 4ES
61	Mr & Mrs R Jefferies The Venture, TORCROSS, Nr Kingsbridge, Devon, TQ7 2TQ	01548 580314 823 421 £20.00	D PL CP 1DR 1T 1F
62	Mrs V Mercer Old Walls, SLAPTON, Nr Kingsbridge, Devon, TQ7 2QN	01548 580516 £16.00	O D PL CP DW 2DR 1T 1ES

Section	Name and Address	Phone No./ Map reference/ Starting Price	Facilities Offered
62	Mr B Wood and Mr Colin Smith The Slide House, Hynetown Road, STRETE, Nr Dartmouth, Devon, TQ6 0RS	01803 770378 £25.00	O D EM PL CP LSP 2DR 1T 3ES
62	Mrs J Wright Camelot, 61 Victoria Road, DARTMOUTH, Devon, TQ6 9RX	01803 833805 875 514 £16.00	O D CL LSP 3DR 2T 2F
62	Tourist Information Centre Newcomen Engine House, Mayors Avenue, DARTMOUTH, Devon, TQ6 9YY	01803 834224	
63	Carlton House Higher Street, KINGSWEAR, Devon, TQ6 0AG	01803 752244 £14.00	O D EM PL DW 2DR 1T 1S 1F 1ES
63	Mr & Mrs P Hancock Melville Hotel, 45 New Road, BRIXHAM, Devon, TQ5 8NL	01803 852033 £15.00	D EM PL CP 3DR 2T 2S 2F 2ES
63	Mr & Mrs T Boulton Sampford House, 57/59 King Street, BRIXHAM, Devon, TQ5 9TH	01803 857761 £16.00	O D PL CP LSP DW 5DR 1T 6ES
63	Mr I Hayhurst Richmond House Hotel, Higher Manor Road, BRIXHAM, Devon, TQ5 8HA	01803 882391 £18.00	D PL CP DW 4DR 2F 5ES
63	Tourist Information Centre The Quay, BRIXHAM, Devon, TQ5 8TB	01803 852861	
64	Mrs P Kingdon Bruce Lodge Guest House, 2 Elmsleigh Rd, PAIGNTON, Devon, TQ4 5AU	01803 550972 £14.00	D EM PL CP LSP 3DR 2T 1S 1F
64	Mrs M McHolm 5a Fortescue Road, PAIGNTON, Devon, TQ3 3BZ	01803 550667 894 616 £12.00	O D EM PL CP LSP 1DR 1F 2ES
64	Mrs P Whitlam Cheltor Hotel, 20 St Andrews Road, PAIGNTON, Devon, TQ4 6HA	01803 551507 £14.00	D EM PL CP LSP DW 3DR 1T 1S 4F 5ES
64	Tourist Information Centre Festival Hall, Esplanade Road, PAIGNTON, Devon	01803 558383	
64	Mr D Day Sunray Hotel, Aveland Road, TORQUAY, Devon, TQ1 3PT	01803 328285 £18.00	O D EM PL CP LSP 10DR 6T 3S 3F
64	Torquay Backpackers Hostel 119 Abbey Road, TORQUAY, Devon, TQ2 5NP	01803 299924 £7.00	O D PL CP 1DR 1T 30S 1F 2ES
64	Tourist Information Centre Vaughan Parade, TORQUAY, Devon	01803 297428	
64	Mr & Mrs K James Suite Dreams Hotel, Steep Hill, MAIDENCOMBE, Nr Torquay, Devon, TQ1 4TS	01803 313900 £20.00	O D PL CP DW 6DR 3T 3F 12ES
64	Mrs F Gowens Barn Hayes Country Hotel, Brim Hill, MAIDENCOMBE, Nr Torquay, Devon, TQ1 4TR	01803 327980 £25.00	D EM PL CP LSP DW 4DR 2T 2S 4F 10ES
65	K Underwood Glenside Hotel, Ringmore Road, SHALDON, Devon TQ14 0EP	01626 872448 £19.00	O D EM PL CP LSP 4DR 4T 1S 1F 8ES
66	Mr & Mrs J New Lalla Rook, 1 Bitton Ave, TEIGNMOUTH, Devon, TQ14 8HD	01626 779653 £13.00	O D CP 3DR 1T 1S
66	Mr & Mrs Ward Glenthorne Guest House, 99 Bitton Park Road, TEIGNMOUTH, Devon, EX14 9BZ	01626 776650 937 731 £13.00	O D PL DW 1DR 1T 2ES

Section	Name and Address	Phone No./ Map reference/ Starting Price	Facilities Offered
66	Tourist Information Centre The Den, TEIGNMOUTH, Devon, TQ14 8BE		
66	Mr & Mrs D Badcock West Hatch Hotel, 34 West Cliff, DAWLISH, Devon, EX7 9DN	01626 864211 962 763 £21.00	O D CP 7DR 1T 2F 10ES
66	Tourist Information Centre The Lawn, DAWLISH, Devon, EX7 9AP	01626 863589	
66	Mrs M Hayes The Old Vicarage, STARCROSS, Nr Exeter, Devon, EX6 8PX	01626 890206 £20.25	O D CP LSP 2DR 2T 1F 3ES
66	Mrs M Lambert Wixels, Ferry Road, TOPSHAM, Devon, EX3 0JH	01392 876785 £15.00	O D CP LSP DW 1DR
66	Barn Hotel Foxholes Hill, EXMOUTH, Devon, EX8 2DF	01395 224411 £30.00	D EM PL CP 4DR 1T 2S 4F
66	Mrs P Garwood St Aubyns, 11 Hartley Road, EXMOUTH, Devon, EX8 2SG	01395 264069 £16.00	O D PL CP LSP DW 2DR 2S
66	Ms A Jones Sholton Guest House, 29 Morton Road, EXMOUTH, Devon, EX8 1BA	01395 277318 £16.00	O D EM PL CP DW 5DR 2T 1S 1F 3ES
66	Mrs Shobrook 30 Withycombe Road, EXMOUTH, Devon, EX8 1TG	01395 277025 £14.50	D EM CP DW 1DR 1T 1S
67	Ms P Bargh Milestone, 39 East Budleigh Road, BUDLEIGH SALTERTON, Devon, EX9 6EW	01395 446197 £16.00	O D CP LSP 2DR 1T
67	Mrs S Freeman 10 Knowle Village, BUDLEIGH SALTERTON, Devon, EX9 6AL	01395 445807 050 825 £15.00	O D PL CP LSP DW 2T 1S
67	J Simmons Chapter House, 6 Westbourne Terrace, BUDLEIGH SALTERTON, Devon, EX9 6BR	01395 444100 £16.50	O D PL CP LSP DW 4DR 2T 3F 2ES
67	Tourist Information Centre Fore Street, BUDLEIGH SALTERTON, Devon, EX9 6NG	01935 445275	
68	Ms D Lee Cheriton Guest House, Vicarage Road SIDMOUTH, Devon,	01395 513810 £16.00	O D EM PL CP LSP 4DR 4T 2S 2F 12ES
68	Royal York & Faulkner Hotel Esplanade, SIDMOUTH, Devon, EX10 8AZ	01395 513043 £22.00	D EM PL CP DW 9DR 29T 22S 8F 68ES
68	Mrs L Lever Canterbury House, Salcombe Road, SIDMOUTH, Devon, EX10 8PR	01395 513373 £20.00	D EM CP DW 2DR 2T 1S 3F 7ES
68	Tourist Information Centre Ham Lane, SIDMOUTH, Devon, EX10 8XR		
69	Mr & Mrs R Hart Hole Mill, BRANSCOMBE, Nr Seaton, Devon, EX12 3BX	01297 680314 192 895 £17.00	O D EM CP LSP DW 2DR 1T
69	Mr & Mrs P Manning Pendennis, South Down Road, BEER, Nr Seaton, Devon, EX12 3AE	01287 23395 £16.50	D EM PL CP LSP 4DR 2T 1S 1F 3ES
69	Tors Guest House 55 Harbour Road, SEATON, Devon, EX12 2LX	01297 20531 £20.00	D PL CP LSP 4DR 2T 2S
69	Mr M Christopher Mariners Hotel, The Esplande, SEATON, Devon, EX12 2NP	01297 20560 £28.00	O D EM PL CP DW 6DR 2T 1S 1F 10ES

Section	Name and Address	Phone No./ Map reference/ Starting Price	Facilities Offered

DORSET

YOUTH HOSTELS - LITTON CHENEY, LULWORTH COVE SEE YHA SECTION PAGE

Section	Name and Address	Phone No./ Map reference/ Starting Price	Facilities Offered
70	Ms M Bolton Cliff Cottage Tea Garden, Cobb Road, LYME REGIS, Dorset, DT7 3JP	01297 443334 £15.50	D EM PL CP DW 3DR 1T 1F 4ES
70	Mrs J Harding Coverdale Guest House, Woodmead Road, LYME REGIS, Dorset, DT7 3AB	01297 442882 £16.00	D CP LSP 2DR 4T 2S 6ES
70	Tourist Information Centre Guildhall Cottage, Church Street, LYME REGIS, Dorset, DT7 3QA	01297 442138	
71	Mrs M Ward Springfield House, Axminster Road, CHARMOUTH, Dorset, DT6 6PB	01297 60509 £19.00	O D EM PL CP DW 6DR 3T 2S 1F 8ES
72	Mr & Mrs R Balchin Park Farmhouse, Main Street, CHIDEOCK, Dorset, DT6 6JD	01297 489157 426 928 £20.00	O D EM PL CP LSP 3DR 2T 1F 6ES
72	Mr K Baylis Seatown Cottage, SEATOWN, Nr Bridport, Dorset, DT6 6JT	01297 489027 420 919 £17.50	O D PL CP LSP DW 1DR 1T 1S
72	Mrs V Vallard Egdon, Third Cliff Walk, WEST BAY, Bridport, Dorset, DT6 4HX	01308 422542 £15.00	O D PL CP DW 1DR 1T 1F
72	Mr & Mrs G Barnes Broadstone Barn, Walditch, BRIDPORT, Dorset, DT6 4LA	01308 427430 £20.00	D CP LSP 1DR 1T 1S 1ES
72	Mrs M Hansowitz Cranston Cottage, 25 & 27 Church Street, BRIDPORT, Dorset, DT6 3PS	01308 456240 467 927 £15.50	O D PL CP LSP DW 4DR 4T 5S 2F 2ES
72	Tourist Information Centre 32 South Street, BRIDPORT, Dorset, DT6 3NO	01309 424901	
73	Mrs J Parr Chesil Coppice, WEST BEXINGTON, Abbotsbury, Dorset, DT2 9DD	01308 897351 £14.00	D EM PL CP 1F
73	Mrs M Harman Linton Cottage, ABBOTSBURY, Dorset, DT3 4JL	01305 871339 £24.00	O D EM PL CP LSP 2DR 1T 1F 4ES
74	Mrs J Baker Aveswood, 5 Bramdon Lane, PORTESHAM, Nr Weymouth, Dorset, DT3 4HW	01305 871413 604 856 £17.00	O D PL CP LSP 1DR 1T
74	Mrs M Adams Corfe Gate Hotel, Coryates, PORTESHAM, Nr Weymouth, Dorset, DT3 4HW	01305 871483 £15.00	O D PL 2DR 1T 1S 2ES
74	Mrs S Andrews Fox Barrow House, LANGTON HERRING, Weymouth, Dorset, DT3 4HT	01305 871463 614 825 £18.00	O D CP LSP DW 2DR 1T 1S 2ES
74	Mrs P Westcott Stonebank, 14 West Street, CHICKERELL, Nr Weymouth, Dorset, DT3 4DY	01305 760120 643 807 £20.00	D PL CP 2DR 2ES
74	Mr G Bisogno Alessandria Hotel & Restaurant, 71 Wakeham Road, PORTLAND, Dorset, DT5 1HW	01305 822270 £25.00	O D EM PL CP LSP 6DR 3T 3S 3F 12ES
74	Mr & Mrs Lees 47 New Street, Easton, PORTLAND, Dorset, DT5 1HG	01305 822879	O D EM PL DW 1DR 1T 1F
74	Mr D Fox The Pulpit Inn, PORTLAND, Dorset, DT5 2JT	01305 821237 £12.50	O D EM PL CP LSP 3DR 1T 1S 1F

Section	Name and Address	Phone No./ Map reference/ Starting Price	Facilities Offered
74	Ms J Coxhill Southbrook, Preston Road, Overcombe, WEYMOUTH, Dorset, DT3 6PU	01305 832208 £17.00	O D PL CP LSP DW 5DR 2T 2S 1F 4ES
74	Mrs Benson Florian, 59 Abbotsbury Road, Westham, WEYMOUTH, Dorset, DT4 0AQ	01305 773836 £21.00	D EM PL CP LSP 3DR 2T 1S 6ES
74	Goldcroft Guest House 6 Goldcroft Avenue, WEYMOUTH, Dorset, DT4 0ET	01305 789953 675 795 £16.00	O D PL CP LSP 2DR 1T 3F
74	Mrs M Wakefield Anchorage, 23 Stavordale Road, WEYMOUTH, Dorset, DT4 0AB	01305 785719 £16.00	O D CP LSP 1DR 1T 1S 1F 3ES
74	Tourist Information Centre The Esplanade, WEYMOUTH, Dorset, DT4 8ED	01305 765221/23	
75	Mrs K Legg Rosedale, Church Lane, OSMINGTON, Nr Weymouth, Dorset, DT3 6EW	01305 832056 £16.00	D CP LSP 1DR 1T 1ES
75	Miss B Leigh Rosthwaite, Church Lane, OSMINGTON, Dorset, ST3 6EW	01305 833621 £15.00	O D PL CP DW 1DR 1T
75	Mr & Mrs R Foote Lulworth Cove Hotel, WEST LULWORTH, Ware, Dorset, BH20 5RQ	01929 400333 £22.00	O D EM PL CP LSP 10DR 1T 3S 1F 10ES
75	Shirley Hotel WEST LULWORTH, Ware, Dorset, Dorset, BH20 5RL	01929 400358 824 806 £30.00	D EM PL CP DW 8DR 4T 3S 3F 18ES
75	Mr D Richards Bishops Cottage, Lulworth Cove, WEST LULWORTH, Dorset, BH20 5RQ	01929 400261 on path £23.00	D EM PL CP LSP 2DR 1T 3S 2F 3ES
75	Mill House Hotel Lulworth Cove, WEST LULWORTH, Dorset, BH20 5RQ	01929 400404 on path £26.00	O D EM PL CP LSP 6DR 4T 2F 12ES
75	Mrs L Simpson Newlands Farm, WEST LULWORTH, Ware, Dorset, BH20 5PU	01929 400376 810 810 £23.00	D PL CP LSP 1DR 1T
76	Mrs E Braisby Blackmanston Farm, Steeple, KIMMERIDGE, Nr Wareham, Dorset, BH20 5NZ	01929 480743 916 808 £15.00	O D PL EM CP LSP 2T 1S
76	Mrs G Hole Bradle Farm, Church Knowle, KIMMERIDGE, Dorset, BH20 5NU	01929 480712 930 805 £19.00	O D PL CP LSP 2DR 1T 3ES
77	Ms E Prior Belros, WORTH MATRAVERS, Dorset	01929 439259 £19.50	O D CP LSP DW
77	Mrs S Amos The West Country Hotel, 12 Rempstone Road, SWANAGE, Dorset, BH19 1DW	£19.50	D EM PL CO 3DR 1T 1S 5ES
77	Mrs C Cruse Purback House Hotel, 91 High Street, SWANAGE, Dorset, BH19 2ΙZ	01929 422872 £45.00	O D EM PL CP LSP 9DR 2T 2S 5F 18ES
77	Mr & Mrs C Davison Penny Farthings, 124 Kings Road West, SWANAGE, Dorset, BH19 1HS	01929 422256 £16.00	O D EM PL CP DW 2DR 1T 1S 2ES
77	Mr & Mrs Preston Sunny Bay, 17 Cluny Crescent, SWANAGE, Dorset, BH19 2BP	01929 422650 £15.00	O CP 1DR 1T 1F
77	Amberlea Hotel 36 Victoria Avenue, SWANAGE, Dorset, BH19 1AP	01929 426213 026 792 £15.50	D EM PL CP 4DR 1T 2F 7ES
77	Ms E Hine Perfick Piece, Springfield Road, SWANAGE, Dorset, BH19 1HD	01929 423178 £15.00	O D EM PL CP LSP 1DR 1T 1F 1ES

Section	Name and Address	Phone No./ Map reference/ Starting Price	Facilities Offered
77	Mrs V Cooper Sunny South, 118 Kings Road West, SWANAGE, Dorset, BH19 1HS	01929 422665 023 790 £14.00	O D PL 1DR 1T 1S 1F 2ES
77	Mrs B Willey Verulam Lodge, 26 Cluny Crescent, SWANAGE, Dorset, BH19 2BT	01929 422079 £15.00	CP 1DR 1T 1F
78	Tourist Information Centre The White House, Shore Road, SWANAGE, Dorset, BH19 1LB	01929 422885	
78	Mrs North The Laurels, 60 Britannia Road, POOLE, Dorset, BH14 8BB	01202 723369 £16.00	O D PL CP LSP 1T 1F
78	Tourist Information Centre The Quay, POOLE, Dorset, BH15 1HE	01202 673322	

YOUTH HOSTEL ASSOCIATION - ACCOMMODATION ADDRESSES

There is an amazing variety of Youth Hostels along the South West Way, 23 in total and all offering comfortable, friendly accommodation. Prices start from £4.00 per night including bed linen, the use ot self-catering kitchens, drying rooms and cycle sheds. The YHA is a membership organisation, non members are welcome to join on arrival at the Youth Hostel. Membership (annual £5.00 Under 18 - £10.00 Adults) enables you to take advantage of the 5000 Youth Hostels world wide, regular member's magazine 'Triangle', annual YHA Accommodation Guides and discounts at YHA Adventure Shops and local tourist attractions. The meals are excellent value, Breakfast £2.95, Packed Lunch £2.55-£3.35, Evening Meal £4.50.

Book directly with the Youth Hostel of your choice or for further assistance please contact South England Regional Office, 11 b York Road, Salisbury, Wiltshire, SP2 7AP Tel: 01722 337494.

Prices range from £4.00 to £9.75 and are for bed and bed linen, available on application to each Hostel.

P	O	D	Name and Address	Telephone No.	Map Ref.	Section
			SOMERSET			
*		*	Minehead Youth Hostel, Alcombe Combe, Minehead, TA24 6EW	Minehead (01643) 702595	973 442	1
			NORTH DEVON			
*		*	Lynton Youth Hostel, Lynbridge, Lynton, EX35 6AZ.	Lynton (01598) 753237	720 487	2
*		*	Ilfracombe Youth Hostel, Ashmour House, Hillsborough Tce., Ilfracombe, EX34 9NR.	Ilfracombe (01271) 865337	524 476	1
*		*	Instow Youth Hostel, Worlington House, New Road,Instow, Bideford, EX39 4LW.	Instow (01271) 860394	483 303	9
		*	Elmscott Youth Hostel, Hartland, Bideford, EX39 6E5. (Self catering only)	Hartland (01237) 441367	231 217	11
			CORNWALL			
*		*	Boscastle Youth Hostel, Palace Stables, Boscastle, PL35 OHD.	Boscastle (01840) 250287	096 915	14
		*	Tintagel Youth Hostel, Dunderhole Point, Tintagel, PL34 0DW (Self catering only)	Tintagel (01840) 770334	047 881	15

TWENTY-THREE OF THE YOUTH HOSTELS IN THE WEST COUNTRY ARE ON THE SOUTH WEST WAY

THEY ARE:-

1	Minehead	15	Golant
2	Lynton	16	Plymouth
3	Ilfracombe	17	Salcombe
4	Instow	18	Maypool (Torbay)
5	Elmscott (Hartland)	19	Exeter
6	Boscastle	20	Beer
7	Tintagel	21	Litton Cheney
8	Treyarnon	22	Lulworth Cove
9	Perranporth	23	Swanage
10	Lands End		
11	Penzance		
12	Coverack		
13	Pendennis Castle		
14	Boswinger		

WE PROVIDE FRIENDLY ACCOMMODATION
AND MEALS FOR YOU AND YOUR FRIENDS
THERE IS NO UPPER AGE LIMIT

YHA SOUTH ENGLAND REGIONAL OFFICE
11B YORK ROAD, SALISBURY, WILTSHIRE, SP2 7AP.
Telephone: (01722) 337494

CORNWALL

*	*	Treyarnon Bay Youth Hostel, Tregonnan, Treyarnon, Padstow PL2B 8JR.	Padstow (01841) 520322	859 741	19
*	*	Perranporth Youth Hostel, Droskyn Point, Perranporth, TR6 OGS. (Self catering only)	Truro (01872) 573812	752 544	23
*	*	Land's End (St Just) Youth Hostel, Letcha Vean, St Just, Penzance, TR197NT.	Penzance (01736) 788437	364 305	30
*	*	Penzance Youth Hostel, Castle Horneck, Alverton, Penzance, TR2O BTF	Penzance (01736) 362666	457 302	34
*	*	Coverack Youth Hostel, Park Behan, School Hill, Coverack, Helaton, TR12 65A.	St Keverne (01326) 280687	782 184	40
*	*	Pendennis Castle Youth Hostel, Pendennis Castle, Falmouth, TR11 4LP.	Falmouth (01326) 311435	823 319	42
*	*	Boswinger Youth Hostel, Boswinger, Gorran, St Austell, PL26 6LL.	Mevagissey (01726) 843234	991 411	49
*	*	Golant Youth Hostel, Penquite House, Golant, Fowey, PL23 1LA	Fowey (01726) 833507	118 557	51

SOUTH DEVON

*	*	Plymouth Youth Hostel, Belmont House, Belmont Place, Stoke, Plymouth, PL3 4DW	Plymouth (01752) 562189	461 555	55
*	*	Salcombe Youth Hostel, 'Overbecks', Sharpitor, Salcombe, T08 8LW.	Salcombe (01548) 842856	728 374	60
*	*	Maypool Youth Hostel, Maypool House, Galmpton, Brixham, TQ5 0ET	Churston (01803) 842444	877 546	64
*	*	Exeter Youth Hostel 47 Countess Wear Road, Exeter, EX2 6LR	Exeter (01392) 873329	942 897	66/67
*	*	Beer Youth Hostel, Bovey Combe, Townsend, Beer, Seaton, EX12 3LL.	Seaton (01297) 20296	223 896	69

DORSET

Bridport Youth Hostel has closed.

*	*	Litton CheneyYouth Hostel, Litton Cheney, Dorchester, OT2 9AT. (No smoking hostel - self-catering only)	Long Brady (01308) 482340	548 900	74
*	*	Lulworth Cove Youth Hostel, School Lane, West Lulworth, Wareham, 8H20 5SA	W. Lulworth (01929) 400564	832 806	75
*	*	Swanage Youth Hostel, Cluny, Cluny Cresc., Swanage, BH19 2BS	Swanage (01929) 422113	031 785	77

CAMPING

A list of Camp Sites has been prepared in path order anti-clockwise. Useful information and free leaflets can also be obtained as follows:

The Exmoor Visitor: A free comprehensive guide (including accommodation). Please apply to Department E.V, Exmoor National Park Authority, Exmoor House, Dulverton, Somerset TA22 9HL.

Tourist Officer, Cornwall County Council, County Hall, Truro.

Devon County Tourist Officer, County Hall, Topsham Road, Exeter.

County Public Relations & Information Officer; County Hall, Dorchester; Dorset DTI 1XJ.

Individuals - but we stress **not parties** - usually find no problem in obtaining leave to camp away from official camp sites if they request permission to do so. In fact, our correspondence has many examples of extra kindnesses extended by farmers and others to campers. We would, however, very much emphasize the requesting of permission first. It would be so easy for the thoughtlessness of a few to undo the good relationships of many others built up over some years.

This list is thin in many areas. Suggestions for inclusions in future lists will always be welcome. Information of any new sites should be addressed to the Membership Secretary.

Section	Name and Address	Telephone No.	Map Ref.	Site Open (Dates inclusive)
	SOMERSET			
1	Camping Club Site North Hill, MINEHEAD, Somerset, TA24 5SF	01643 704138	958 471	23 MAR - 28 SEPT
1	Sparkhayes Farm Camp Site R R Richards & Sons, Sparkhayes Lane, PORLOCK, Somerset, TA24 8NE	01643 862470	886 469	APRIL - OCT
	NORTH DEVON			
3	Newberry Farm Camp Site Woodlands, COMBE MARTIN, Devon, EX34 0AT	01271 882333/4	574 467	EASTER - OCTOBER
4	Mr D L Wassell Big Meadow Camp Site, Watermouth, ILFRACOMBE, Devon, EX34 9SJ	01271 862282	passes through site	EASTER - END OCTOBER
4	Hele Valley Holiday Park Hele Bay, ILFRACOMBE, Devon, EX34 9RD	01271 862460		EASTER - OCTOBER
5	Warcombe Farm Station Road, MORTEHOE, Devon, EX34 7EJ	01271 870690		EASTER - OCTOBER
5	The Owner North Morte Farm, MORTEHOE, Devon, EX34 7EG	01271 871381	461 456	

Section	Name and Address	Telephone No.	Map Ref.	Site Open (Dates inclusive)
8	Chivenor Holiday Centre Chivenor Cross, BARNSTAPLE, Devon, EX31 4BN	01271 812217	504 351	
9	Braddicks Holiday Centre Merly Road, WESTWARD HO! Devon, EX39 1JS	01237 473263	425 290	ALL YEAR
10	Mr Rob Croslegh Steart Farm Touring Park, Horns Cross, BUCK MILLS, Bideford, Devon, EX39 5DW	01237 431836	356 229	4 APRIL - 31 OCTOBER
11	Mrs H Davey Stoke Barton Farm, Stoke, HARTLAND, Devon, EX39 6DU	01237 441238	234 246	EASTER - END SEPTEMBER

NORTH CORNWALL

Section	Name and Address	Telephone No.	Map Ref.	Site Open (Dates inclusive)
12	Bude Holiday Park Maer Lane, BUDE, Cornwall	01288 355955	208 085	APRIL - SEPTEMBER
12	Wooda Farm Caravan and Camping Park Wooda Farm, Poughill, BUDE, Cornwall, EX23 9HJ	01288 352069	229 078	APRIL - OCTOBER
12	Upper Lynstone Camping & Caravan Park, BUDE, Cornwall, EX23 0LP	01288 352017	205 053	EASTER - SEPTEMBER
13	Coxford Meadow St Gennys, CRACKINGTON HAVEN, Cornwall, EX23 0NS	01840 230707	162 967	EASTER - SEPTEMBER
13	Mrs S Weller Hentervene Camping & Caravan Park, CRACKINGTON HAVEN, Cornwall, EX23 0LF	01840 230365	155 944	EASTER - NOVEMBER
15	Mr M Francis The Headland Caravan & Camping Park, Atlantic Road, TINTAGEL, Cornwall, PL34 0DE	01840 770239	056 888	EASTER - 31 OCTOBER
17	Tristram Camping & Caravan POLZEATH, Cornwall, PL27	01208 862215	948 792	EASTER - OCTOBER
17	South Winds Camping & Caravan Park, POLZEATH, Cornwall, PL27 6QU	01208 863267	948 792	MARCH - SEPTEMBER
18	Little Bodieve Holiday Park Bodieve Road, WADEBRIDGE, Cornwall, PL27 6EG	01208 812323	995 734	APRIL - OCTOBER
18	Dennis Cove Campsite Dennis Cove, PADSTOW, Cornwall, PL28 8DR	01841 532349	920 745	EASTER - 30 SEPTEMBER
18	Mother Iveys Bay Caravan Park TREVOSE HEAD, Padstow, Cornwall, PL28 8SL	01841 520990	865 756	EASTER - END OF OCT
20	Carnevas Farm Holiday Park PORTHCOTHAN BAY, Cornwall, PL28 8PN	01841 520230	862 728	APRIL - NOVEMBER
21	Camping & Caravan Club Site Tregurrian, NEWQUAY, Cornwall, TR8 4AE	01637 860448	853 654	23 MARCH - 28 SEPT
21	Trevornick Holiday Park Holywell Bay, NEWQUAY, Cornwall	01637 830531		EASTER - 30 SEPTEMBER
24	Beacon Cottage Farm Touring Park, Beacon Drive, ST AGNES, Cornwall, TR5 0NU	01872 552347	705 505	MAY - SEPTEMBER

Section	Name and Address	Telephone No.	Map Ref.	Site Open (Dates inclusive)
26	H Williams & Son Magor Farm Caravan Site, Tehidy, PORTREATH, Camborne, Cornwall	01209 713367	632 427	EASTER - SEPTEMBER
29	Mr M Osborne Trevalgan Family Camping Park, ST IVES, Cornwall, TR26 3BJ	01736 796433	490 402	MAY - END SEPTEMBER
29	The Old Chapel Backpackers Hostel, ZENNOR, Cornwall	01736 798307	455 385	ALL YEAR
29	Mr J Boyns Levant House Camp Site, Trewellard, PENDEEN, Cornwall, TR19 7SX	01736 788795	375 338	APRIL - 31 OCTOBER
30	Trevaylor Camp Site Botallack, ST JUST, Penzance, Cornwall, TR19 7PU	01736 787016	370 328	MID MARCH - 31 OCT
30	Kelynack Caravan & Camping Park, Kelynack, ST JUST, Penzance, Cornwall	01736 787633	374 301 Bunkhouse now open	ALL YEAR

SOUTH CORNWALL

Section	Name and Address	Telephone No.	Map Ref.	Site Open (Dates inclusive)
33	Mr J Hall Treen Campsite, Treen, ST LEVAN, Nr Penzance, Cornwall	01736 810526	392 228	APRIL -END OCTOBER
34	Bone Valley Caravan Park Heamoor, PENZANCE, Cornwall, TR20 8UJ	01736 60313	462 318	1 MARCH - 13 DECEMBER
35	Wheal Rodney Gwallon, MARAZION, Cornwall, TR17 0HL	01736 710605		1 APRIL - 31 OCTOBER
38	Criggan Mill MULLION COVE, Cornwall, TR12 7EU	01326 240496	667 180	ALL YEAR
39	J Lyne Henry's Campsite, THE LIZARD, Nr Helston, Cornwall, TR12 7NX	01326 290596		ALL YEAR
40	Silver Sands Holiday Park Gwendreath, KENNACK SANDS, Helston, Cornwall, TR12 7LZ	01326 290631	729 169	MAY - SEPTEMBER
40	Gwendreath Farm Caravan Park, KENNACK SANDS, Helston, Cornwall, TR12 7LZ	01326 290666	729 167	EASTER - OCTOBER
42	J B Jewell Pennance Mill Farm Chalet & Camping, Maenporth, FALMOUTH, Cornwall, TR11 5HJ	01326 312616	791 307	EASTER - END OCTOBER
42	Tremorvah Tent Park Swanpool, FALMOUTH, Cornwall, TR11 5BE	01326 312103	799 312	MAY - END SEPTEMBER
44	Trewince Manor PORTSCATHO, Truro, Cornwall, TR2 5ET	01872 580289	868 338	EASTER - 30 OCTOBER
47	Mrs M Parkhouse Treveor Farm, GORRAN, HAVEN, Cornwall, PL26 6LW	01726 842387	987 418	EASTER - END OCTOBER
47	Trelispen Camping Park GORRAN HAVEN, Cornwall	01726 843501	005 421	APRIL - OCTOBER
50	Sun Valley Holiday Park Pentewan Road, ST AUSTELL, Cornwall, PL26 6DJ	01726 843266		APRIL - OCTOBER

Section	Name and Address	Telephone No.	Map Ref.	Site Open (Dates inclusive)
51	Penhale Caravan & Camping Polkerris, FOWEY, Cornwall, PL23 1JU	01726 833425	103 526	APRIL - OCTOBER
52	Kiligarth Manor Hols. Est. POLPERRO, Cornwall, PL13 2JQ	01503 72216	215 516	EASTER - OCTOBER
53	Tencreek Caravan Park LOOE, Cornwall, PL13 2JR	01503 262447	234 525	ALL YEAR
54	Ms Stocker Carbeil Caravan & Camping Park, Treliodon Lane, DOWNDERRY, Cornwall	01503 250636		EASTER - 31 OCTOBER

SOUTH DEVON

Section	Name and Address	Telephone No.	Map Ref.	Site Open (Dates inclusive)
56	Plymouth Backpackers Hotel 172 Citadel Road, The Hoe, PLYMOUTH, Devon, PL31 3DB	01752 225158		ALL YEAR
59	Mr S Chapman Fryer Tucks Takeaway, CHALLABOROUGH, Devon, TQ7 4HZ	01548 810425		MARCH - OCTOBER
60	Mr J Tucker Mount Jolly Farm, BIGBURY ON SEA, Devon, TQ7 4AR	01548 810267	661 469	MARCH - OCTOBER
60	Mr P Higgin Karrageen Camping Site, BOLBERRY, Nr Kingsbridge, Devon, TQ7 3EN	01548 561230	689 394	15 MARCH - 15 NOV
60	Mr B Sweetman Sun Park, Soar, MALBOROUGH, Devon, TQ7 3DS	01548 561378		EASTER - OCTOBER
60	Higher Rew Farm Camping Park, MALBOROUGH, Devon, TQ7 3DW	01548 842681	713 383	EASTER - OCTOBER
60	Ilton Farm Camp Site MALBOROUGH, Devon, TQ7 3BZ	01548 842858	722 403	EASTER - OCTOBER
61	Mr S Bradney Old Cotmore Farm, STOKENHAM, Torcross, Devon, TQ7 2LR	01548 580240	804 415	MARCH - NOVEMBER
61	Camping & Caravanning Club Site, Middle Grounds, SLAPTON, Torcross, Devon, TQ7 1QW	01548 580538	825 450	24 MARCH - 3 NOV
63	W Hosking Upton Manor Farm Camping, St Mary's, BRIXHAM, Devon, TQ5 9QH	01803 882384	549 926 path $\frac{1}{2}$ mile	SPRING BH TO MID SEPT
64	Beverly Park Holiday Park Goodrington Road, PAIGNTON, Devon, TQ4 7JE	01803 843887	888 588	EASTER - DECEMBER
64	Marine Park Holiday Centre Grange Road, PAIGNTON, Devon, TQ4 7JR	01803 843887	888 587	EASTER - OCTOBER
66	Lady's Mile Touring Exeter Road, DAWLISH, Devon, EX7 0LX	01626 863411	968 784	MARCH - END OCTOBER
66	Devon Cliffs Holiday Centre Sandy Bay, EXMOUTH, Devon, EX8 5BT	01395 223000	035 805	EASTER - OCTOBER
68	Ladram Bay Holiday Centre Nr BUDLEIGH SALTERTON, Devon, EX9 7BX	01395 568398	096 854	1 APRIL - 30 SEPTEMBER

Section Name and Address	Telephone No.	Map Ref.	Site Open (Dates inclusive)
68 Oakdown Caravan Parks Weston, SIDMOUTH, Devon, EX10 0PH	01297 680387	167 902	APRIL - OCTOBER
69 Manor Farm Camping & Caravan Site, Seaton Down Hill, SEATON, Devon, EX12 2JA	01297 21524		MARCH - OCTOBER
70 Mr R K Webber Axmouth Camping Site, Axe Farm, Pound Hill, SEATON, Devon, EX12 4BG	01297 24707	256 911	EASTER - END OCTOBER
DORSET			
71 Wood Farm Caravan & Camping Park, Axminster Road, CHARMOUTH, Dorset, DT6 6BT	01297 560697	355 940	APRIL - NOVEMBER
71 Manor Farm Holiday Centre CHARMOUTH, Dorset, DT6 6QL	01297 560226	368 937	ALL YEAR
72 Golden Cap Holiday Park Seatown, CHIDEOCK, Bridport, Dorset, DT6 6JX	01308 422139	424 919	MARCH - OCTOBER
72 Mr K G Mundy Eype House Caravan & Camping Park, EYPE, Nr Bridport, Dorset, DT6 6AL	01308 424903	446 912	EASTER - MID OCTOBER
73 Freshwater Beach Holiday Park, BURTON BRADSTOCK, N Dorset, DT6 4PT	01308 897317	898 479	20 MARCH - 15 NOV
74 Sea Barn Farm Camping Fleet, WEYMOUTH, Dorset, DT3 4ED	01305 782218	624 814	EASTER - OCTOBER
75 Osmington Mills Holidays Ltd, The Ranch House, OSMINGTON MILLS, Dorset, DT3 6HB	01305 832311	733 822	EASTER - SEPT
77 Ulwell Cottage Caravan Park Ulwell, SWANAGE, Dorset, BH19 3DG	01929 422823		MARCH - JANUARY

SOUTH WEST WAY ASSOCIATION - HISTORY

We are sometimes asked what we have done and we set out below some of the things in which we have been involved in one way or another. We do as well send a steady flow of reports on path deficiencies, both as regards maintenance and the route of the path to the local authorities and the Countryside Commission.

1973 Official Formation in May.
Attendance Cornish Opening at Newquay.
Comments to Sports Council on proposed Countryside Park at Northam Burrows.
First Information Sheets produced.

1974 Evidence submitted to Mr Yepp for his report to the Countryside Commission on Long Distance Footpaths.
We welcomed Devon N.F.U. representation on our Committee.
Attendance at South Devon and Dorset Opening in September at Beer.
Registration as a Charity.
First Description issued.

1975 Mark Richard's book "Walking the North Cornwall Coastal Path" published - a work in which we may fairly say we played a part.
Small new section of Coast Path agreed at Clematon Hill, Bigbury at S.W.W.A.'s instigation.
Article on S.W.W. in Rucksack.
Attendance at Opening of so-called Exmoor Coastal Path.
Bideford Public Enquiry - successful opposition to Golf Course on the Coastal Path at Abbotsham.
Success at last in getting path south from Hartland Point over Blagdon and Upright Cliffs.
Walk over new Lulworth Range Walk.

1976 First Footpath Guide issued.
Diversion at Thurlestone opposed.
Evidence submitted to House of Commons Expenditure Committee Environment sub-committee.
Improvements at North Cliffs between Portreath and Hayle secured, thanks to National Trust.
Public Enquiry with R.A. at Kingswear on the section Kellys Cove to Mann Sands.
Consulted by Devon County Council on path at Watermouth and Dorset County Council about Abbotsbury.
Goodbye to our first Chairman, Mr Walter - we lose a tower of strength.

1977 S.W.W.A. mentioned in the YH. Handbook.
Publications of Letts Guides in three volumes. The first satisfactory books to whole path in which we can say our information helped a little.
Attendance at Coverack Youth Hostel official opening.
Evidence presented to Lord Porchester's Exmoor Study.
Badges produced.
Evidence given to Devon County Council for Taw/Torridge Estuary Survey.

1978 First Printed Footpath guide.
Attendance at Westward Hol Somerset/North Devon Opening.
Opposition to diversion at Dean Quarry, St Keverne, Cornwall.
Lack of Path at Pentewan submitted to Local Ombudsman.
New path seaward of Radar Station at Hartland obtained, thanks to South West Way Association.

1979 Evidence given at Public Enquiries at Abbotsbury and Lulworth Cove.
Submission to Mr Himsworth for his report on Areas of Outstanding Natural Beauty.
First printed News Letters and Descriptions, and the first illustrated description.
Pine Haven to Port Duin gap submitted to Local Ombudsman.
Assistance to Letts for their Guide reprint.

1980 Result of 1976 Public Enquiry at Kingswear published.
Discussion Dean Quarry, St Keverne, Cornwall.
Dialogues with Countryside Commission about path deficiencies.
Alternative coastal path open Glenthorne Estate, Somerset and we submit proposals for rerouting in Exmoor National Park.
Special report submitted on St Loy, Cornwall.
Attendance at Widmouth Head, North Devon, Public Enquiry.
Opinions expressed to Department of Environment on draft "Wildlife and Countryside Bill".

1981 Annual Guide "State of the Path" section improved.
Attendance at second Kingswear Public Enquiry.
Countryside Commission decide that path wardenship will be greatly extended.
Bridge provided at Duckpool, North Cornwall.
Path improvements at Watermouth; Braunton to Barnstaple; Dean Quarry; Clematon Hill;
Bigbury; Mothecombe and Maidencombe.

1982 Wardenship of coastal path in Cornwall completed.
Further openings at: Cleave Farm in North Cornwall, Pentewan with its unfortunate execution and Mount Edgecombe in South Cornwall, Higher Brownstone Farm, Kingswear and a short section west of Berry Head in South Devon.
Agreement was also reached for a high tide route at Mothecombe in South Devon.
The 1982 Guide incorporates a new `Itinerary Suggested' section.

1983 Opening of the Widmouth Head section in North Devon and a second long section in South Devon between Kingswear and Mann Sands.
Major improvements to the Path on the western side of Crackington Haven, North Cornwall.
Cornwall's 10th Anniversary Walk.

1984 **New Section**
A new section of the Path opened on the east bank of the mouth of the River Dart close to Kingswear and giving access to Mill Bay Cove and a splendid stretch of coastal walking.

Improvement
A coastal route was opened westwards from Trebarwith Strand to Backways Cove in North Cornwall.

1985 **Culbone - Foreland Point**
The alternative coastal path at the Glenthorne Estate was waymarked as the official route, which is a great improvement.

Pinehaven - Port Quin (North Cornwall)
The new path was opened and is a vast improvement, although the substantial fence and barbed wire detracts from the scene.

1986 **Minehead to Porlock Weir** New alternative path between North Hill and Hurlstone Point signposted and waymarked.

Black Head, Cornwall Now purchased by the National Trust.

1987 **Barnstaple/Bideford/Northam** The new route completed along the railway lines and open.

Bude Attendance at Public Enquiry to prevent development adjacent to footpath.

Chynhalls Point Coast path moved to seaward of hotel.

Branscombe Attendance at Public Enquiry to urge true coast path instead of inland route. Preferred route adopted.

Bidna/Northam Owing to breach in sea wall an acceptable diversion negotiated.

1988 **Woody Bay to Trentishoe** Devon County Council adopts our recommended, nearer the coast route as the official coast path.

1989 **Culbone** On site exploration with Countryside Commission and Exmoor National Park Authority to discover an acceptable alternative to the long unnecessary Culbone diversion.

Chynhalls Cliff On site exploration for a more coastal trail.

Fire Beacon Point/pentargon Cornwall County Council install grand new path.

Wembury Attend public meeting at Down Thomas to successfully oppose erection of locked gates across Coast Path by Royal Navy.

Strete Gate/Warren Cove Attend public meeting and give evidence to support proposals by Countryside Commission and Devon County Council for an improved and more true coast path.

1990 **Membership** Now over 1000.

1991 **Buckator** At our request Cornwall County Council re-route official path around the headland.

Worthy/Culbone On site explorations for a preferable diversion to that proposed by Exmoor National Park Authority.

Strete Gate/Warren Cove Continuing our strong argument with Devon County Council for a coast path.

Lyme Regis Continued pleas to Dorset County Council to reinstate the coast path along the golf course.

Total length we estimate the Coast Path to be about 613 miles long.

1992 Our recommended route between Watcombe and Maidencombe put in by Devon County Council.

Our suggested path at Worthygate Wood installed by National Trust.

Commenced discussions with Countryside Commission to examine sections of coast suitable for 'Set Aside'.

1993 Successful opposition to an application to close path on west side of Foreland Point.

Success with our request for a coast path avoiding the holiday complex at Buck's Mills.

Our suggested path installed by National Trust at Port Quin.

Write and produce the `trail description' in this book the 'Other Way Round'.

1994 Invited by the Countryside Commission to become a member of the South West Coast Path Steering Group to review the management of our Coast Path.

Association acquires a computer.

1995 Membership reaches 2,000
Culbone section re-opened by Exmoor National Park.
Strete Gate/Warren Point - continuous pressure causes Devon County Council to explore again for a route that will provide an acceptable coast path.
Continuing involvement in the 'Coast Path Project'.
Association details on the Internet. See Web addresses on page 2.

1996 Path descriptions for the whole SWW written and printed.
Continuing involvement in the coast path project and production of the strategy document.
Lyme Regis - Golf Course Route reinstated by Dorset County Council.
Strete Gate/Warren Point - Devon County Council decide to install our preferred route but rejected by Countryside Commission.

1997 A new footbridge put in by Cornwall County Council across the Red River at Gwithian).
The SWCP Project published it strategy for the future management of the Coast Path.
The Association becomes a member of the SWCP Management Group.

OFFA'S DYKE: MORE THAN A PATH!

For 1,200 years the term 'Offa's Dyke' has meant the great earthwork thrown up by the powerful ruler of Mercia (central England to mark the boundary with the Welsh and as such it has also colloquially come to refer to the Anglo-Welsh boundary. In the last forty years a new meaning has come to the term with the designation of the Offa's Dyke Long Distance Footpath in 1949. It took 22 years from designation to the opening in 1971 and here lies the origin of another meaning to 'Offa's Dyke', the Association. This was originally set-up to act as a pressure group to push for the necessary works and the opening to take place. Since 1971 Offa's Dyke Path has become one of the best used of the National Trails, and a name known to most 'serious' walkers. The Association has had no mean success itself with, now, over 1,000 members.

But why have a long distance footpath along this particular route? The historic border it may be but it follows no obvious physical feature. Offa's Dyke Path as a walking route is something else, in one word, Variety. The Welsh Border is, for Britain, lonely country and some of the most attractive and unspoilt moorland, rolling hills and farmland are crossed by the Path between the tourist areas of the Wye Valley and the North Wales coast. Across the plains of Gwent, over the Black Mountains, the river valleys and hills of Radnor, the Severn and Dee valleys, the limestone hills round Llangollen and the Ciwyddian ridges: the list of varied attractions is long. For nearly half the route the earthwork is your companion, often 20 feet from ditch to top even after twelve centuries of erosion. Many castles and abbeys lie near the route and though the 177 miles can be covered in a week, most visitors will sensibly prefer a more leisurely walk.

But why an Offa's Dyke Association? And, in particular what was the need for this voluntary pressure group to continue beyond the official opening of the Path? We foresaw some of the needs of visitors to the Path that official facilities and services could not meet and we correctly anticipated a minor boom in walking and other tourism where there had been little before. Also inevitably there would be a different approach to the Path from walkers and from historians, from visitors and from those who lived and worked there. If we could cover this range of interests then harmony in development, rather than areas of conflict would be more likely.

We run the Offa's Dyke Centre at Knighton, which also serves as the town's T.I.C., and thus receives some local authority aid. It helps nearly 30,000 people each year. Most want to know about accommodation and so we publish annual 'where to stay' and camping lists. Additionally we issue guides, 'strip maps' of the route, point to point route notes in both directions, circular walks and alternative routes based on the Path, also town trails and history notes. We sell non-ODA maps and guides. Association members were commissioned to write the 'official' guides to the Path. Finally, we send a wide-ranging journal three times a year to members.

Maintenance and erosion of the Path with the attendant problem of vandalism, are constant sources of concern. We have a system of volunteers, each watching over a stretch of the route and negotiating with farmers over access etc., and local authorities over necessary maintenance; even doing minor works themselves. Since 1982 this work has been in co-operation with an 'Offa's Dyke Development Officer' (ODDO); now expanded into a full scale Path Management Service, this is financed by the Countryside Council for Wales and works via Powys County Council from our Knighton Centre. A new purpose built centre, adjacent to the present crumbling building, will be developed during 1988.

We are pleased to be regarded as a body to be consulted on policy matters by national and local government and their agencies.

A strong membership and flourishing sales are the key to our public recognition and to our strength as a pressure group: please write, with S.A.E., to Offa's Dyke Association (S.W.I, West Street, Knighton, Powys, Wales. Tel: 01547 528753.

ERNIE KAY - Hon General Secretary

NTRODUCTION TO SOUTH WEST WAY ASSOCIATION

hilst walking the path, or on any other occasion, should you meet
meone interested in this book, the Association, or the coast path, do
t worry it no one has a pencil and paper - just tear off one of these:

---✂-----

e South West Way Association was formed 24 years ago to promote the interest of users
our coast path. We continue to press the authorities to maintain it properly and to
mplete the path. we produce guide books which are issued to members.

embership Secretary, Mary Macleod, 1 Orchard Drive, Kingskerswell, Newton Abbot,
von, TQ12 5DG (01803 873061)

cretary, Eric Wallis, Windlestraw, Penquit, Ermington, Devon, PL21 OLU (01752 896237)

---✂-----

e South West Way Association was formed 24 years ago to promote the interest of users
our coast path. We continue to press the authorities to maintain it properly and to
mplete the path. we produce guide books which are issued to members.

embership Secretary, Mary Macleod, 1 Orchard Drive, Kingskerswell, Newton Abbot,
von, TQ12 5DG (01803 873061)

cretary, Eric Wallis, Windlestraw, Penquit, Ermington, Devon, PL21 OLU (01752 896237)

---✂-----

e South West Way Association was formed 24 years ago to promote the interest of users
our coast path. We continue to press the authorities to maintain it properly and to
mplete the path. we produce guide books which are issued to members.

embership Secretary, Mary Macleod, 1 Orchard Drive, Kingskerswell, Newton Abbot,
von, TQ12 5DG (01803 873061)

cretary, Eric Wallis, Windlestraw, Penquit, Ermington, Devon, PL21 OLU (01752 896237)

---✂-----

e South West Way Association was formed 24 years ago to promote the interest of users
our coast path. We continue to press the authorities to maintain it properly and to
mplete the path. we produce guide books which are issued to members.

embership Secretary, Mary Macleod, 1 Orchard Drive, Kingskerswell, Newton Abbot,
von, TQ12 5DG (01803 873061)

cretary, Eric Wallis, Windlestraw, Penquit, Ermington, Devon, PL21 OLU (01752 896237)